BRITISH AIRCRAFT AT WAR 1939-45

Gordon Swanborough

HPC Publishing, East Sussex, England

Front cover photographs: Clockwise from top left, Hawker Typhoon IB of No 609 Sqn, Blackburn Rocs, de Havilland Mosquito FB.6 of No 248 Sqn, Supermarine Spitfire VBs of No 601 Sqn, Bristol Blenheim IVFs of No 235 Sqn, Bristol Beaufighter X of No 455 Sqn, Vickers Wellington VIII of No 172 Sqn. Back cover: Fairey battles of No 218 Sqn.

First published in 1997

British Library Cataloguing in Publication data
A Catalogue record of this book is available from the British Library.

ISBN 0 9531421 0 8

Published by HPC Publishing, Drury Lane, St Leonards-on-Sea, East Sussex TN38 9BJ.

Printed in Great Britain by Hastings Printing Company Ltd.

Introduction

Between September 1939 and August 1945, no fewer than 265 different types of British aircraft flew somewhere in those parts of the world that became involved in World War II, either directly or indirectly. Now, more than 50 years on, the wartime use of those types - many of which had originally been intended for the most peaceful of purposes - continues to exert a fascination on 'aircraft enthusiasts' of several generations.

Many books have been devoted - some might say too many - to the most famous of Britain's military aircraft of the wartime period. As more and more information has become available through the release of official files and through personal reminiscences, details of the design, manufacture, development, deployment and operational exploits of such famous types as the Spitfire, Hurricane, Mosquito, Lancaster and others have been recorded down to the last final item.

The same cannot be said, though, of many of the less warlike types - elderly RAF and FAA survivors of the 'twenties and 'thirties; civil types impressed for military service and those that operated in far-flung corners of the combat zones, where circumstances did not require, or did not allow, deployment of more up-to-date front-line aircraft. This book sets out - for the first time between single covers - to summarise the use made of **every** one of these British types. Only those few that flew exclusively in neutral skies during the wartime period are excluded.

Throughout the pages that follow I have sought to record the way in which each type served; but more than that, to summarise such information as first flight dates, intended and actual roles, production quantities, mark number variations, dates and units for service introduction, user services, areas of use, and so on. Brief data are included for power plant, performance, weights and dimensions.

As would be expected in a book of this size, some of the entries (notably for the multi-variant front-line types) can be little more than concentrated notes: information on 43 marks of Mosquito, for instance, or 24 marks of Spitfire, is not easily digested into a page or even three! Nevertheless, the basic information is all there, as it is also for the less multi-varied types, and can be used as a starting point for further study and research. That, indeed, is one of the intended purposes of this volume. In other cases, the information to be found here is more surprising (and less well-known): there are the Gladiators sold to Latvia and Lithuania, that passed into Soviet hands only to end up serving the *Luftwaffe* as glider tugs; the Blenheims built in Yugoslavia used to equip the embryonic Croatian Air Force; the Cierva W.9 helicopter that was hovering in Britain before the war ended, and the engineless BA Swallows towed into the air as gliders to test radar effectiveness. Also included, for the sake of completeness, are those types that were only at the start of their flight testing programmes as the war ended - some of which would suffer peremptory cancellation while others would be produced to serve in the RAF and FAA or were intended, even then, for use in the civil field.

The contents of this volume (now slightly amended and with additional photographs) first appeared in *AIR Pictorial* from January 1994 to December 1996. I am grateful to that paper's editor, Barry Wheeler, for his willingness to devote so much space to the series in the first place, and to its publisher, Derek Knoll, for having faith in this book version. Other acknowledgments appear below.

Gordon Swanborough
Bromley, Kent, 1997.

Acknowledgements

Much of the content of this volume is based on facts, figures and photographs accumulated in a lifetime of recording and collecting - a process that began, in the author's case, before the Second World War had come to an end. It is impossible to acknowledge all those individuals who have contributed, either directly or indirectly, to this book by providing information and/or photographs over that long period.

I can, and gladly do, acknowledge, on the other hand, the many friends and fellow enthusiasts who have given specific help during the preparation of this work by digging out facts or loaning photographs. They are: Peter Amos; Chris Ashworth; David Godfrey; Peter Green; James Halley; John Havers; Mike Hirst; Roger Jackson; Derek James; Philip Jarrett; Alec Lumsden; Tim Mason; Jim Oughton; Richard Riding; Eric Myall; Mike Stroud (Aerospace Publishing Ltd); Ray Sturtevant; Andy Thomas and Stewart Wilson.

AIRSPEED AS.4 FERRY

Prototype of this three-engined (one 360 hp Gipsy III and two Gipsy II) 10-seat biplane impressed by RAF in 1940 (as AV968) and used by Halton Station Flight until late 1941. One other impressed (as DJ715) as ground instruction airframe only.
Max speed, 112 mph (180 km/h). Gross weight, 5,400 lb (2,452 kg). Span, 55 ft 0 in (16.78 m). Length, 39 ft 8 in (12.09 m).

AIRSPEED AS.5 COURIER

One example of this six-seat light aircraft, designed by A Hessell Tiltman and first flown at Portsmouth on April 10, 1933, acquired by Air Ministry in February 1934, with 360 hp Cheetah IX, and used at RAE Farnborough (as K4047) until 1943. Nine Couriers with 240 hp Lynx IVc engines impressed in 1939 for use by National Air Communications unit, later assigned to ATA station comm flights.
Max speed, 153 mph (246 km/h). Gross weight, 3,900 lb (1,771 kg). Span, 47 ft 0 in (14.36 m). Length, 28 ft 6 in (8.69 m).

AIRSPEED AS.6 ENVOY

A twin-engined six/eight passenger light transport designed to complement the Courier, the Envoy first flew on June 26, 1934 at Portsmouth, with 200 hp Wolseley AR.9 Mk II engines. Last five of 82 Envoys built were against an Air Ministry contract (to Specification 24/38) and taken on charge in March 1939 for

Above: One of three AS.6JM(II) Convertible Envoys, No 253 (also ZS-ALF) served with the SAAF Air Survey Flight. Below: Envoy N9108 (also G-AFJE), bought by RAF August 1938, crashed at Rangoon February 24, 1942.

communications duties. Two others acquired by RAF August 1938 and assigned to similar duties in India, serving until 1942. Four more, ex-civil, impressed for RAF use in UK, including one (to Specification 6/37) used by Royal Flight from 1937. Three with dorsal gun turrets (to Specification 39/35) purchased by SAAF in 1936 and four more impressed from SAA in 1938; surviving examples used for reconnaissance and survey flights over Ethiopia and Somaliland, 1940. Production Envoys powered by 240 hp Armstrong Siddeley Lynx IVC or 350 hp Cheetah IX engines; data apply to latter version, known as Envoy III.
Max speed, 210 mph (338 km/h) at 7,300 ft (2,226 m). Cruising range, 650 mls (1,045 km). Gross weight, 6,300 lb (2,860 kg). Span, 52 ft 4 in (15.94 m). Length, 34 ft 6 in (10.53 m).

Above: Ferry G-ABSI was impressed as AV968 and used at Halton until November 1940, then became an ATC instructional airframe as 2758M. Below: Courier K4047, used at the RAE, crashed July 14, 1943.

AIRSPEED AS.10 OXFORD

Developed from the AS.6 Envoy to meet Specification T.23/36, the AS.10 was named Oxford in January 1937 and became the RAF's standard multi-engined trainer throughout WWII. Powered by two 375 hp Cheetah Xs, the first Oxford flew at Portsmouth on June 19, 1937, and production deliveries to the RAF began in November 1937, in two versions: Mk I general purpose, bombing and gunnery trainer with provision for an AW dorsal turret mounting one 0.303-in (7.7-mm) Vickers K gun; and Mk II pilot, navigation and radio trainer, without turret provision. Oxford Mk V (AS.46) was as Mk II, with 450 hp R-985-AN6 Wasp Junior engines. Mk III was a single prototype in March 1940 with Cheetah XV engines and Rotol constant-speed propellers, and Mk IV was projected pilot-training version of Mk III. Undesignated experimentals included one (AS504) with 250 hp Gipsy Queen in-line engines, one (N6327) with twin fins-and-rudders and one (L4539) with McLaren 'drift-correcting' undercarriage to counteract crosswinds during landings. Production contracts totalled 8,751, of which 165 are

Below: This AS.6E Envoy II was originally OK-BAL, one of four sold to the Czech airline CSA in 1935/36. Captured by invading German forces, it was used by the Luftwaffe as shown here, but was passed on to the Finnish Air Force in March 1942 and then operated with the serial EV-1 from March 1942 until destroyed in an accident on July 31, 1943. (Photo courtesy Karl Schmitz via Jean-Louis Ruba).

Above: Oxford II HN386 survived the War, flying with Nos 25 and 234 Sqns. Below left: Oxford Is at 14 FTS include N4587, N4340 and P1927 (No 19). Next in line (No 26) is minus the dorsal turret. Right: Oxford V AS592 flew in Canada with 1 IFS until early 1945.

believed cancelled before completion: Airspeed built 4,411 at Portsmouth and 550 at Christchurch; de Havilland built 1,515 at Hatfield; Standard Motors 750 at Coventry and Percival 1,360 at Luton, final delivery being made at Portsmouth on July 14, 1945. RAF use included, in addition to training, such duties as communications, air experience, air ambulance and radar calibration. A few operated as light bombers carrying 20-lb (9.1-kg) bombs during Iraqi rebellion at Habbaniya, May 1941; later, Oxfords of RNZAF adapted to carry 250-lb (114-kg) bombs for defence against possible Japanese invasion of New Zealand. RNZAF received 297 Oxfords from 1938 onwards; more than 500 to South Africa and Southern Rhodesia for the Empire Pilot Training Scheme; 25 Mk Is supplied to RCAF followed by 606 RAF Mk Is and IIs and 188 Mk Vs used in Canada at Service Flying Training Schools, etc; 391 to RAAF from 1940 onwards for EATS schools; others served with RAF in Middle East, with USAAF in Europe, and with Portuguese and Free French Air Forces. Data for Mk II.

Max speed, 188 mph (301 km/h) at 8,300 ft (2,530 m). Rate of climb at 6,300 ft (1,920 m), 960 ft/min (4.9 m/sec). Service ceiling, 19,500 ft (5,945 m). Endurance, 5¹/₂ hrs. Gross weight, 7,600 lb (3,447 kg). Span, 53 ft 4 in (16.25 m). Length, 34 ft 6 in (10.50 m).

AIRSPEED AS.30 QUEEN WASP

Designed under the direction of A Hessell Tiltman at Portsmouth, the AS.30 Queen Wasp originated to the requirements of Specification Q.32/35 for a radio-controlled target aircraft to be operated as a landplane or a seaplane for live ground-to-air gunnery practice. First of two prototypes (K8887), powered by a 350 hp Cheetah IX engine, flown on June 11, 1937, as a landplane and second (K8888) on October 19, 1937, as a seaplane. Fitted with R1127 radio-control equipment plus provision for a safety pilot. Contract for 65 production Queen Wasps with Cheetah XIIs placed in 1939 but reduced to 12 in 1940 and only five of these completed and delivered, the first (P5441)

being flown on March 29, 1940; a second contract for 258 also cancelled. Projected AS.38 communications variant and AS.50 trainer to specification T.24/40 were unbuilt derivatives.

Max speed, 172 mph (277 km/h) at 8,000 ft (2,400 m). Gross weight, landplane, 3,500 lb (1,588 kg), seaplane, 3,800 lb (1,724 kg). Span, 31 ft 0 in (9.46 m). Length, landplane, 24 ft 4 in (7.42 m), seaplane, 29 ft 1 in (8.86 m).

AIRSPEED AS.39

Designed (with General Aircraft GAL.38) to Specification S.23/37 to provide the FAA with a carrier-based slow-flying reconnaissance aircraft with a long duration for 'fleet shadowing' duties, the AS.39 was powered by four 130 hp Niagara V radials and featured folding wings and a special BLG long-travel tailwheel to achieve 'level-landing' characteristics. Two prototypes ordered but only one (N1323) flown, initially on October 18, 1940. No production.

Max speed, 126 mph (202 km/h) at 5,000 ft (1,525 m). Stalling speed, 37.5 mph (60 km/h) at full throttle at 5,000 ft (1,525 m). Endurance, approx 6 hr. Gross weight, 6,935 lb (3,146 kg). Span, 53 ft 4 in (16.25 m). Length, 40 ft 0 in (12.2 m).

AIRSPEED AS.45

Provisionally named the Cambridge, the AS.45 was designed to Specification T.4/39 as an advanced trainer for possible production to supplement the NA Harvard and Miles Master. First of two prototypes

Below left: Second prototype Queen Wasp K8888 crashed March 20, 1941, in the hands of the Pilotless Aircraft Unit. Below right: The sole AS.39 N1323 (Experimental Aeroplane 117) was never delivered to the RAF.

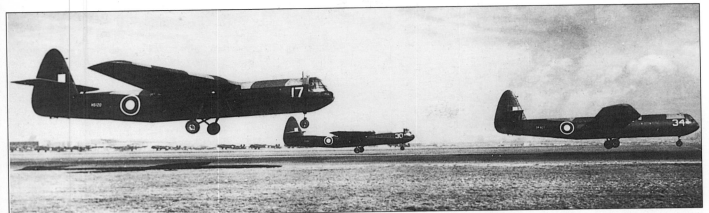

(T2449 and T2453) with a 730 hp Mercury VIII engine, flown at Portsmouth on February 19, 1941; both delivered in July 1942 but no production ordered, and prototypes assigned to RAE Farnborough.
Max economical cruising speed, 237 mph (381 km/h) at 16,000 ft (4,880 m). Span 42 ft 0 in (12.81 m). Length, 36 ft 1 in (11.0 m).

AIRSPEED AS.51 HORSA

Hessell Tiltman designed the AS.51 Horsa to Specification X.26/40 as Britain's first major troop-carrying glider. Of all-wood construction, the Horsa was designed for dispersed production by companies outside the aircraft industry. Design and construction of first two prototypes (DG597 and DG603) at Salisbury Hall, London Colney, for assembly at Fairey's Great West Aerodrome and first flight on September 12, 1941, behind a Whitley tug; five more prototypes built and test-flown at Portsmouth .

Horsa Mk I: Initial production version to carry 20-25 troops. 470 built by Airspeed at Christchurch, 300 by Austin Motor Co and 1,461 by Harris Lebus and Associates. First operation November 19, 1942 (two Horsas towed by Halifaxes) against Norwegian heavy water plant in Norway; first major deployment, invasion of Sicily, July 1943. Projected AS.52 to specification X.3/41 designed (but not built) to carry up to 8,000 lbs (3,632 kg) of bombs. Powered version with two 375 hp Cheetah Xs also projected, along with AS.53 vehicle-carrying glider.
Normal max towing speed, 150 mph (241 km/h). Normal gliding speed, 100 mph (161 km/h). Gross weight, 15,500 lb (7,030 kg). Span, 88 ft 0 in (26.8 m). Length, 67 ft (20.4 m).

Horsa Mk II: Version of AS.53 further developed in 1943 as AS.58 with hinged nose and reinforced floor to carry vehicles; twin nose wheels, and twin tow-rope attachment moved from underwing to nosewheel strut. 225 built by Airspeed at Christchurch; 65 by Austin Motor Co; 1,271 by Harris Lebus Group. Extensively used (some in USAAF markings) in D-Day landings and subsequent operations up to crossing of the

Above: Atlas IAC 409 (ex-RAF K1531) in RCAF service. Below: Siskin IIIA 210, delivered June 1931, served with 113(F) Sqn in 1939, was struck off September 1942.

Rhine in March 1945. A few to India for trials. Tugs included Stirling, Halifax, Albemarle, Whitley and, rarely, Dakota. Gross weight increased to 15,750 lb (7,144 kg).

ARMSTRONG WHITWORTH ATLAS I

Two-seat army co-operation biplane produced for RAF in late-1920s. RCAF acquired five Atlas I, one Atlas I dual (with 400 hp Jaguar IVB) and 10 ex-RAF Atlas IAC Jaguar VIB); a few served with 2 (AC) Squadron flying offshore patrols in late 1939 and with No 118 (Combat Alert Centre) Squadron in 1940.

Above: Horsa Is at the Heavy Glider Conversion Unit in 1943 included DP807 (No 34, right), destined to be lost at Arnhem on September 18, 1944, and HS120 (No 17). Left: The first of two AS.45 trainers, T2449 (Experimental Aeroplane 112), completed in 1941.

Max speed, 142 mph (229 km/h) at sea level. Gross weight, 4,020 lb (1,824 kg). Span, 39 ft 7 in (12.07 m) . Length, 28 ft 7 in (8.71 m).

ARMSTRONG WHITWORTH SISKIN IIIA

Single-seat biplane fighter of mid-'twenties origin. Twelve supplied to RCAF (two Mk III, eight Mk IIIA, two Mk III dual), with Jaguar IV engine, of which at least three still with 113(F) Sqn in 1939 and not finally struck off strength until war's end.
Max speed, 153 mph (246 km/h) at 10,000 ft (3,050 m). Gross weight, 3,012 lb (1,367 kg). Span, 33 ft 2 in (10.11 m). Length, 25 ft 4 in (7.72 m).

ARMSTRONG WHITWORTH AW.15 ATALANTA

Four-engined high-wing 17-seat transport built for Imperial Airways and Indian National in 1932. Five survivors of original fleet of eight impressed (as DG450-DG454) April 1941 in India and used to evacuate civilians during Iraqi rebellion, then operated by No 1 (Madras) and No 3 (Calcutta) Flights, IAF on coastal patrols, with defensive armament of one 0.303-in (7.7-mm) machine gun and crew of three. Retired August 1942. Four 340 hp Serval III engines.
Max speed, 156 mph (251 km/h) at 3,000 ft (914 m). Gross weight, 21,000 lb (9,525 kg). Span, 90 ft 0 in (27.43 m). Length, 71 ft 6 in (21.79 m).

ARMSTRONG WHITWORTH A.W.23

Single prototype (K3585) bomber/transport to C.26/31, first flown on June 4, 1935, became a tanker for Flight Refuelling Ltd in 1937. Registered G-AFRX in April 1939. stored at Ford Aerodrome, Sussex, before War started and destroyed there in enemy air raid on August 18, 1940.

ARMSTRONG WHITWORTH A.W.27 ENSIGN

Four-engined 27-40 passenger airliner designed by J Lloyd to an Imperial Airways

Below: A.W.15 Atalanta, originally G-ABTL 'Astraea', impressed as DG450 to serve with No 1 (Madras) and No 3 (Calcutta) Flights, IAF, until August 1942.

Above: Ensign II G-ADSV 'Explorer' on wartime service with BOAC at Takoradi, West Africa until the War ended. Left: Ninth production Whitley I K7191, delivered 1937, flew with nos 10 and 166 Sqns before being struck off October 1940. Below: Whitley II K7244 G:George of No 7 Sqn, crashed in Abersoch Bay February 19, 1941.

specification in 1934, and first flown on January 24, 1938, at Hamble. Twelve Ensign Mk 1 (935 hp Tiger IXC engines) built, all used by National Air Communications service (with civilian crews and registrations) from September 1939 to June 1940.

Max speed, 182 mph (293 km/h). Gross weight, 49,000 lb (22,226 kg). Span, 123 ft 0 in (37.5 m). Length, 114 ft 0 in (34.8 m).

Ensign II: Eight surviving Ensign Is converted 1941-43 to have 950 hp Cyclone GR-1820-G102A engines plus two new-built aircraft to similar standard, with gross weight of 55,500 lb (25,174 kg) and max speed of 210 mph (338 km/h). Based in Middle East to operate BOAC routes from East Africa to India until end of War. One force-landed in French West Africa February 1942, then used by Vichy French forces and Air France until impressed for service with *Luftwaffe*.

ARMSTRONG WHITWORTH A.W.38 WHITLEY

The A.W.38 was designed under the direction of J Lloyd to the requirements of Specification B.3/34 for a five-seat 'heavy bomber' replacement for the Heyford and Hendon, to carry a 2,500-lb (1,135-kg) bomb load over 1,250 mls (2,010 km) at 225 mph (362 km/h) at 15,000 ft (4,575 m). First of two prototypes (K4586) with 795 hp Tiger IX engines flown at Whitley, Coventry, aerodrome on March 17, 1936. Second prototype (K4587) with Tiger XIs flown February 11, 1937.

Whitley I: First contract for 80 Whitley Mk Is placed 'off the drawing board' in June 1935. First example flown December 23, 1936; deliveries to No 10 Sqn, RAF, on March 9, later to Nos 51 and 78 Sqns. Tiger IX engines; armament of single 0.303-in (7.7-mm) Lewis gun each in front (A.W. or Nash and Thompson) and rear (A.W.) manual turrets. Production terminated at 34th aircraft.

Whitley II: Final 46 aircraft on initial contract completed with 920 hp Tiger VIIIs with two-speed superchargers, to

Specification B.21/35. Deliveries mid-1938, to Nos 7, 51, 58 and 97 Sqns. One Whitley II (K7243) test-bed for AS Deerhound 21-cyl air-cooled radial engine, flown Jan 1939-March 1940.

Whitley III: Second production batch of 80, to Specification B.20/36, similar to Whitley Mk II but with powered Nash and Thompson single-gun nose turret and retractable ventral 'dustbin' turret with two 0.303-in (7.7-mm) Brownings. Bomb-bay and racks modified for larger bombs. Deliveries second half of 1938 to replace Mk Is and IIs and also to Nos 77, 97, 102 and 166 Sqns. Early marks of Whitley from Nos 51 and 58 Sqns flew first RAF *Nickel* (leaflet) raid over Germany on night of September 3/4, 1939.

Max speed, 193 mph (311 km/h) at 14,250 ft (4,343 m). Cruising speed, 164 mph (264 km/h) at 15,000 ft (4,575 m). Time to 15,000 ft (4,575 m), 44 min. Service ceiling, 17,000 ft (5,182 m). Range with standard fuel, 1,190

mls (1,914 km). Gross weight, 26,500 lb (12,031 kg). Span, 84 ft 0 in (25.60 m). Length, 69 ft 4 in (21.12 m).

Whitley IV: Final 40 aircraft on second production contract (additional to 80 Mk IIIs) fitted with Merlin in-line engines and extra fuel tanks. Prototype (converted Mk I K7208) first flown at Hucknall on February 11, 1938; first production Whitley IV flown on April 5, 1939 with Merlin IVs; final seven aircraft had 1,070 hp Merlin Xs and designated Whitley IVA.

Whitley V: Contracts placed in 1938 for 312, in 1939 for 150 and in 1940 for 1,150 Whitleys, of which 1,466 completed as Whitley Mk V and 146 as Whitley Mk VII (see below). As Mk IV with Nash and Thompson powered tail turret mounting four 0.303-in (7.7-mm) Browning guns; 15-in (38.1-cm) rear fuselage extension to improve rear gunner's field of fire; modified fin shape; wing leading-edge rubber de-icers and fuel capacity increased to 837 Imp gal (3,805 l). First production Mk V flown August 8, 1939, and initial deliveries to No 77 Sqn in September. Many Whitley Vs (and some earlier marks) used as glider tugs, with towing gear in place of rear turret or fitted beneath rear fuselage, and as paratroop transports; also used to drop agents into occupied territory. Fifteen Whitley Mk Vs transferred (with civil registrations) to BOAC for Gibraltar-Malta supply flights, 1942/43.

Max speed, 230 mph (370 km/h) at 16,400 ft (5,000 m). Cruising speed, 210 mph (338 km/h) at 15,000 ft (4,575 m). Time to 15,000 ft (4,575 m), 16 min. Service ceiling, 26,000 ft (7,925 m). Range with standard fuel, 1,500 mls (2,414 km). Gross weight, 33,500 lb (15,196 kg). Span, 84 ft 0 in (25.60 m). Length, 70 ft 6 in (21.60 m).

Whitley VII: Total of 146 Whitley Mk VII built on final production contract, plus some Mk V conversions, to serve with Coastal Command squadrons on maritime reconnaissance duties, carrying ASV Mk II radar (with four dorsal radar masts plus lateral and underwing aerials), sixth crew member and extra fuel in bomb bay and fuselage to a total of 1,100 Imp gal (5,000 l) for a range of 2,300 mls (3,700 km). Initial CC squadrons were Nos 502 (GR) and 612 (GR), using standard Whitley Vs from 1940 and 1941 respectively, with Whitley VIIs introduced 1942.

Above: Whitley V Z6640, here as Y:York in service with No 1484 Flight, survived until April 1945. Below: Whitley VII BD622, delivered July 1942 to serve with No 612 Sqn, and struck off May 12, 1944.

ARMSTRONG WHITWORTH A.W.41 ALBEMARLE

The Albemarle originated to an Air Ministry requirement for a medium bomber of composite construction, combining welded steel tube and plywood structures to permit sub-contract manufacture by light engineering and woodworking industries. Initial Specification P.9/38 revised as B.18/38 to cover design proposal by AW team under J Lloyd, for twin-engined aircraft to carry 1,500-lb (681-kg) bomb load for 2,000 mls (3,200 kg) and cruise at 250 mph (402 km/h) at 5,000 ft (1,525 m). Contract for 200 including two prototypes placed 1939; two subsequent contracts for total of 880 but 478 cancelled. Prototypes with 1,590 hp Hercules XI engines and wing span of 67 ft (20.44 m) assembled by AST at Hamble where first flown on March 20, 1940; second prototype with span of 77 ft (23.47 m) flown on April 20, 1941. Six hundred production aircraft assembled by A W Hawksley Ltd at Brockworth, Glos, from parts supplied by more than 1,000 sub-contractors; Hercules XI engines and increased-span wing; first delivery October 1941. Bomber role discontinued by late 1941 and production continued in transport and glider-tug roles in variants listed below. Entered service with No 295 Sqn early 1943; first operations during invasion of Sicily, July 1943. Equipped four RAF troop-carrying squadrons (Nos 295, 296, 297 and 570), one freighting squadron (No 511) and one special duties squadron (No 161). Data that follow are for B Mk I.

Max speed, 265 mph (427 km/h) at 10,500 ft (3,200 m). Cruising speed, 170 mph (274 km/h). Service ceiling, 18,000 ft (5,486 m). Range with normal fuel, 1,300 mls (2,092 km). Gross weight (ST), 36,500 lb (16,556 kg). Span, 77 ft (23.47 m). Length, 59 ft 11 in (18.26 m).

Albemarle I: Initial bomber-reconnaissance version with BP powered dorsal turret carrying four 0.303-in (7.7-mm) Brownings and provision for two similar guns in retractable dorsal manual turret. Fuel tanks in wing and centre fuselage.

Albemarle ST Mk I: Special transport version (troop carrier) with operational bombing equipment, ventral turret and

Above: The homebuilt Arpin A-1 — sometimes known as the 'Safety Pin' — was evaluated unsuccessfully for AOP use late in 1939. Below left: The A.W.52G glider, first flown behind a Whitley in March 1945, was a scale model of the post-war A.W.52 tailless twin-jet prototypes.

fuselage fuel tanks removed; dorsal turret replaced by hand-operated Rose two-gun installation with sliding hood. Freight loading doors in starboard fuselage side and paratroop jump doors in rear fuselage floor. Malcolm glider towing hook at rear of fuselage. Built in Srs 1, Srs 2 and Srs 3 versions with small equipment changes. 12 supplied to Soviet Union, 1943/44.

Albemarle GT Mk I: Glider towing version with similar modifications to ST Mk I but with paratroop provision. Built in Srs 2 and Srs 3 versions.

Albemarle GT Mk II: Single example of glider tug variant similar to GT Mk I.

Albemarle ST Mk II: Similar to ST Mk I special transport with equipment changes and dorsal turret re-introduced. Ninety-nine built.

Albemarle IV: Single prototype with R-2600-A5B Double Cyclone engines and dorsal turret, flown on December 12, 1942, and one production conversion.

Albemarle ST Mk V: Special transport similar to ST Mk II with changed fuel jettison system, flown July 27, 1943. Fifty built.

Albemarle ST Mk VI: Final production special transport version, with dorsal turret. One hundred and thirty-three Srs 1 built.

Albemarle GT Mk VI: Final production glider tug version, with dorsal turret. One hundred and seventeen Srs 2 built.

ARMSTRONG WHITWORTH A.W.52G

The A.W.52G flying wing glider (RG324) was built as a scale model of the A.W.52 twin-jet tailless research aircraft, two prototypes of which were built to Specification E.9/44 and flew after the end of the war. First flight of glider on March 2, 1945, with Whitley tug.

Gross weight, 6,000 lb (2,724 kg). Span, 53 ft 10 in (16.41 m). Length, 19 ft 4 in (5.89 m).

ARPIN A-1 Mk 2

A homebuilt (by M B Arpin) two-seat twin-boom cabin monoplane first flown May 7, 1938, the Arpin A-1 (G-AFGB) after conversion to have a 90 hp Cirrus Minor I as Mk 2, was evaluated by School of Army Co-operation at Old Sarum in December 1939 as a potential AOP, but Taylorcraft Plus D selected instead.

Cruising speed, 95 mph (153 km/h). Gross weight, 1,300 lb (590 kg). Span, 31 ft 6 in (9.61 m). Length, 23 ft 3 in (7.09 m).

AVRO 504N

An *ab initio* training biplane powered by a 215 hp Lynx IVC derived from an original design of pre-WWI origin, the Avro 504N had been retired by the RAF by early 1939 but seven civil examples (all ex-RAF) were impressed in 1940 and used primarily as glider tugs by Special Duty Flight, particularly in connection with radar development. Three 504s were still at Thame in October 1944 on formation of 1 GTS, and were towing such sailplanes as Minimoa and Kirby Kite, but were then replaced by Hinds and Hectors. Believed to be only aircraft of World War I vintage to serve with RAF in World War II. Twelve Avro 504Ns in service with Belgian *Aéronautique Militaire* until May 1940 were then evacuated to France. One or two survived in Greece until 1940.

Above: One of 12 Albemarle ST Mk I troop transports supplied to the Soviet Union, showing the sliding hood over the dorsal guns. Below: Here seen in service with No 297 Sqn, Albemarle ST Mk V V1823 was transferred to 22 HGCU and crashed while glider-towing on December 22, 1944.

Above: One or two Avro 504Ns, originally supplied for Greek Naval service, were still flying with the EVA (Royal Hellenic Air Force) in 1940. Below left: The first production Avro Avian, G-EBQN converted to Mk II, was among 14 Avians impressed for RAF use in 1940. Below right: Avro Five G-ABBY served as a navigation trainer until 1941.

Max speed, 100 mph (160 km/h). Gross weight, 2,240 lb (1,017 kg). Span, 36 ft 0 in (10.98 m). Length, 28 ft 6 in (8.69 m).

AVRO 616 AVIAN IVM

The South African Air Force impressed five Avian IVMs, with 100 hp Genet Major engines in 1939 for communications duties; they had been purchased new in 1929 and sold subsequently to private owners. Fourteen assorted Avians including 10 wooden Avro 594s and four metal Avian IVMs were impressed by the RAF in 1940 but were used only as instructional airframes for ground engineer training.

Max speed, 115 mph (185 km/h). Gross weight, 1,600 lb (726 kg). Span, 28 ft 0 in (8.54 m). Length, 24 ft 3 in (7.39 m).

AVRO 619 FIVE

A scaled-down derivative of Avro's licence-built Fokker F.VIIB/3m (the Avro 618 Ten), the Avro 619 Five was designed by Roy Chadwick in 1930, powered by three 105 hp Genet Majors. One example, G-ABBY, used by AST pre-war as navigation

trainer at No 3 E & RFTS, Hamble, transferred for use by No 11 Air Observers' Navigation School until March 1941.

Max speed, 118 mph (190 km/h). Gross weight, 4,620 lb (2,097 kg). Span, 47 ft 0 in (14.3 m). Length, 35 ft 9 in (10.9 m).

AVRO 621 TUTOR

The Chadwick-designed Avro 621, flown in 1929, provided the RAF with a replacement for the Avro 504N basic trainer, leading to production of 381 Tutors and 15 Avro 646 Sea Tutors. Some 200, plus five Sea Tutors, still on RAF strength when WWII began, and extensively used initially in training role, later as station hacks, etc. At least one each used in Hong Kong and Singapore. Three civil Tutors also impressed, 1940/41. Six Tutors acquired 1931 by RCAF, flown until 1943. Danish Navy had five (three-locally-built) at time of German occupation,

but stored without use. Survivors of 29 Tutors bought by Greek Air Force survived until 1941. SAAF still flying many Tutors in 1939, of some 60 acquired, primarily from local production. Standard Tutor powered by 240 hp Lynx IVC.

Max speed, 122 mph (196 km/h). Gross weight, 2,548 lb (1,115 kg). Span, 34 ft 0 in (10.37 m). Length, 26 ft 4¹/₂ in (8.04 m).

AVRO 626 and PREFECT

The Avro 626 was developed in 1930 from the Tutor with an optional third seat in a rear cockpit with provision for a gun ring. Numerous sales were made to foreign air

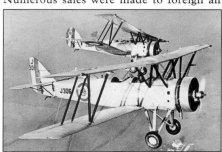

Above: Avro 626s of the Egyptian Army Air Force, where the type equipped No 1 (GP) Sqn. Below: One of the three-seat Avro 626s used by the RNZAF as instrument trainers until 1942.

Below: Tutor K6100 photographed in November 1941. Delivered to No 615 Sqn in 1935, it flew with a variety of RAF units until struck off in June 1944. Above right: Avro 621 — with long chord cowling — of the Danish Naval Air Service, one of several put into store when Germany occupied Denmark and not flown again.

forces up to 1939, some of which survived in second-line service until 1945. At least two 626s survived in Belgium's *Aéronautique Militaire* until 1940.

Max speed, 130 mph (209 km/h). Gross weight, 2,667 lb (1,211 kg). Span, 34 ft 0 in (10.37 m). Length, 26 ft 6 in (8.08 m).

Prefect: The RAF bought seven Tutor/Avro 626 hybrids, two-seaters with Lynx IVC engines, to Specification 32/34 as navigation trainers for service at School of Air Navigation, Andover. Delivered in 1935, they operated during WWII on miscellaneous duties. Four Lynx-engined Prefects supplied to RNZAF in 1935 were three-seaters; one survived to 1945.

Max speed of the Prefect was 112 mph (180 km/h), gross weight, 2,735 lb (1,242 kg), dimensions as Avro 626.

AVRO 631 and 643 CADET

This two-seat (in tandem) open cockpit biplane designed by Roy Chadwick appeared in 1932. Avro built 36 Type 631s and eight improved Type 643 Cadets, all with 135 hp Genet Major 1 radial engines, principally for civil users pre-war. Of these, 14 Type 631s used by AST at Hamble joined No 3 E & RFTS in September 1939 and were in use for about a year before being transferred to Watchfield and then impressed for further use, mostly as non-flying instructional airframes. Avro also built 27 Type 643 Mk II Cadets, with 150 hp Genet Major IA and lengthened nose, for civil use, of which 18 served similarly with No 3 E & RFTS at Hamble and No 9 E & RFTS at Ansty until transfer to Watchfield in 1940 and subsequent impressment. RAAF purchased 34 Type 643 Mk II Cadets in 1935-1939 and these served with No 1 FTS, Point Cook, and Nos 21 (City of Melbourne) and 22 (City of Sydney) squadrons for most of the war, 16 surviving to 1945.

Max speed, 116 mph (187 km/h). Gross weight, 2,000 lb (908 kg). Span, 30 ft 2 in (9.19 m). Length, 24 ft 9 in (7.54 m).

AVRO 638 CLUB CADET

An improved version of the Avro Cadet, the Type 638 Club Cadet appeared in 1933 with Genet Major I engine. Re-engined with an in-line 130 hp Gipsy Major, a single example, G-ACHP, was impressed as HM570 in July 1942 and operated throughout the war as a communications aircraft for Saunders-Roe, flying between Eastleigh on the mainland and Cowes on the Isle of Wight.

Max speed, 115 mph (185 km/h). Gross weight, 2,000 lb (908 kg). Span, 30 ft 2 in (9.19 m). Length, 24 ft 9 in (7.54 m).

AVRO 641 COMMODORE

A four/five-seat cabin biplane designed by

Above: A Type 643 Mk II Cadet in RAAF service in 1939. Sixteen survived to 1945, of 34 purchased as primary trainers. Below left: The sole Club Cadet impressed by the RAF, which survived the war and is seen here in 1952.

Roy Chadwick in 1934, the Commodore was powered by the 240 hp Lynx IVC engine. Of six built, two were impressed in 1941, one, DJ710, being used by the ATA at White Waltham until August 1941 and the other, HH979, by No 17 OTU, Cranfield, until August 1942. Two others in Egypt in 1936 were acquired by Egyptian Army Air Force and at least one was still in use for communications in 1941.

Max speed, 130 mph (209 km/h). Gross weight, 3,500 lb (1,588 kg). Span, 37 ft 4 in (11.38 m). Length, 27 ft 3 in (8.31 m).

AVRO 652

The Avro 652 was designed by Roy Chadwick to meet an Imperial Airways specification for a long-range twin-engined light transport, combining Avro and Fokker structural principles with a one-piece wooden mainplane and a welded steel tube fuselage. Powered by 270 hp Cheetah V engines and with hand-worked retractable undercarriage, two prototypes were built at Manchester and first flight was made at Woodford on January 7, 1935. Both aircraft acquired by AST as navigation trainers for No 11 Air Observers' Navigation School in 1938; impressed February 1941 as DG655 and DG656 for use by No 1 School of Photography and then served with No 811 Squadron, RN.

Max speed, 195 mph (314 km/h). Gross weight, 7,400 lb (3,360 kg). Span, 56 ft 6 in (17.23 m). Length, 42 ft 3 in (12.89 m).

AVRO 652A ANSON

The Avro Type 652A Anson was evolved by a design team headed by Roy Chadwick in 1934, responding to a specification calling for a coastal patrol landplane. The RAF requirements indicated an aeroplane of similar characteristics to the Avro 652 (see previous entry) already designed for Imperial Airways, and the Type 652A was of similar size and configuration, with 295 hp Cheetah VI engines in helmeted cowlings; larger, square, windows; provision for an Armstrong Whitworth hand-operated dorsal turret with a single 0.303-in (7.7-mm) gun, a single forward-firing Vickers gun of similar calibre in the fuselage, and a 360-lb (163-kg) bomb-load in the centre section. A single prototype was flown on March 24, 1935, and production was ordered on May 25 to Specification 18/35, with later batches to 16/37 and 34/37.

Anson Mk I: Initial production version, differing from prototype in having 350 hp Cheetah IXs and increased cabin windows. First example flown December 31, 1935; deliveries to RAF began in February 1936 and first squadron, No 48, commissioned at Manston on March 6, the Anson thus becoming the first monoplane and first aircraft with retractable undercarriage to reach RAF squadron service. Served operationally with Coastal Command squadrons until 1940, and on air-sea rescue duties until 1942; thereafter as a trainer for pilots, navigators and air gunners, mostly with no dorsal turret but including 313 fitted with Bristol B.1 Mk VI powered turrets. Also widely used for communication duties by RAF and other air forces, including USAAF in the UK.

Total of 1,026 exported to Australia starting in 1936, 48 initially to equip RAAF general reconnaissance squadrons and 978 later primarily for use in Empire Air Training

Below left: Of six Avro Commodores built, two went to the Egyptian Army Air Force, and saw some wartime service. Below right: The Avro 652 G-ACRN, built for Imperial Airways, was eventually impressed for the training of air photographers.

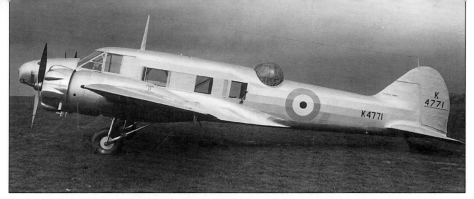

Above: The prototype Anson, based on the civil Type 652, as flown in March 1935, with AW dorsal turret. Left: An early production Anson I in the pre-war markings of No 233 Sqn, one of the Coastal Command squadrons that flew the type briefly on operations in 1939. Below: A late production Anson I, with Bristol dorsal turret, serving with No 1 AGS.

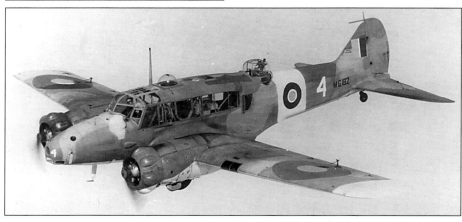

Anson Mk IV: As Anson Mk I with 300 hp Whirlwind R-760-E1 engines. Prototype conversion, R9816, in England and 169 Mk Is and IIIs converted in Canada in 1943.

Anson Mk V: Improved Canadian production version with Vidal-mounted plywood fuselage in place of original Fokker-type steel tube fuselage construction. Used 450 hp R-985-AN12B or -AN14B engines with constant speed propellers. No dorsal turret. Prototype flown in 1942; 1,049 built for RCAF service, deliveries ended 1945.
Max speed, 190 mph (306 km/h). Cruising speed, 145 mph (233 km/h). Initial climb, 1,500 ft/min (7.63 m/sec). Service ceiling, 21,450 ft (6.542 m). Gross weight, 9,460 lb (4,295 kg). Span, 56 ft 6 in (17.23 m). Length, 42 ft 3 in (12.89 m).

Anson Mk VI: Gunnery trainer, as Mk V with Bristol B Mk VI dorsal turret. One only, serial 13881.

Anson X: British production version, as Mk I with strengthened floor for heavy freight; many fitted with transparent nose cap and smooth engine cowlings. Production of 120 by Avro at Yeadon, 1943, included Series Is with Cheetah IXs and Series 2s with 395 hp Cheetah XIXs and hydraulic u/c operation. Some Mk I conversions.

Anson XI: Improved Mk X transport with deepened fuselage and individual square windows in cabin; hydraulically-operated u/c as Canadian Mk II; 395 hp Cheetah XIXs with fixed-pitch Fairey-Reed metal propellers. Some fitted as ambulances, with stretcher-loading doors in port side. Total of 90 delivered, 1944/45.

Anson XII: Similar to Anson Mk XI with 420 hp Cheetah XVs and Rotol cs propellers with spinners. Prototype first flown September 5, 1944; 271 built.
Max speed, 190 mph (306 km/h). Cruising speed, 167 mph (269 km/h). Gross weight, 10,500 lb (4,767 kg).

Scheme; also supplied to Canada (1,528), Rhodesia (79), New Zealand (23) and South Africa (768) for the EATS. Three to Finnish Air Force, 1937; one to Estonian Air Force, 1937; four to Irish Army Air Corps, 1938; six to Turkish Air Force, 1939; 12 to Greek Air Force, 1939 of which some captured by *Luftwaffe* in 1941 and five transferred to Egyptian Army Air Force to equip a light Bomber Squadron, joining one Avro 652 Mk II and several Anson Is previously supplied; several to Royal Iraqi Air Force 1938/39, destroyed May 1941; 48 to Imperial Iranian Air Force 1943/44; 17 to Free French Air Forces up to 1945, others post-War. Total Mk I production, 6,726 by Avro at Newton Heath and Yeadon.
Max speed, 188 mph (302 km/h). Cruising speed, 158 mph (254 km/h). Initial climb, 960 ft/min (4.88 m/sec). Service ceiling, 19,000 ft (5,795 m). Range, 660 mls (1,062 km). Gross weight (coastal patrol), 9,300 lb (4,222 kg); (gunnery trainer), 9,850 lb (4,472 kg). Span, 56 ft 6 in (17.23 m). Length, 42 ft 3 in (12.89 m).

Anson Mk II: Canadian production version of Anson Mk I, under direction of Federal Aircraft Ltd with participation by de Havilland, Canadian Vickers, CCF, National Steel Car Co, Ottawa Car and Aircraft Co and Macdonald Bros. Fitted with faired plastic-bonded Vidal nose, Dowty hydraulic u/c retraction and 330 hp Jacobs L6MB engines with smooth cowlings. Total of 1,832 built; all served in Canada for CATP except 50 supplied to USAAF in 1942/43 as AT-20 navigation trainers.
Max speed, 178 mph (286 km/h). Gross weight, 7,660 lb (3,477 kg). Span, 56 ft 6 in (17.23 m). Length, 42 ft 3 in (12.89 m).

Anson Mk III: Total of 150 British-built Anson Mk Is converted in Canada to have 330 hp Jacobs L6MB engines. Prototype flown May 1941.

Above: The first production Anson V, serial 11581, which reached the RCAF in February 1943 and survived until mid-1947. Right: Anson II serial 11371 served in RCAF's 2 Training Command from 1943 to 1948. Below: The first Anson XII, MG159, showing the deepened fuselage and square cabin windows.

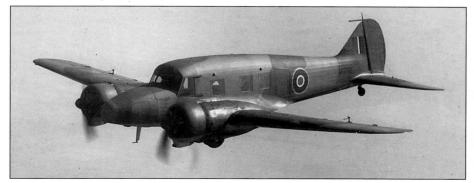

AVRO 671 ROTA

The Rota was the name given to the Cierva C.30A by the RAF, for which it was built under licence by Avro. It is described later under the Cierva heading.

AVRO 674

This type number was given to a version of the Hawker Audax developed by Avro in 1936 to an Egyptian Government requirement, having a 750 hp Panther VIA engine and other improvements. Six delivered in March 1937 plus 18 more with Panther Xs in February-May 1938, some being in service on border patrols up to the time of the Italian invasion in 1940. No precise specification details are available.

AVRO 679 MANCHESTER

Designed under the direction of Roy Chadwick, the Avro 679 Manchester was a twin-engined medium bomber to Specification P.13/36, ordered in 1937 for competitive evaluation with the Handley Page H.P.56. Powered by two 1,760 hp Vulture I X-type engines, the first of two prototypes flew on July 25, 1939, unarmed and with twin fins and rudders; a third, central fin was added after early flight tests. The second prototype flew on May 26, 1940, with two 0.303-in (7.7-mm) machine guns each in nose, tail and ventral Frazer Nash turrets, and wing span increased from 80 ft 2 in (24.45 m) to 90 ft 1 in (27.48 m). The ventral turret was later replaced by a dorsal FN 7 turret, also with two guns, and production aircraft to this configuration were ordered to Specification 19/37.

Manchester Mk I: Initial production batch of 200 ordered from Avro, Manchester, in December 1937, and 100 ordered from Metropolitan-Vickers Ltd, Trafford Park, in 1939. Deliveries began on July 31, 1940, from Avro assembly line and on March 10, 1941, from Metrovick, production terminating at 157 Avro and 43 Metrovick aircraft for a total of 200. Initial deliveries to No 207 Sqn, RAF, November

Above: An adaptation of the Hawker Audax, the Panther-engined Avro 674 was built only for the Egyptian Army Air Force, many of the 24 delivered in 1937/38 seeing wartime service alongside the RAF.

1940 and first operation February 24/25, 1941.

Manchester Mk IA: Later production aircraft were delivered with a tailplane of increased span (33 ft/10.1 m), taller fins and rudders and no central fin. These were designated Manchester Mk IA and all Mk Is were eventually converted to this standard. *Cruising speed, 205 mph (330 km/h). Ceiling, 19,200 ft (5,856 m). Range, 1,200 mls (1,930 km) with 10,350 lb (4,699 kg) bomb load, 1,630 mls (2,188 km) with 8,100-lb (3,677-kg) bomb load. Gross weight (Mk I), 50,000 lb (22,700 kg), (Mk IA), 56,000 lb (25,424 kg). Span, 90ft 1 in (27.48 m); length, 68 ft 10 in (20.99 m).*

AVRO 683 LANCASTER

Avro's design team under Roy Chadwick evolved a scheme for a Manchester III powered by four 1,145 hp Rolls-Royce Merlin Xs, to overcome difficulties with the Vulture engine installation in the earlier twin-

Above: First Lancaster prototype (BT308) with Manchester I-type tail unit and no dorsal turret. Below: The second prototype (DG585) showing definitive tail unit, no dorsal turret fairing, and retracted ventral turret.

The third Lancaster prototype (DT810) was the Hercules-engined Mk II, shown (above) in original guise and (below) with dorsal turret fairing and deepened bomb-bay.

engined bomber. With a new wider centre section and re-named Lancaster, a prototype flew on January 9, 1941, at first with standard Manchester I triple-fin tail unit and later with Manchester IA enlarged twin fins and wider tailplane. Second prototype, with 1,280 hp Merlin XXs, flown May 13, 1941.

Lancaster B Mk I: Production initiated 1941, replacing final 243 Manchesters on A V Roe contracts and 57 on Metropolitan-Vickers contracts, and then continuing on major new contracts placed with Avro (Chadderton and Yeadon), Vickers-

Above: The seventh production Manchester I (L7248) in service with the first user squadron, No 207 at RAF Waddington, showing original tail unit and early lack of dorsal turret. Below: Also serving with No 207, Manchester IA (L7515) displays the dorsal turret and later tail unit.

Above: An early Lancaster I (R5556), flown by No 44 Sqn on two missions to Essen before transfer to No 1661 CU. Left: Lancaster II (DS689) was lost on a mission to Stuttgart in Dec 1943, flying with No 426 (Canadian) Sqn. Below: The first Lancaster B Mk I (Special) (PB995), carrying a 22,000-lb Grand Slam bomb on trials from the A & AEE, early 1945, with nose and dorsal turrets retained.

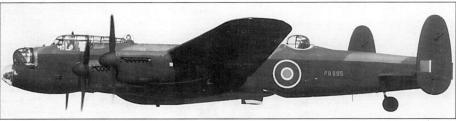

Armstrong (Chester and Castle Bromwich), Armstrong Whitworth (Baginton), Austin (Longbridge) and Metrovick (Manchester). Initially with 1,280 hp Merlin XXs; Merlin 22s and Merlin 24s later, with higher boost ratings. Armament comprised two 0.303-in (7.7-mm) Browning guns each in nose and dorsal turrets, four in tail turret and provision for two in remotely-sighted ventral barbette, little used, especially after ventral H2S radome fitted; turrets by Frazer Nash or Rose. Some later Mk Is had a single 0.303-in (7.7-mm) or 0.50-in (12.7-mm) ventral gun, manually operated, and a two-gun tail turret. Initial design bomb load, 4,000 lb (1,816 kg), later increased to 18,000 lb (8,172 kg) without special mods, including standard 8,000 lb (3,632 kg) and 12,000 lb (5,448 kg) bombs. Aircraft of Nos 9 and 617 Sqn modified in 1944 to carry 12,000-lb (5,448-kg) 'Tallboy' bomb and used to attack and sink *Tirpitz* on November 12, 1944. Lancaster entered service with No 44 (Rhodesia) Sqn, Waddington, and used for first operational sortie on March 3, 1942. Total production, 3,434 (including special Mk I variants noted below).
Max speed, 275 mph (442 km/h) fully loaded at 15,000 ft (4,572 m). Service ceiling, 24,500 ft (7,468 m). Range, 1,660 mls (2,670 km) at 210 mph (338 km/h) with 14,000-lb (6,356-kg) bomb load. Gross weight, initially, 60,000 lb (27,240 kg); later 65,000 lb (29,510 kg). Span, 102 ft 0 in (31.09 m). Length, 68 ft 11 in (21.0 m).
Lancaster B Mk I (Special): 33 aircraft with Merlin 24s modified 1945 for 617 Sqn to carry 22,000-lb (9,988-kg) 'Grand Slam' bomb, with no bomb-bay doors, and nose and dorsal turrets and H2S removed. First operation March 14, 1945, against Bielefeld Viaduct. Gross weight, 72,000 lb (32,688 kg).
Lancaster B Mk I (FE): Late production aircraft for Tiger Force operation against Japanese targets in the Far East, with modified radio, radar and navaids, and white top/black underside finish. Two Lancaster Is tested (by No 1577 SD Flight)

in India and Australia in 1945 with long range saddle tank in upper fuselage aft of cockpit, for possible Tiger Force application. Two other Mk Is used by No 1577 SD Flight to tow Horsa and Hamilcar gliders in trials for India-Burma operations.
Lancaster II: Similar to Mk I but with four 1,725 hp Hercules VI or XVI radial air-cooled engines. Single prototype by Avro, first flown on November 26, 1941, and 300 built by Armstrong Whitworth. Deliveries starting October 1942. Performance, armament and bomb load similar to Mk I.
Lancaster B Mk III: Similar to Mk I but with Packard-built 1,300 hp Merlin 28, 1,390 hp Merlin 38 or 1,620 hp Merlin 224 engines supplied from USA. Armament and bomb load similar to Mk 1. Production totalled 3,020 including 136 by Metrovick and 110 by Armstrong Whitworth, the remainder by Avro. Twenty-three Mk IIIs converted by Avro in 1943 to carry Vickers Type 464 spinning bomb for use by No 617 Sqn with front and dorsal turret and bomb doors removed, small VSG hydraulic motor

in fuselage to spin weapon before release, and single 0.303-in (7.7-mm) ventral gun fitted. First bomb drop on April 16, 1943, and used to attack Mohne, Eder and Sorpe dams on May 17/18, 1943.
Max speed, 270 mph (434 km/h) at 19,000 ft (5,791 m). Cruising speed, 210 mph (338 km/h). Initial rate of climb, about 600 ft/min (3.05 m/sec). Time to 20,000 ft (6,100 m), 43.5 min. Service ceiling, 21,500 ft (6,553 m). Range, 2,230 mls (3,588 km) with 7,000-lb (3,178 km) bomb load. Empty weight, 41,000 lb (18,614 km). Normal loaded weight, 53,000 lb (24,062 kg). Maximum take-off weight, 65,000 lb (29,510 kg). Span, 102 ft 0 in (31.09 m). Length, 68 ft 11 in (21.02 m). Height, 19 ft 6 in (5.95 m). Wing area, 1,297 sq ft (120.5 m²).
Lancaster VI: Nine Lancaster IIIs fitted with 1,635 hp Merlin 85 engines and four-blade propellers for general engine development by Rolls-Royce (including other two-stage Merlin marks in due course) and as potential successor to the Mks I and II. First conversion June/July 1943, service trials by Nos 7 and 635 Sqn (with nose and dorsal turrets removed) until November 1944.
Lancaster B Mk VII: Similar to B Mk III, with Packard Merlin engines but with Martin 250 CE 23A dorsal turret mounting two 0.50-in (12.7-mm) machine guns. 180 built by Austin, deliveries starting April 1945; some equipped for Tiger Force in Far East and designated Lancaster B Mk VII (FE).
Lancaster B Mk X: Similar to B Mk III, built in Canada by Victory Aircraft with Merlin 38 or 224, deepened bomb-bay and (later aircraft) Martin dorsal turret. First flown on August 6, 1943; 430 built.
Lancaster XPP: Two Lancaster Xs converted by Victory Aircraft as passenger and mail carriers (CF-CMT, CF-CMU), for TCA, with fairings over nose and tail turret positions, no dorsal turret, extra fuel in bomb bay and ten seats, following similar initial conversion of one Mk I (CF-CMS).

AVRO 685 YORK
Military transport version of the Lancaster, evolved by Roy Chadwick in parallel with the bomber prototype, having the same wings, power plant, undercarriage and tail unit with a square-section fuselage providing double the capacity. Prototype flown July 5, 1942, followed by three more prototypes of varying standard and introducing a third central fin. Production deliveries to

Above: A Canadian-built Lancaster B Mk X (KB783), showing Martin dorsal turret and deepened bomb-bay of this version. After service in Britain, this example became A451 as a ground instructional airframe in Canada. Below: Austin-built Lancaster B Mk VII(FE) serving with 1689 Flight in mid-1945.

Specification C.1/42 began 1944, and total of 208 eventually built for RAF by 1948. Used by RAF as York C Mk I in all-passenger, all-freight and combined passenger/freight versions, initially by No 24 Sqn (from April 1944). Also used as VIP transport. Five transferred to BOAC in 1944 and used with 12 seats plus freight compartment to open UK-Cairo route on April 22, 1944. One prototype converted to York C Mk II with 1,650 hp Hercules VI; basic York C Mk I had 1,620 hp Merlin T24s. One York C Mk I Special built by Victory Aircraft for RCAF, first flown November 1944.

Max speed, 298 mph (479 km/h). Cruising speed, 233 mph (375 km/h). Initial rate of climb, 1,500 ft/min (25.0 m/sec). Ceiling, 26,000 ft (7,925 m). Range, 2,700 mls (4,344 km). Empty weight, 42,040 lb (19,086 kg). Gross weight, 68,000 lb (30,872 kg). Span, 102 ft 0 in (31.09 m). Length, 78 ft 6 in (23.93 m). Wing area, 1,205 sq ft (111.9 m²).

AVRO 691 LANCASTRIAN

Following development of the Lancaster XPP for TCA, six more Lancaster Mk Xs were more extensively converted with elongated nose and tail cones, 3½-ton (3 560-kg) mail capacity, windows in the rear fuselage and ten passenger seats. Operated by TCA on North Atlantic route, 1944/45, and known as Lancastrians.

Lancastrian C Mk I: Basic Lancaster I airframe adapted for transport duties to Specification 16/44, similar to Victory Aircraft conversion in Canada. Nine passengers, plus freight and mail. 1,635 hp Merlin T.24/2 engines. Twenty-three built, 1944/45, on RAF contract and transferred to BOAC for operation on UK-Australia route, commencing May 31, 1945. Subsequent marks built post-war.

Max speed, 310 mph (499 km/h). Cruising speed, 230 mph (370 km/h). Range, 4,150 mls (6,677 km). Gross weight, 65,000 lb (29,510 kg). Span, 102 ft 0 in (31.09 m). Length, 76 ft 10 in (23.43 m).

AVRO 694 LINCOLN

Designed by Roy Chadwick to Specification B.14/43 as a Lancaster variant (originally Lancaster IV and Lancaster V with Merlin 85 and Merlin 68A respectively) with greater wing span, enlarged fuselage and increased performance. Prototype first flown June 9, 1944, with Merlin 85s; armament of paired 0.50-in (12.7-mm) machine guns in nose, dorsal and tail turrets, and bomb-load up to 14,000 lb (6,356 kg). Production Lincoln B Mk Is entered service

Above: An early production Avro York in its original Transport Command camouflage, which was giving way to an overall natural metal finish by the time the war ended.

with No 57 Sqn at East Kirkby in August 1945 in preparation for joining Tiger Force in the Far East.

Max speed, 295 mph (475 km/h) at 15,000 ft (4 572 m). Cruising speed, 215 mph (346 km/h) at 20,000 ft (6,100 m). Initial climb, 800 ft/min (4.06 m/sec). Service ceiling, 30,500 ft (9,296 m). Time to 20,000 ft (6,100 m), 26½ min. Range, 1,470 mls (2,365 km) with max bomb load. Empty weight, 43,778 lb (19,875 kg). Gross weight, 82,000 lb (37,228 kg). Span, 120 ft 0 in (36.58 m). Length, 78 ft 3½ in (23.85 m). Wing area, 1,421 sq ft (132.0 m²).

AVRO 688 TUDOR

Intended for post-war commercial use, the Tudor was the first British transport aircraft with a pressurised cabin. Although it had no military applications, it qualifies for a men-

Above: British-built Lancaster I (R5727) after its conversion to transport configuration (as CF-CMS) by Victory Aircraft in Canada. Below: Canadian-built Lancaster KB702 partially converted as Mk XPP; it later became CF-CMT for use by TCA.

Below: Avro Lancastrian 1 G-AGLV (allocated serial VF163) was certificated in April 1945 for service with BOAC, and operated the first service to Australia at the end of May.

tion in this review as it flew before VJ-Day, on June 14, 1945. This first flight was made by the first of two prototypes ordered in September 1944 (as TT176 and TT181) carrying neither its military nor its civil registration, G-AGPF.

BAC DRONE DE LUXE

One example of this powered glider, G-AEKT, with a Carden Ford engine, was flown (in full RAF colours and coded PR-?) for light relief by pilots of No 609 Sqn until

April 1941, when it was destroyed. One other Drone (G-AEKM) was used briefly in 1941/42 by various establishments at Ringway.

Max speed, 73 mph (117 km/h). Gross weight, 720 lb (327 kg). Span, 39 ft 8 in (12.09 m). Length, 21 ft 2 in (6.45 m).

Below: Lincoln I (RA638) was delivered by Metrovick early in 1945 and retained Bomber Command European night bomber finish as it was assigned to trials at the BBU and LRWE. Right: The BAC Drone G-AEKT bearing the codes of No 609 Sqn in 1940/41.

BAYNES BAT

The Bat was a one-third scale model of a proposed Carrier Wing, comprising a set of wings to be attached to a tank to permit it to be towed as a glider. Designed by L E Baynes, the Bat was built by Slingsby Sailplanes and first flown at Sherburn-in-Elmet, HQ of Airborne Forces Experimental Establishment, by Flt Lt Robert Kronfeld in July 1943. Later used at RAE for stability and control investigations on tailless aircraft.

Max free flight speed, fully loaded, 90 mph (145 km/h). Gross weight, 963 lb (437 kg). Span, 33 ft 4 in (10.16 m). Length, 11 ft 4'/2 in (3.46 m). Wing area, 160 sq ft (14.86 m²).

BLACKBURN B-2

Side-by-side trainer first flown 1932, the B-2 was built in small numbers until 1937 and usually powered by a 120 hp Cirrus Hermes IVA or 135 hp Cirrus Major I engine; some with 120 hp Gipsy III or 130 hp Gipsy Major. Equipped No 4 Elementary Flying Training School at Brough until February, 1942, when 26 surviving examples were impressed and given to ATC units as instructional airframes.

Max speed, 112 mph (180 km/h). Gross weight, 1,850 lb (840 kg). Span, 30 ft 2 in (9.19 m). Length, 24 ft 3 in (7. 39 m).

BLACKBURN T.5 RIPPON IIF

Designed in 1925 by Major F A Bumpus as a replacement for the Dart, the two-seat Rippon torpedo-bomber served in the Fleet Air Arm until 1934. A single specimen with a Jupiter VIII engine was sold to the Finnish Air Force in 1929 as the Rippon IIF and 25 more were built by the Valtion

Above: The Baynes Bat successfully demonstrated - in small scale - the feasibility of adding a 'carrier wing' to an armoured vehicle, but the tank-carrying Hamilcar was preferred. The Bat was identified as Experimental Aeroplane 209 in the contemporary AP. 1480X recognition manual. Below: Blackburn B-2 G-ACBJ, with Gipsy III engine, serving at No 4 EFTS, Brough, in 1940.

Lentokonetehdas at Tampere under licence between 1931 and 1934 — seven with 480 hp Gnome-Rhone Jupiter VI 9AK, eight with 535 hp Panther IIA and ten with 580 hp Pegasus II.M3. Single trial installations were made of the 525 hp Cyclone R-1750, 525 hp BMW-132A, 525 hp Hornet B, 650 hp Tiger I and 600 hp Hispano-Suiza 12Nbr. Armament comprised one forward and one aft 0.303-in (7.7-mm) machine gun, with provision for a torpedo under the fuselage and bombs under the wings. The Rippon IIFs operated primarily in a recon-

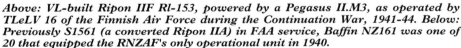

Above: VL-built Ripon IIF Rl-153, powered by a Pegasus II.M3, as operated by TLeLV 16 of the Finnish Air Force during the Continuation War, 1941-44. Below: Previously S1561 (a converted Ripon IIA) in FAA service, Baffin NZ161 was one of 20 that equipped the RNZAF's only operational unit in 1940.

naissance role, serving with LeLv 16, 36 and 39 in the Winter War and then with LeLv 6 and 16 in the Continuation War, for anti-shipping patrols, casualty evacuation and supply carrying. Some operated on skis or floats, as required.

Max speed, 118 mph (190 km/h) at sea level, 128 mph (206 km/h) at 5,000 ft (1,525 m). Initial rate of climb, 510 ft/min (2.60 m/sec). Service ceiling, 8,700 ft (2,650 m). Range, 1,127 mls (1,813 km). Empty weight, 3,850 kg) . Gross weight, 7,000 lb (3,178 kg). Span, 45 ft 6'/2 in (13. 87 m). Length, 36 ft 9 in (11.2 m). Wing area, 683 sq ft (63.5 m²).

BLACKBURN B-5 BAFFIN

The B-5 Baffin was evolved under the direction of Major F A Bumpus in 1932 as a version of the earlier Ripon torpedo bomber, with a 545 hp Pegasus I.MS engine. Armament of the two-seat Baffin comprised one fixed forward-firing 0.303-in (7.7-mm) Vickers gun and one free-mounted Lewis gun in rear cockpit, plus one 2,000-lb (908-kg) bomb or 1,576-kg (716-kg) Mk VIII or Mk IX torpedo or three 530-lb (241-kg) or six 250-lb (114-kg) bombs. Starting in 1937, a total of 29 Baffins, with 565 hp Pegasus I.M3 or 580 hp Pegasus II.M3 engines, was acquired ex-RAF service by the RNZAF and used to equip the newly-formed Territorial Squadrons at Wellington, Christchurch and Auckland, all of which were fully operational by September 1939. First operations November 16, 1939. The Baffin squadrons were merged in March 1940 as the NZ General Reconnaissance Squadron, renamed No 1 GR Squadron in

Above: After pre-war service at Gosport and Lee, Shark II K8485 found its way to the A & AEE, Boscombe Down, where – with deck arrester hook deleted – it was photographed in November 1941. Right: Delivered to the FAA early in 1937 as a Shark II, K8513 was converted to Mk III with a cockpit canopy and is seen here in floatplane configuration. Far right: Tiger-engined Shark II serial 504 in (pre-war) service with No 6(TB) Sqn of the RCAF at Trenton, Ontario.

1941 when half the Baffins were transferred to No 3 GR Squadron.

Max speed, 125 mph (201 km/h) at sea level and 136 mph (219 km/h) at 6,500 ft (1,981 m). Initial rate of climb, 480 ft/min (2.44 m/sec). Service ceiling, 15,000 ft (4,572 m). Endurance, 4¹/₂hr. Gross weight, 7,610 lb (3,455 kg). Span, 45 ft 6¹/₂ in (13.87 m). Length, 38 ft 3³/₄ in (11.67 m). Wing area, 649 sq ft (60.29 m²).

BLACKBURN B-6 SHARK

The B-6 Shark was designed and built, initially as a private venture, to Specification S.15/33 for a torpedo-spotter-reconnaissance aircraft to be operated by the Fleet Air Arm. It had a crew of three, with observer/wireless operator and gunner sharing the second cockpit (open on Mks I and II, enclosed on Mk III). Armament com-

prised one fixed forward-firing 0.303-in (7.7-mm) Vickers gun plus a ring-mounted Vickers K in the rear cockpit, plus provision for a 1,500-lb torpedo or equivalent bombload externally. Prototype with 700 hp Tiger IV flown at Brough on August 24, 1933. Production for Fleet Air Arm totalled 16 Mk I (Tiger IV), 126 Mk II (760 hp Tiger VI) and 95 Mk III (760 hp Tiger VI); at least 22 Mk IIs and IIIs (all brought up to Mk III standard) were converted 1937/38 as target tugs and operated in this role and for training and communications until 1942. Sharks based in Seletar as target tugs operated against Japanese invaders over Malaya in January 1942.

Data for Shark III (Tiger VI): Max speed, 162 mph (261 km/h) at 5,500 ft (1,676 m). Initial rate of climb, 1,350 ft/min (6.86 m/sec). Service ceiling, 20,400 ft (6,218 m). Range 680 mls (1,094 km). Empty weight, 4,153 lb (1,885 kg). Gross weight, 7,323 lb (3,325 kg). Span, 46 ft 0 in (14.02 m). Length, 35 ft 3 in (10.74 m). Wing area, 489 sq ft (45.43 m²).

Canadian Sharks: The RCAF purchased seven Shark II (760 hp Tiger VI) in 1936 for service with No 6 (TB) Squadron, later operating as No 6 (BR) Sqn on shipping patrols off the Canadian west coast. Two Shark IIIs (800 hp Pegasus III) were supplied to RCAF by Blackburn in 1939 as forerunners of 17 similar aircraft built by Boeing Aircraft of Canada at Vancouver, with 840 hp Pegasus IX and used by Nos 6 and 4 (BR) Squadrons. RCAF Sharks, some of which operated as floatplanes, were withdrawn from service in August 1944 and five were then transferred to the RN Air Observers' School in Trinidad.

BLACKBURN B-24 SKUA I

Designed by G E Petty to Specification O.27/34, the B-24 Skua was the first deck-landing monoplane fighter-bomber produced for the Fleet Air Arm. The prototype, with 840 hp Mercury IX, flew on February 9, 1937, and production aircraft to Specification 25/36, with the 890 hp Perseus XII engine, began to appear in 1938, the first being flown on August 28. Production totalled 190 and was completed by March 1940. The Skua had an armament of four 0.303-in (7.7-mm) Browning machine guns in the wings plus one Lewis gun of the same calibre on a pillar mounting in the rear cockpit, and carried one 500-lb (227-kg) bomb on a retractable ejector arm under the fuselage for dive bombing plus eight 30-lb (13.6-kg) practice bombs under the wings. First deliveries were made to Nos 800 and 803 Sqns in late 1938, and Nos 801 and 806 equipped on the type in 1939, but the Skua was withdrawn from front-line service by August 1941, whereafter several continued in use for advanced training and for target-towing, for which latter role the final production batches were equipped from the outset.

Max speed, 225 mph (362 km/h) at 6,500 ft (1,980 m). Cruising speed, 114-187 mph

Below: Blackburn Skua I L2928 serving with No 801 Sqn at Donibristle in the summer of 1939. In May/June 1940 this unit flew its Skuas from RAF Detling to give air cover over the Dunkirk evacuation.

(183-301 km/h). Initial rate of climb, 1,580 ft/min (26.3 m/sec). Service ceiling, 20,200 ft (6,157 m). Max range, 435 mls (700 km). Empty weight, 5,496 lb (2,495 kg). Gross weight, 8,124 lb (3,688 kg). Span, 46 ft 2 in (14.07 m). Length, 35 ft 7 in (10.84 m). Wing area, 319 sq ft (29.64 m²).

BLACKBURN B-25 ROC I

The B-25 Roc, designed in 1936 to Specification O.30/35 by G E Petty, was a direct derivative of the Skua, adapted as a two-seat turret fighter and the first aircraft in such a category to enter service with the Fleet Air Arm. Armament was concentrated in a BP Type A Mk II power-operated turret with four 0.303-in (7.7-mm) Browning guns, with provision for eight 30-lb (13.6-kg) bombs under the wings. Production of 136 was ordered to Specification 26/36 in April 1937, without prototypes, and the first flight was made on December 23, 1938. The engine was a 890 hp Perseus XII, and three Rocs were also built to Specification 20/37 as floatplanes. A few Rocs served operationally with Nos 801 and 806 Sqns (alongside Skuas) for a few months in 1940 but most remained in second-line squadrons, usually with turrets removed, for training and target towing.

Max speed, 196 mph (315 km/h) at 6,500 ft (1,982 m). Gross weight, 8,800 lb (3,995 kg). Span, 46 ft 0 in (14.02 m). Length, 35 ft 7 in (10.84 m).

BLACKBURN B-26 BOTHA I

Under G E Petty, the Blackburn design team projected the B-26 Botha to the requirements of Specification M.15/35 for a land-based general reconnaissance/torpedo-bomber. The four-seat high-wing monoplane powered by two 880 hp Perseus X engines was ordered into production to Specification 10/36 with an initial order for 442, increased to 580 in 1940 with contracts for 676 more eventually cancelled. The first Botha flew on December 28, 1938, and deliveries were completed by June 1941, later batches having the 930 hp

Above: Inherited from No 801 Sqn, these Roc Is were flown by No 769 Sqn in the role of Fighter Deck Landing Training at Donibristle in late 1939. Note the retracted rear fuselage decking on L3114 (foreground) and L3118 (background). Right: With turret removed, this Roc served in the target towing role with No 770 Sqn at Crail, 1941-43. Below: Roc L3057 was one of at least three modified as floatplanes and briefly planned to have been used by No 805 Sqn in Norway in May 1940.

Perseus XA engine. Armament comprised one forward-firing Vickers 0.303-in machine gun and two similar Lewis guns in a dorsal turret; internal loads could include one Mk XII or Mk XIV torpedo or up to 2,000-lb (908-kg) of bombs, plus provision for underwing bomb racks. Deliveries began in May 1940 to No 608 (North Riding) Sqn and others served briefly with No 502 Sqn; No 608 operated the Botha until November 1940 but it was seriously underpowered and was then assigned to second-line units, such as No 3 School of General Reconnaissance, No 11 Radio School and other training units until declared obsolete in 1944. A few served as target tugs, with winch gear replacing the dorsal turret.

Max speed, 220 mph (354 km/h) at 15,000 ft (4,575 m). Initial rate of climb, 355 ft/min (1.80 m/sec). Service ceiling, 18,400 ft (5,610 m). Range, 1,270 mls (2,043 km). Empty weight, 12,036 lb (5,464 kg). Gross weight, 18,450 lb (8,376 kg). Span, 59 ft 0 in (17.98 m). Length, 51 ft 0½ in (15.56 m). Wing area, 518 sq ft (48.12 m²).

BLACKBURN B-20

The B-20 was designed by Major J D Rennie to meet the requirements of Specification R.1/36 for a reconnaissance flying-boat, a unique feature of the design being a retractable planing bottom that formed part of the hull when retracted, and was used in association with retractable wing-tip floats to obtain adequate propeller clearance on the water. Powered by two 1,720 hp Vulture X engines, the B-20 was designed to have two 0.303-in (7.7-mm) guns in the nose, two in a dorsal turret and four in a tail turret, and to carry four 500-lb (227-kg) bombs in wing cells. The prototype (V8914) was ready to fly by the end of March 1940 but was lost on April 7, within a few days of the first flight, probably as a result of aileron flutter.

Max speed, 306 mph (492 km/h) at 15,000 ft (4,572 m). Gross weight, 35,000 lb (15,890 kg). Span, 82 ft 2 in (25.04 m). Length, 69 ft 7½ in (21.22 m).

Above: Botha I L6250 serving with No 3 School of General Reconnaissance, Squires Gate, in the training role to which this type was rapidly relegated after brief unsatisfactory operational experience. Below: The intriguinely unconventional Blackburn B-20 V8914, which sadly was destroyed on a test flight a few days after it had first flown.

BLACKBURN B-37 FIREBRAND

To meet the requirements of Specification N.11/40, G E Petty's design team began development of a heavily-armed single-seat fleet fighter during 1940. The first of three prototypes, with a 2,305 hp Sabre III engine, flew on February 27, 1942, and was unarmed, the second prototype having the definitive armament of four 20-mm British Hispano cannon in the wings and provision for one 500-lb (227-kg) bomb under each wing. Initial production aircraft designated Firebrand I were used only experimentally and were followed by 12 Firebrand TF Mk IIs with provision for carrying a 1,850-lb (840-kg) 18-in (46-cm) torpedo beneath a widened centre-section. The prototype TF Mk II flew on March 31, 1943, and the production aircraft went to No 708 Sqn to form a trials unit in September/October 1944.

Max speed, 355 mph (571 km/h) clean. Cruising speed, 274 mph (441 km/h). Initial rate of climb, 2,300 ft/min (11.7 m/sec) with torpedo. Range, 770 mls (1,239 km). Gross weight, 15,050 lb (6,833 kg). Span, 51 ft 3¹/₂ in (15.60 m). Length, 38 ft 2 in (11.63 m). Wing area, 383 sq ft (35.58 m²).

Firebrand TF Mk III: To overcome a shortage of Sabre engines, the Firebrand was re-engined with a 2,400 hp Centaurus VII radial, a prototype of this TF Mk III version flying on December 21, 1943. The first of 27 production examples flew in November 1944 and served as trials aircraft in preparation for the Firebrand TF Mk IV. The latter differed from the TF Mk III in having a 2,520 hp Centaurus IX, improved controls and ability to carry a 2,000-lb (908-kg) bomb under each wing. The first TF Mk IV, of 102 built, flew on May 17, 1945, service introduction proceeding after the end of the war.

Max speed, 319 mph (513 km/h) clean. Cruising speed, 272 mph (438 km/h). Initial rate of climb, 2,480 ft/min (12.6 m/sec). Service ceiling, 29,400 ft (8,960 m). Range, 530 mls (853 km). Empty weight, 11,375 lb (5,164 kg). Gross weight, 15,753 lb (7,152 kg). Span, 51 ft 3¹/₂ in (15.60 m). Length, 37 ft 7 in (11.45 m). Wing area, 383 sq ft (35.58 m²).

BOULTON PAUL P.75 OVERSTRAND

A twin-engined biplane bomber designed by J D North to the requirements of Specification 23/34 (originally as Sidestrand Mk V), the Overstrand served with RAF bomber squadrons 1935-1937. Of 24 aircraft delivered (plus some Sidestrand con-

Above: The fifth of nine Firebrand F Mk I production aircraft, DK367, in use at the A & AEE in 1944 for the development of rocket projectiles. Below right: The 10th Mk I airframe, DK 372, was completed as the prototype Firebrand TF Mk III and is shown on test at the A & AEE in March 1944.

versions), a few continued in service as gunnery trainers until 1940 at No 10 Bombing and Gunnery School at Dumfries, and two on special duties survived into 1941. The engines were 580 hp Pegasus II.M3.

Max speed, 153 mph (246 km/h) at 6,500 ft (1,981 m). Gross weight, 12,000 lb (5,443 kg). Span, 72 ft 0 in (21.95 m). Length, 46 ft 0 in (14.02 m).

BOULTON PAUL P.82 DEFIANT

The P.82 Defiant was designed by a team headed by J D North to meet requirements of Specification F.9/35 for a two-seat interceptor fighter with armament concentrated in powered dorsal turret with 360° traverse. First of two prototypes flown August 11, 1937 (without turret fitted until February 1938), powered by Merlin I engine. Second prototype, with turret and Merlin II, flown May 18, 1939. Prototype trials later with single 20-mm cannon in place of machine guns, and as single-seat 'stop-gap' fighter minus turret but with four wing guns.

Defiant Mk I: Initial contract for 87 Defiant Mk Is placed March 1937. First example flown July 30, 1939, with Merlin III rated at 1,030 hp at 16,250 ft (4,953 m). Boulton Paul A.Mk.IID turret with four 0.303-in (7.7-mm) Browning guns. First day fighter unit (of two) to receive Defiant Is, No 264 Sqn, received first aircraft December 8, 1939; first operational deployment May 1940. Philosophy of turret-equipped single-engined fighter proved ill-founded for day fighting role, and Defiant (Mks I & II) assigned to night fighting. First night operations (No 141 Sqn) September

1940 and 11 NF squadrons eventually Defiant-equipped. AI Mk IV radar added on Mk I night fighters from autumn 1941, with designation Defiant IA. Some 76 modified Defiants (Mks I & II) used by five air-sea rescue squadrons, carrying two M-type dinghies in underwing containers, 1942/43. Total Mk I contracts for 930 aircraft.

Max speed, 250 mph (402 km/h) at sea level 304 mph (489 km/h) at 17,000 ft (5,182 m). Initial climb, 1,900 ft/min (9.65 m/sec). Service ceiling, 28,100 ft (8,565 m). Range 465 mls (748 km). Loaded weight, 8,318 lb (3,773 kg). Span, 39 ft 4 in (11.99 m). Length, 35 ft 4 in (10. 77 m).

Defiant Mk II: Final contract for Mk I amended to call for 210 Defiant Mk IIs with 1,280 hp Merlin XX engine, slightly enlarged rudder and additional fuel. Prototype (Mk I conversion) first flown July 20, 1940. Normal loaded weight increased to 8,424 lb (3,821 kg) and max speed to 315 mph (507 km/h) at 16,000 ft (4,877 m). Seven Mk Is also converted to Mk IIs on assembly line, with deliveries commencing February 1941. Mk IIs initially replaced Mk Is in night fighter squadrons, mostly equipped with AI Mk VI radar. Some for air-sea rescue duty alongside Mk Is, and 35 used by No 515 Sqn 1942/43 specially equipped with *Moonshine* and *Mandrel* radar jamming equipment. All Defiants withdrawn from other operational roles by end of 1942.

Defiant T.T.Mk I and T.T.Mk III: One

Overstrand I K4552 was in use at No 1 Air Armament School at RAF Manby until the end of 1939, when it became 1822M ground instructional airframe.

Above: Defiant Is of No 264 Sqn at RAF Kirton-in-Lindsey in August 1940, on the eve of operations in the Battle of Britain. Below left: The Defiant prototype K8310 in single-seat form as a 'stop-gap' fighter in 1940. Below right: Defiant II AA436 serving in the night fighter role with No 151 Sqn in 1942.

hundred and forty examples of a target-towing version ordered July 1941 as T.T.Mk I. Turret removed and replaced by fixed canopy over winch operator's cockpit. Based on Defiant II, first T.T.Mk I delivered January 31, 1942. Last 40 Mk II fighters on order built as T.T.Mk Is and, subsequently, 150 Merlin III-engined Defiant Mk Is converted similarly as T.T.Mk IIIs. Some 60 Defiant target tugs transferred to Admiralty for FAA use; others used by RAF in European and (suitably 'tropicalised') Middle East and Far East theatres.

BOULTON PAUL P.92/2

The P.92 was a design to Specification F.11/37 for a large twin-engined three-seat long-range escort fighter with armament of four 20-mm cannon in a dorsal turret faired

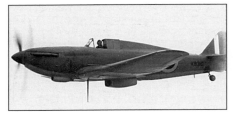

into the upper surface of the high wing. Two prototypes were ordered in March 1938, one with 1,760 hp Vulture IIs and one with 2,055 hp Sabre Is, plus a third (with Vultures) ordered later, but all three were cancelled in May 1940 when construction had only just begun. A half-scale flying model of the design was authorised for construction in May 1939 as the P.92/2

(V3142) and was built under contract to BP by Heston Aircraft (with that company's type number JA.8), making its first flight in the Spring of 1940 powered by two 130 hp Gipsy Major IIs.
Max speed, 152 mph (245 km/h). Gross weight, 2,778 lb (1,261 kg). Span, 33 ft 1¹/₂ in (10.10 m). Length, 27ft 6 in (8.38 m).

BRISTOL TYPE 105 BULLDOG IVA

The single-seat Bulldog fighting biplane was designed by Frank Barnwell in 1925 to meet RAF requirements and was produced in a number of versions for the RAF and other countries. In 1934 the Finnish Air Force (*Ilmavoimat*) acquired 17 Bulldog IVAs with 640 hp Mercury VIS.2 engines and armament of two 0.303-in (7.7-mm) Vickers Mk II machine guns. A few were still in front-line service with LLv 26 during the Winter-War of 1939-40 and the survivors, supplemented by two Bulldog IIAs with 440 hp Jupiter VIIF engines donated by the Swedish Air Force (*Flygvapnet*), flew as station hacks and trainers throughout the Continuation War, 1941-1944, often on skis.
Max speed, 225 mph (362 km/h) at 16,000 ft (4,877 m). Time to 10,000 m (3,050 m), 4.68 mins. Empty weight, 2,690 lb (1,220 kg). Gross weight, 4,100 lb (1,861 kg). Span, 33 ft 8in (10.26 m). Length, 25 ft 2¹/₂ in (7.68 m). Wing area, 293.6 sq ft (27.27m²).

BRISTOL TYPE 130 BOMBAY

Design of the Bristol Type 130 was initiated by Frank Barnwell to meet the requirements of Specification C.26/31 for a bomber/transport to carry up to 24 equipped troops or bombs and primarily intended for service in the Middle and Far East. A prototype first flew on June 23, 1935, and 50 production Bombay Is were built to Specification 47/36 by Short and Harland Ltd in Belfast, with 1,010 hp Pegasus XXII engines and a single Vickers 'K' 0.303-in (7.7-mm) gun each in Bristol nose and tail turrets. Deliveries to No 216 Sqn, RAF, began in

Above: Defiant TT Mk I AA507, a converted Mk II, in service with 26 Anti-Aircraft Co-operation Unit, in overall yellow finish with black striping to identify its use as a target-tug. Below: The P.92/2 at the A & AEE in August 1943. V3142 was Experimental Aeroplane 127 in AP.1480X.

Above: Bulldog IVA BU-66, one of 17 acquired by Finland in 1934, was in service with LLv 26 until March 1940. Right: The Bristol 142 'Britain First' at the RAF Display in 1936. Below: The Bombay L5831 operating in Italy in the casevac role with No 1 Air Ambulance Unit.

September 1939 and three other squadrons also flew the type on bomber, transport and casevac duties, chiefly in the Middle East in 1940-41. Declared obsolete 1944.

Max speed, 192 mph (309 km/h). Service ceiling, 25,000 ft (7,620 m). Range, 2,230 mls (3,588 km). Empty weight, 13,800 lb (6,265 kg). Gross weight, 20,000 lb (9,080 kg). Span, 95 ft 9 in (29.18 m). Length, 69 ft 3 in (21.10 m). Wing area, 1,340 sq ft (124.5 m²).

BRISTOL TYPE 142

The Bristol Type 142 was designed by Frank Barnwell during 1933-34 as a high-speed transport with possible applications as a bomber and was built in civil guise with seats for two pilots and six passengers to the order of Lord Rothermere. First flown on April 12, 1935, the Type 142 was powered by two 650 hp Mercury VIS2 radials and, named Britain First, was presented to the Air Ministry in July 1935 and, with the serial K7557 replacing the original R-12 marking, subsequently operated on experimental and transport duties at RAE Farnborough until 1942.

Max speed, 307 mph (494 km/h). Gross weight, 9,357 lb (4,248 kg). Span, 56 ft 4 in (17.17 m). Length, 39 ft 9 in (12.12 m).

BRISTOL TYPE 142M BLENHEIM I

The Bristol team headed by Frank Barnwell designed the Type 142M during 1935 as a three-seat light bomber derivative of the Type 142 *Britain First*, the major differences being raising the wing to a mid position to make room for a bomb-bay in the fuselage, adding nose and dorsal armament plus a bomb-aiming station in the nose, the raising

and enlarging the tailplane. A contract for 150 Type 142Ms to Specification 28/35 was placed by the Air Ministry in September 1935 and the name Blenheim was adopted in April 1936.

Blenheim I: Production contracts for 150 in 1935 and 434 in 1936, and 134 in 1937 to make a total of 718 built by Bristol, plus 250 by Avro at Chadderton and 422 by Rootes Securities at Speke. Two 840 hp Bristol Mercury VIII engines. One fixed forward-firing 0.303-in (7.7-mm) Browning gun in port wing and one 0.303-in (7.7-mm) Lewis gun in Bristol B.I Mk I powered dorsal turret. Internal bomb-load, 1,000 lb (454 kg). First production Blenheim I flown June 25, 1936; initial deliveries to No 114 (B) Squadron in March 1937, and 16 other home bomber squadrons and 13 overseas bomber squadrons equipped, 1937-39. Blenheim I bombers out of front-line service in UK by September 1939 but operational overseas, notably in the Western Desert and Greek theatres. Bristol built 18 Blenheim Is

for the Finnish Air Force (*Ilmavoimat*) in 1937-38, adapted to carry Swedish bombs and to operate on skis, supplemented early-1940 by 12 ex-RAF Blenheim Is, and Finland's Valtion Lentokonetehdas at Tampere built 45 Blenheim Is under licence, the type being operational in the Winter War and Continuation War with LLv 42, 44, 46 and other units. The Yugoslav government purchased two Blenheim Is in 1937 and a licence to build 50, of which 16 had been completed by Ikarus AD at Zemun by the time of the German invasion in 1941, being supplemented by another 20 ex-RAF in 1940, some adapted to have two 20-mm forward firing cannon. A few of the Blenheim Is that survived the fighting in 1941 later served with the Croat Air Force. The Turkish government purchased 30 Blenheim Is, delivered late 1937-February 1939, and in November 1939, 13 ex-RAF machines were supplied to Romania.

Max speed, 285 mph (459 km/h). Cruising speed, 200 mph (322 km/h). Initial rate of climb, 1,540 ft/min (7.82 m/sec). Service ceiling, 32,000 ft (9,754 m). Range, 1,125 mls (1,810 km). Empty weight, 8,100 lb (3,677 kg). Gross weight, 12,250 lb (5,561 kg). Span, 56 ft 4 in (17.17 m) . Length, 39 ft 9 in (12.12 m) . Wing area, 469 sq ft (43.57 m²).

Blenheim IF: About 200 bomber Blenheims adapted as twin-engined fighters, with a pack of four fixed forward-firing 0.303-in (7.7-mm) Browning guns under the fuselage. Initial deliveries to No 25 Sqn, December 1938, and used by several squadrons at home and overseas for day and night fighting. Some fitted with AI Mk III radar for operational trials, gaining a first success on 2/3 July 1940.

Blenheim II: A single Blenheim I (L1222) with long-range tanks and gross weight of 14,000 lb (6,356 kg), with provision for extra bombs externally under inner wings.

Above: Blenheim I BL-135 was part of the 'Srs IV' batch of Blenheims taken into the Finnish Air Force, here serving with 3/LeLv 48 in 1942.

Below: A Blenheim IF fighter of No 601 County of London Sqn, AAF, on the eve of war, still carrying its 'Munich' code of YN. Above right; Blenheim IF K7159 in night fighter finish and with AI Mk III radar, flying in September 1941 with No 54 Night Fighter Operational Training Unit.

Above: Blenheim I L6670, with tropical filters on its Mercury engines, photographed in Greece in 1940 whilst serving with No 211 Sqn. It was transferred to the R Hellenic AF in April 1941. Below: A Blenheim IVF fighter in service with No 235 Sqn for convoy protection and reconnaissance during 1940; note bombs on under fuselage racks.

Below: Several Blenheim Is were acquired by German forces in Yugoslavia after the collapse of organised resitance there, and were transferred to the embryonic Croatian Air Force, whose markings are seen on this example. Right upper: A Blenheim IV, of unknown origin, under evaluation by the Luftwaffe after capture. Right lower: One of 12 Blenheim IVs equipping 32 Mira of the R Hellenic AF in 1940.

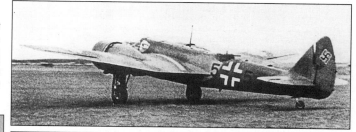

BRISTOL TYPE 149 BLENHEIM IV

The Bristol 149 was developed in 1935 to Specification G.24/35 for a general reconnaissance and coastal bomber, being basically a Blenheim I airframe with nose lengthened by 3 ft (0.91) to provide space for a navigator/radio operator ahead of pilot. Initially named Bolingbroke I and 134 ordered to Specification 11/36. Prototype (Blenheim I K7072 converted) flown September 24, 1937, and entered production after changes to nose shape and introduction of long range tanks in wings. Renamed Blenheim IV for RAF service; Bolingbroke name retained for Canadian production versions.

Blenheim III: Projected variant of Blenheim I with Blenheim Mk IV long nose but without extra fuel tankage of Mk IV.

Blenheim IV: Contracts for 312 with Bristol in 1937-38, plus 750 built by Avro at Chadderton and 2,060 by Rootes Securities at Speke and Blythe Bridge. Two 920 hp Mercury XV engines. Initial armament of one fixed forward firing Browning and one Lewis or Vickers K gun in dorsal turret, both of 0.303-in (7.7-mm) calibre, later one gimbal-mounted nose gun, one or two rearward-firing Brownings in blister under nose and two Vickers 'K' or Browning guns in dorsal turret; bomb load 1,000 lb (454 kg) internal and 320 lb (145 kg) external. Deliveries began March 1939, to No 90 Squadron; equipped 18 RAF squadrons by August 1939 and one aircraft of No 139 Sqn flew first RAF sortie of World War II to cross enemy lines, on September 3, 1939. Six Blenheim IV squadrons attached to BEF in France, 1939-40. Used extensively for day and night bombing and reconnaissance operations from the UK and in North Africa and Greece. Twelve Blenheim IVs (ex-RAF) supplied to Finnish Air Force, 1940, and ten

built under licence in Finland, used alongside Mk Is in Winter War and Continuation War. Twelve (ex-RAF) supplied to Greece, October 1939-February 1940.

Max speed, 266 mph (428 km/h) at 11,800 ft (3,597 m). Cruising speed, 198 mph (319 km/h). Initial rate of climb, 1,500 ft/min (7.82 m/sec). Service ceiling, 27,260 ft (8,309 m). Max range, 1,460 mls (2,350 km) at 169 mph (272 km/h). Empty weight, 9,790 lb (4,445 kg). Gross weight, 14,500 lb (6,583 kg). Span, 56 ft 4 in (17.17 m). Length, 42 ft 7 in (12.98 m). Wing area, 469 sq ft (43.57 m²).

Blenheim IVF: Bomber Blenheims adapted to serve as long-range fighters, primarily with Coastal Command squadrons in 1940, carrying a pack of four fixed forward-firing 0.303-in (7,7-mm) guns under the fuselage.

BRISTOL (FAIRCHILD) BOLINGBROKE

The Bristol-developed Blenheim IV adopted by RCAF for coastal reconnaissance, with original British name retained, and licence for production obtained by Fairchild Aircraft Ltd at Longueuil, Quebec. Bolingbroke prototype K7072 first flew in Britain on September 24, 1937, later shipped to Canada. Total of 676 built in following versions:

Bolingbroke I: First 18 aircraft assembled by Fairchild, using British drawings, British equipment and some British components. 840 hp Mercury VIII engines. First aircraft flown at Lonqueuil on September 14, 1939. A few fitted with ventral gun packs served with No 115(F) Sqn; others with Nos 8 and 147(BR) Sqns.

Bolingbroke II: A single Bolingbroke I (705) rebuilt with US equipment and instruments after it had crashed.

Bolingbroke III: One Bolingbroke I

Above: The Bolingbroke prototype K7072 before despatch to Canada. Below: Bolingbroke I fighter with locally-produced ventral gun pack, in the markings of No 119 Sqn, RCAF, before transfer to No 115.

Above: Bolingbroke IV 9021, with Twin Wasp engines. Below: The sole Bolingbroke III seaplane.

(717) for trials as a seaplane, with twin Edo floats. Operational evaluation by No 5(BR) Sqn, 1940-41.

Bolingbroke IV: Standard Canadian-built version for RCAF with US equipment, dinghies for overwater reconnaissance role, wing de-icing boots and interchangeable wheel and ski gear. Production of 185 with 920 hp Mercury XVs. Used by Nos 8(BR), 115(BR), 119(BR) and 147(BR) Sqns, mostly on patrols from Canadian west coast and in Alaska. Also some photo-recce use by No 163(AC) Sqn.

Bolingbroke IV-W: Fifteen aircraft as Bolingbroke IV but with 835 hp R-1535-SB4G Twin Wasp Junior engines. Used by No 119(BR) Sqn.

Bolingbroke IV-C: A single airframe (9074), as Bolingbroke IV with 900 hp

Above: Blenheim IVF – note the ventral gun tray – in service with No 254 Sqn, a Coastal Command unit engaged in shipping protection. Below: Blenheim IV V6083 from No 13 OTU at Bicester in 1941, showing twin guns under the nose and B.I Mk IV dorsal turret with twin Brownings.

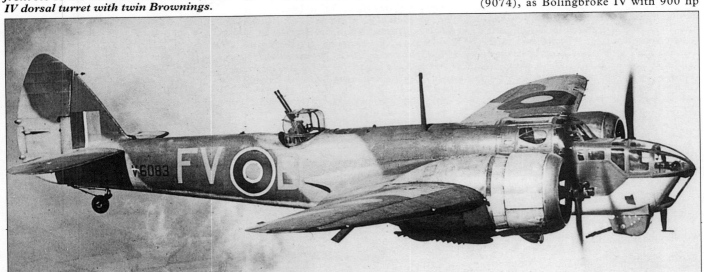

Above: The Bisley I prototype (Type 160CS) AD657, with Mercury XVI engines, and the original nose design to contain four Brownings with 1,000 rpg. Below: Blenheim V BA491 of No 162 Sqn at Fayid in 1942, showing the definitive bomb-aiming nose with FN54 rear-defense Brownings incorporated in the 'bath' fairing.

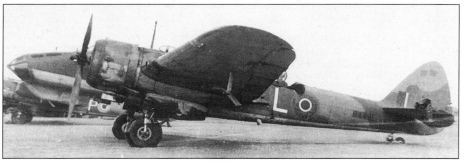

Cyclone R-1820-G3B engines.

Bolingbroke IV-T: Final 457 Canadian airframes (including 51 spare) with 920 hp Mercury XX engines, equipped as navigation and gunnery trainers and used in Canada until 1945. Boulton Paul Type C dorsal turret in place of Bristol B.I. Some used also in target-towing role.

BRISTOL TYPE 160 BLENHEIM V AND BISLEY

The Bristol 160 was proposed during 1940 as a variant of the Type 149 Blenheim IV specifically intended for short-range bombing operation in support of the Army, with a secondary role as a bomber. Specification B.6/40 was written round the proposal and two prototypes were ordered, initially as Bisley I but renamed Blenheim V before the first flight on February 24, 1941. Production totalled 942, by Rootes at Blythe Bridge, with 950 hp Mercury 25 or 30 engines. Direct-support version armed with four Browning 0.303-in (7.7-mm) guns in redesigned nose, plus two similar guns in Bristol B.X dorsal turret. High-altitude bombing version had navigation/bomb-aiming station in redesigned nose with two rearward-firing Brownings in Frazer Nash mount. Initial deliveries to No 18 Sqn, summer 1942, for operations in North Africa (where some were later transferred to the Turkish Air Force); also used in Malayan campaign. Some Blenheim Vs with dual controls and without dorsal turrets used by Fighter Command OTUs.

Max speed, 260 mph (418 km/h). Service ceiling, 31,000 ft (9,450 m). Range, 1,600 mls (2,574 km). Empty weight, 11,000 lb (4,994 kg). Gross weight, 17,000 lb (7,718 kg). Span, 56 ft 1 in (17.09 m). Length, 43 ft 11 in (13.38 m). Wing area, 469 sq ft (43.57 m²).

BRISTOL TYPE 152 BEAUFORT

The Bristol design team under Frank Barnwell evolved the Type 152 as a variant of the Blenheim to meet the combined requirements of Specifications M.15/35 and G.24/35, as a land-based twin-engined torpedo-bomber and general reconnaissance aircraft. With a crew of four, the Type 152 could carry an 18-in (45.7-cm) torpedo partially exposed in the fuselage, and an initial contract (for 78 aircraft) was placed in August 1936 to Specification 10/36, the name Beaufort being adopted. From total UK production of 1,429 against Air Ministry contracts, 64 Mk I and 40 Mk II to FAA, 20 Mk I and 40 Mk II to SAAF for No 16 Sqn in North Africa, 1942/44; 13 Mk I and 12 Mk II to Turkish Air Force, eventually to 105th Torpedo and Reconnaissance Group in 1945, and 12 Mk I to RCAF for No 149(TB) Sqn on Vancouver Island, 1942-43. One Mk I to Australia as pattern aircraft for Mk V production. Remainder to RAF torpedo-reconnaissance squadrons in UK, Malta, Middle East, India and Ceylon; and in large numbers for training.

Beaufort I: Two 1,035 hp Taurus III or VI, or 1,130 hp Taurus XII or XVI engines and armament of one or two Vickers 'K' guns in a Bristol B.IV dorsal turret (or two Brownings in later B.I Mk V turret) plus one or two Vickers guns in nose and one or, later, two Brownings in wings; some later aircraft with two Vickers 'K' beam guns and optional rearward-firing Browning under nose, all guns of 0.303-in calibre. First flown October 15, 1938, and delivery of 1,014 Mk Is began November 1939, initially to No 22 Sqn; first (minelaying) operations April 1940.

Max speed, 260 mph (418 km/h). Cruising speed, 200 mph (322 km/h). Service ceiling, 16,500 ft (5,030 m). Range, 1,035-1,600 mls (1,665-2,574 km). Endurance, 6 hrs. Empty weight, 13,100 lb (5,947 kg). Gross weight, 21,230 lb (9,638 kg). Span, 57 ft 10 in (17.63 m). Length, 44 ft 3 in (13.49 m). Wing area, 503 sq ft (46.73 m²).

Below: Beaufort Is in service with No 22 Sqn, the first RAF unit to operate the type, at Thorney Island in 1940. Above: radar-equipped Beaufort II DD906 of No 39 Sqn, operating from North African bases in 1942. Right: Beaufort II ML625 as used by FAA units for multi-engine training, minus armament.

Above: Beaufort A9-102, one of 60 Mk VIIs built in Australia and serving with No 1 Bombing and Gunnery School, East Sale, Vic, in 1943. Right: The first Beaufort assembled in Australia, T9540 later A9-1. Below: Beaufort VIII or 'Beaufreighter' special transport conversion.

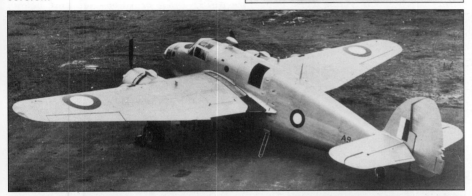

Above: Beaufighter R2153, an early-production Mk I, in service with coastal fighter squadron No 252 in early 1941. Below: Beaufighter Mk X NE548 from No 455 Sqn, an RAAF unit in Coastal Command flying from RAF Langham, Lincs, in 1944, firing a salvo of rocket projectiles.

Beaufort II: Designation first used for Mk Is with Taurus II in place of Taurus III engines, 1939. Reallocated in 1940 to Beaufort I with 1,200 hp R-1820-S3C4G Twin Wasp engines. Prototype flown November 9, 1940, and first production Mk II on August 17, 1941; production totalled 415, last 250 of which were delivered as Mk II(T) trainers, without dorsal turrets.

Beaufort III: Projected variant of Mk I with R-R Merlin XX engines. Merlin installation in W6518 as prototype did not proceed.

Beaufort IV: A single Beaufort II (AW372) converted to have 1,250 hp Taurus XX engines and a four-gun Bristol B.XV dorsal turret.

Beaufort V: Version of Beaufort II built by Beaufort Division of Australian Dept of Aircraft Production, at Mascot and Fishermen's Bend, for RAAF. One British Mk I (L4448) fitted in Australia with Twin Wasp engines flown May 5, 1941, and first of 50 production aircraft flown August 22, 1941, followed by 30 Mk VA in 1942 with enlarged fin and Curtiss in place of Hamilton-Standard propellers. Operational use began June 1942 with No 100 Sqn RAAF; Mk VAs used primarily by No 14 Sqn.

Beaufort VI: Forty Australian-built aircraft in 1942 with imported 1,200 hp R-1820-S1C3G Twin Wasps and Curtiss Electric propellers. Enlarged fin. First in service with No 100 Sqn.

Beaufort VII: Sixty Australian-built aircraft with R-1820-S1C3G engines and Hamilton-Standard propellers. Enlarged fin. Served with No 7 Sqn.

Beaufort VIII: Final 520 Australian-built Beauforts, with R-1820-S3C4G engines, B.I Mk V (first 380) or Australian-made B.I Mk VE twin-Browning 0.50-in (12.7-mm) dorsal turrets, LORAN and extra fuel. Enlarged fin. Deliveries November 1942-August 1944 and extensively used in nine RAAF operations against Japanese targets in the SW Pacific.
Max speed, 268 mph (431 km/h). Service ceiling, 22,500 ft (6,858 m). Range, with auxiliary fuel, 1,450 mls (2,333 km). Empty weight, 14,070 lb (6,382 kg). Gross weight, 22,500 lb (10,215 kg).

Beaufort IX: Forty-six Beaufort VIIIs converted as unarmed transports with dorsal turret faired over, in 1944-45. Gross weight of 20,000 lb (9,080 kg) and nine seats including pilot.

BRISTOL 156 BEAUFIGHTER

The Bristol Type 156 was designed by L G Frise as a two-seat four-cannon long-range fighter using the wings, tail unit and landing gear of the Beaufort for speed of production. First of four prototypes, with Hercules I-SM radials, flown on July 17, 1939; second prototype had Hercules I-M, third had Hercules III and fourth had Hercules II.

Beaufighter I: First production contract placed July 1939, for 300 aircraft (including the four prototypes) with 1,400 hp Hercules IIIs. First 50 armed with four 20-mm Hispano cannon in nose; subsequent aircraft also had six 0.303-in (7.7-mm) guns in wings; Hercules XI engines in last 120 Filton-built Mk Is. Deliveries to RAF began July 27, 1940, initial deliveries being to Nos 25, 29, 219, 600 and 604 Squadrons. Most fitted with AI Mk IV 'arrowhead' radar for night-fighting role in retrospective programme starting September 1940. During 1941, Beaufighter Is adopted for Coastal Command service with long-range fuel tanks in place of wing guns and revised crew arrangements; deliveries began to No 252 Sqn in March 1942. Coastal Command version subsequently designated Mk IC and Fighter Command version Mk IF. Production totals, 272 Mk IF and 78 Mk IC at Filton, 240 Mk IF by MAP Shadow Factory at Weston-super-Mare; 25 IF and 300 Mk IC by Fairey at Stockport including 72 Mk IC supplied to RAAF, of which one re-engined in Australia with 1,600 hp Wright GR-2600-A5B radials, and flown in August 1944. First operational with No 30 Sqn, RAAF, in September 1942.
Max speed, 306 mph (492 km/h) at sea level, 323 mph (520 km/h) at 15,000 ft (4,575 m). Max cruise, 272 mph (437 km/h) at 15,000 ft (4,575 m). Initial rate of climb, 1,850 ft/min (9.4 m/sec). Time to 20,000 ft (6,100 m), 14.1 min. Service ceiling, 26,500 ft (8,077 m). Normal range, 1,170 mls (1,883 km) at 182 mph (293 km/h) at 5,000 ft (1,525 m). Empty weight, 14,069 lb (6,381 kg). Gross weight, 21,100 (9,435 kg). Span, 57 ft 10 in (17.63 m). Length, 41 ft 4 in (12.60 m). Wing area, 503 sq ft (46.73 m²).

Much use was made of early Beaufighter marks for night fighting. Equipped with AI Mk IV 'arrowhead' radar were, above, the Mk IF T4638 of No 604 Sqn and, below, the Mk IIF R2402 of No 255 Sqn – both photographed in 1941. Note the flat tailplane.

Beaufighter II: As Mk IF with 1,250 hp Merlin XX liquid-cooled in-line engines. Prototype (with Merlin Xs) flown at Hucknall July 1940 and first production Mk IIF at Filton on March 22, 1941, with first deliveries to No 600 Sqn in April. Production totalled 450 (including prototypes converted from Mk Is), used exclusively to equip a total of 11 UK-based night-fighter squadrons.

Max speed, 283 mph (455 km/h) at 15,000 ft (4,575 m), 301 mph (484 km/h) at 20,200 ft (6,157m). Range, 1,040 mls (1,673 km) at 10,000 ft (3,050m) at 177 mph (285 km/h). Span, 57 ft 10 in (17.63 m). Length, 42 ft 9 in (31.03 m).

Beaufighter III: Projected Bristol Type 158 with slimmer fuselage and Hercules engines.

Beaufighter IV: As Beaufighter III with Griffon engines, not built.

Beaufighter V: Two Mk IIs modified March 1941 to have Boulton Paul BPA.1 dorsal turret with four 0.303-in machine guns and wing guns removed.

Beaufighter VI: As Mk I with 1,670 hp Hercules VI engines and progressively-introduced improvements including dihedral on tailplane, underwing bombracks, AI Mk VIII radar in 'thimble' nose (in Mk VIF) and bellows-operated dive brakes (in Mk VIC). First Beaufighter with Hercules VI engines flown early 1941; deliveries of Mk VIF early 1942 and thereafter operational in fighter role in UK, Europe, North Africa and Burma. Also equipped four USAAF night fighter squadrons in North Africa, and 63 supplied to RAAF for operation in Pacific area. Production totals, 669 Mk VIF at Filton, 175 Mk VIC by Fairey at Stockport, 260 Mk VIF and 518 Mk VIC at Weston-super-Mare and 150 Mk VIF by Rootes at Stoke-on-Trent.

Max speed, 333 mph (536 km/h) at 15,600 ft (4,755 m). Max cruise, 276 mph (444 km/h) at 15,000 ft (4,575 m). Range, 1,480 mls (2,381 km) at 243 mph (391 km/h) at 15,000 ft (4,575 m). Empty weight, 14,600 lb (6,628 kg). Gross weight, 21,600 lb (9,806 kg).

Beaufighter VI (ITF): Mk VIC adapted as torpedo-carrier for Coastal Command service, following prototype trials April/May

Above: Serving with No 255 Sqn in Italy, a Beaufighter VIF displays AI Mk VIII in the nose and dihedral on the tailplane. Below: On test with rocket projectiles and an overload fuel tank, NE343 is a Beaufighter TF Mk X in initial configuration. The AI Mk VIII installation and a long dorsal fin came later.

1942. One British 18-in (46-cm) or US 22.5-in (57-cm) torpedo externally under fuselage; otherwise as standard Mk VIC with Hercules VIs. Sixty built at Weston, entered service with No 254 Sqn early 1943.

Beaufighter VII: Proposed production of Beaufighter VIC in Australia by DAP at Fishermen's Bend, with Hercules 26 engines.

Beaufighter VIII: Proposed Australian production version with GR-2600-A5B Cyclone engines.

Beaufighter IX: Similar to Beaufighter VIII proposal.

Beaufighter TF Mk X: Similar to Beaufighter VI (ITF), with Hercules XVII engines for improved low altitude performance. One 0.303-in Browning or Vickers

The Beaufighter 21 was the standard Australian production model, 365 examples being built by the Government Aircraft Factory. Unique to the Mk 21 was the fairing ahead of the windscreen, to cover a Sperry autopilot. Delivered late in 1945, A8-358 was later converted as a target tug.

'K' gun in observer's cupola for rear defence; AI Mk VIII in 'thimble' nose, long dorsal fin, enlarged tailplane, increased ammunition load for nose cannon, provision for third crewman behind pilot to assist in aiming torpedo and provision for underwing rocket projectiles and/or 1,000-lb (454-kg) bombs, and for two 500-lb (227-kg) bombs under fuselage in lieu of torpedo. Operational from early 1944 with Beaufighter Strike Wings in Coastal Command, including RAF, RCAF, RAAF and RNZAF units operating from UK bases and in Mediterranean area,

including two SAAF units as part of Balkan Air Force. Production totals, 2,095 built at Weston and 110 by Rootes at Stoke-on-Trent, including 62 supplied to RAAF.

Max speed, 303 mph (488 km/h) at 1,300 ft (396 m). Max cruise, 249 mph (401 km/h) at 5,000 ft (1,525 m). Range, 1,470 mls (2,365 km) at 205 mph (330 km/h) at 5,000 ft (1,525 m). Service ceiling, 15,000 ft (4,575 m). Empty weight, 15,600 lb (7,082 kg). Gross weight, 25,200 lb (11,440 kg).

Beaufighter XIC: Similar to TF Mk X, but no provision to carry torpedo. Production total, 163 by Weston factory, of which 20 supplied to RAAF.

Beaufighter XII: Projected variant with Hercules 27 engines and 1,000-lb bomb under each wing.

Beaufighter 21: Australian production version similar to British Mk XIC, with Hercules XVIIIs, Sperry autopilot, four 20-mm nose cannon and four 0.50-in (12.7-mm) guns in the wings, provision for two 250-lb (113-kg) bombs and eight 60-lb (27-kg) rocket projectiles under wings. No dorsal fin and no nose radar. Produced by Government Aircraft Factory at Fishermen's Bend. First flown May 26, 1944, and 365 built for RAAF up to end-1945 (of which one not delivered). Equipped five RAAF squadrons operational against Japanese targets in Pacific area.

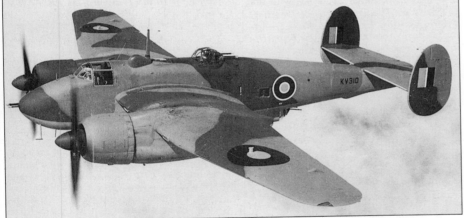

Above: A production Buckingham B Mk I, KV310. None of the bomber Buckinghams reached squadron service, most being converted to transports before being scrapped. Left: The first Buckingham prototype, unpainted, at Filton. Below: An unarmed Buckingham C Mk I, KV313, in January 1945.

BRISTOL TYPE 163 BUCKINGHAM

The Bristol Type 163 was evolved during 1941 as a fast four-seat medium bomber for day and night use, to the requirements of Specification B.2/41, and four prototypes were ordered in July 1941. Two 2,400 hp Centaurus IV engines were used and design armament comprised four 0.303-in (7.7-mm) guns in Bristol B.XIV nose mounting with four more in a B.XII dorsal turret and two in a ventral position; the bomb load was 4,000 lb (1,816 kg). Prototype first flown on February 4, 1943.

Buckingham B Mk I: First 54 of a production order for 400, first flown February 12, 1944, and all delivered in 1944 in bomber configuration with 2,400 hp Centaurus VIII or XI engines. Did not become operational.

Max speed, 335 mph (539 km/h). Gross weight, 36,900 lb (16,753 kg). Span, 71 ft 10 in (21.89 m). Length, 46 ft 10 in (14.27 m).

Buckingham C Mk I: Seventy-five delivered as fast courier transports, after requirement for bomber version dropped, and most of the B Mk Is converted to this standard, with no armament or armour, seats for four passengers and three crew, and fuel for 3,000-ml (4,827-km) range. Few used by Transport Command Development Unit, 1945, but most put into storage and then scrapped.

BRISTOL 164 BRIGAND TF Mk I

The Bristol Type 164 was designed by a team led by C W Tinson to serve in the role of a replacement for the Beaufighter torpedo-bomber, to the requirements of Specification H.7/42. Four prototypes were ordered in April 1943, to use basically the same wings and tail unit as the Type 163 Buckingham, with a new fuselage carrying AI Mk VIII radar and four 20-mm cannon in the nose and one 0.303-in dorsal gun, with a torpedo slung beneath. Prototype first flown December 4, 1944, with 2,400 hp Centaurus VIII; production deliveries and RAF service post-war.

Max speed, 360 mph (579 km/h). Gross weight, 39,000 lb (17,706 kg). Span, 72 ft 4 in (22.05 m). Length, 46 ft 5 in (14.14 m).

BRISTOL 166 BUCKMASTER T Mk I

The Bristol Type 166 was derived during 1943 from the Type 163 Buckingham as an unarmed dual control trainer, to Specification T.13/43. All armament and armour were removed, and a wider front fuselage seated two pilots side-by-side and a wireless operator behind. First of two prototypes flown October 27, 1944, and 110 production aircraft, using components laid down as part of original Buckingham contract, delivered from 1945 onwards, with 2,400 hp Centaurus VII or XI engines.

Max speed, 352 mph (565 km/h). Gross weight, 33,700 lb (15,300 kg). Span, 71 ft 10 in (21.89 m). Length, 46 ft 10 in (14.27 m).

BRITISH AIRCRAFT B.K.1 EAGLE

A three-seat lightplane designed by G H Handasyde for British Aircraft Klemm Aeroplane Co Ltd (later British Aircraft Manufacturing Co Ltd), the Eagle first flew in 1934 and was powered by a 130 hp Gipsy Major. Seven impressed in 1941 used for communications duties in the UK; two impressed in India and one in Kenya.

Max speed, 148 mph (238 km/h). Gross weight, 2,400 lb (1,090 kg). Span, 39 ft 3 in (11.96 m). Length, 26 ft 0 in (7.92 m).

Below: The Burnelli OA-1 G-AFMB – built in the UK by Cunliffe Owen for the British Burnelli company – ended up in West Africa and was used by the Free French forces there. Above right: BA Double Eagle ZS-AIY (later ZS-AOC) exported to South Africa in 1937, served the SAAF's No 60 Sqn in East Africa.

Above: The second Brigand TF Mk I prototype MX991, at the A & AEE in July 1945 and, right, MX988, the first prototype, in November 1944. Production deliveries began after the war ended. Below: The first of the Buckmaster T Mk Is in November 1944.

Although impressed in some numbers for communications and other duties, the BA Swallow II (above) and BA Eagle (below) appear to have evaded the photographer during the war. Both are depicted here in pre-war civil guise.

BRITISH AIRCRAFT BA IV DOUBLE EAGLE

A six-seat light twin powered by two 130 hp Gipsy Majors, the Double Eagle first flew in 1936 and three were built. One (ES949) impressed by RAF and used for communications duties by Armstrong Whitworth and then Parnall Aircraft until 1944. Second example (ES950) impressed as instructional airframe only. Third aircraft impressed (as 1415) in South Africa 1940 by SAAF and used for photo-reconnaissance by No 60 Sqn.

Max speed, 165 mph (265 km/h). Gross weight, 3,500 lb (1,589 kg). Span 41 ft 0 in (12.50 m). Length, 29 ft 10 in (9.09 m).

BRITISH AIRCRAFT SWALLOW II

A modified licence-built version of the Klemm L-25e, built by British Aircraft Manufacturing Co Ltd from 1935 onwards, with 90 hp Pobjoy Cataract radial or 90 hp Cirrus Minor I in-line engine. Nine examples impressed for flying duties 1940/41 and several of these flown as gliders for RAE trials in multiple tows, up to four Swallows being towed simultaneously by Heyfords and Whitleys. Four Klemm L-25Cs built by British Klemm (predecessor of British Aircraft Manufacturing Co) also impressed by RAF, with Pobjoy engine. One other Swallow II, ex-civil, purchased in Ceylon for naval communications duty as NP491.

Max speed, 112 mph (180 km/h). Gross weight, 1,500 lb (681 kg). Span, 42 ft 8 1/2 in (13.01 m). Length, 26 ft 3 in (8.00 m).

BRITISH BURNELLI OA-1

Prototype lifting fuselage transport (G-AFMB) based on American Burnelli UB 14 design and built in 1938 by Cunliffe Owen Aircraft Ltd, with two 710 hp Bristol Perseus XIVC radials. Delivered from UK to West Africa in 1941 for use by Free French forces.

Max speed, 225 mph (362 km/h). Gross weight, 19,000 lb (8,626 kg). Span, 73 ft 6 in (22.40 m). Length, 44 ft 0 in (13.41).

CIERVA C.30A (ROTA I)

The C.30A was the production version of a two-seat autogiro designed by Juan de la Cierva and flown in prototype form in 1933. Under Cierva licence, Avro built 78 in Britain including 12 for RAF to specification 16/35 as Avro Type 671 Rota I, with 140 hp Civet I (Genet Major) engine. Delivered 1934-35, they were used by No 1448 Flight at Duxford from 1940 and No 529 Sqn until 1945 on calibration duties, primarily along South coast, together with 13 impressed civil machines.

Max speed, 100 mph (161 km/h). Initial climb, 700 ft/min (3.56 m/sec). Service ceiling, 8,000 ft (2,438 m). Range, 250 mls (402 km). Empty weight, 1,220 lb (554 kg). Gross weight, 1,900 lb (863 kg). Rotor diameter, 37 ft 0 in (11.28 m). Length, 19 ft 8¹/₂ in (5.99 m).

CIERVA C.40A (ROTA II)

An improved version of the C.30 evolved in 1938 with side-by-side seating for two and 175 hp Salmson engine. One built by British Aircraft Manufacturing Co Ltd and six by Oddie, Bradbury and Cull, of which five supplied to RAF, and other two impressed, as Rota IIs for service with Rota Is.

Max speed, 120 mph (193 km/h). Gross weight, 1,950 lb (885 kg). Rotor diameter, 40 ft 0 in (12.19 m).

CIERVA W.9

The Cierva Autogiro Co — formed in 1943 out of the rotary-wing department of G & J Weir — obtained a contract for two experimental helicopters to Spec E.16/43. Completed late-1944, the first W.9 (eventually to be marked PX203) had a manually-controlled tilting main rotor hub and used a jet of warm air from an engine-driven blower for torque control. The engine was a 210 hp DH Gipsy Queen II. After being damaged in ground running, the W.9 was rebuilt, slightly modified, and entered full flight testing in mid-1945. No data available for early version.

COMPER CLA 7 SWIFT

Single-seat light aircraft designed by Flt Lt Nick Comper and first flown 1930. At least two flown as squadron 'hacks' up to 1942, attached to Nos 25 and 247 Sqns, with 75 hp Pobjoy R radials. A third flew in civil markings (G-ACTF), used throughout the war by Portsmouth Aviation.

Max speed, 140 mph (225 km/h). Gross weight, 985 lb (447 kg). Span, 24 ft 0 in (7.32 m). Length, 17 ft 8¹/₂ in (5.38 m).

DE HAVILLAND D.H.50A

One of 14 D.H.50A four-seat light transport biplanes originally built by DH at Stag Lane

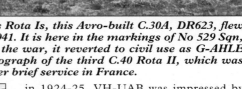

Above: Externally similar to the RAF's Rota Is, this Avro-built C.30A, DR623, flew as G-ACWH until impressed in June 1941. It is here in the markings of No 529 Sqn, at Hethel, Norfolk, in 1943. Surviving the war, it reverted to civil use as G-AHLE until 1947. Below left: A pre-war photograph of the third C.40 Rota II, which was written off at Odiham in April 1940 after brief service in France.

Below: The Cierva W.9 as completed and ready for tests, late-1944.

Above right: The Comper Swift G-ACTF, which flew throughout the war in civil guise and is shown here in a post-war photograph. Below: The fourth D.H.50, built in 1924 as G-AUAB for service in Australia, where it became VH-UAB. Re-engined in November 1942 with a P&W Wasp, it is seen here serving with the RAAF in New Guinea shortly before acquiring the serial A.10-1 in 1943.

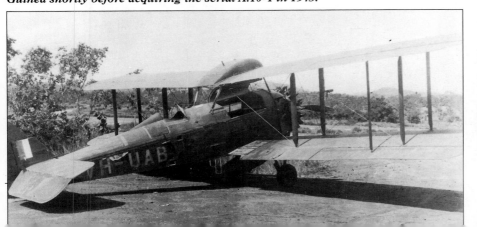

in 1924-25, VH-UAB was impressed by RAAF in April 1943 (as A10-1) for general duties, with 450 hp R-985-C Wasp, but retained for only two months.

Max speed, 126 mph (203 km/h). Gross weight, 4,200 lb (1,907 kg). Span, 42 ft 9 in (13.03 m). Length, 28 ft 9 in (8.76 m).

DE HAVILLAND D.H.60 MOTH

Two-seat lightplane originally flown on February 22, 1925 and built in large numbers and several distinct versions up to 1931. Military customers included Egyptian Air Force (six D.H.60T Moth Trainers), Royal Iraqi Air Force (five D.H.60T and five D.H.60M), RCAF (89 assorted D.H.60M, D.H.60G, D.H.60X and Genet-Moths, some Canadian-built), SAAF (one D.H.60M), RAAF (D.H.60, D.H.60G and D.H.60M), RNZAF (four D.H.60G and four D.H.60M), the air forces of Denmark, Norway and others. Examples of the Moth were still serving in many of these countries in 1939 and were joined by civil machines impressed as trainers and for communications duties, including over 140 in the UK and 15 in India for the RAF, 48 in Australia for RAAF and at least 16 for SAAF in South Africa. Data are for D.H.60G with 120 hp Gipsy II engine.

Max speed, 102 mph (164 km/h). Gross weight, 1,750 lb (795 kg). Span, 30 ft 0 in (9.14 m). Length, 23 ft 11 in (7.29 m).

DE HAVILLAND D.H.80 PUSS MOTH

A three-seat cabin monoplane designed during 1929 and first flown on September 9 that year, the standard D.H.80A Puss Moth was powered by a 130 hp Gipsy Major. Total of 47 civil examples impressed for military service in UK 1940-41 and attached to RAF units and Air Transport Auxiliary for communications/ferry duties throughout the war. Six impressed in India and Middle East for similar use, at least eight in South Africa for SAAF, and five in New Zealand for RNZAF.

Max speed, 128 mph (206 km/h). Gross weight, 2,050 lb (931 kg). Span, 36 ft 9 in (11.20 m). Length, 25 ft 0 in (7.62 m).

DE HAVILLAND D.H.82A TIGER MOTH

The D.H.82A training biplane was designed by Capt Geoffrey de Havilland during 1931 as an improved derivative of the D.H.60

Above: The second Moth to carry the serial J9107 was this D.H.60M which replaced an earlier Cirrus-engined example and was used at Gosport by No 769 Sqn for deck-landing training in the final months of 1939. Below: Puss Moth G-AEIV shortly after its impressment in March 1941 and before acquiring the serial DP853.

Gipsy Moth. Two D.H.60T Tiger Moth prototypes tested late summer 1931 with 120 hp Gipsy III inverted in-line engine, followed by first D.H.82 with increased dihedral and sweep-back flown on October 26, 1931. Entered production for RAF as new standard *ab initio* trainer (as noted below); pre-war production of D.H.82s by de Havilland at Hatfield also included five for Danish Air Force and 20 for Persian Air Force. In 1934, D.H.82A version introduced 130 hp Gipsy Major, plywood rear fuselage decking and blind flying hood over rear cockpit. Pre-war deliveries, apart from (or by diversion from) RAF contracts, included nine for Danish Air Force, 59 for Persian Air Force, 17 for Iraqi Air Force, 12 for Brazilian Air Force, one for RCAF, 110 for RNZAF and 20 for RAAF.

Production transferred to Morris Motors Ltd at Cowley in 1941, subsequent deliveries including (in addition to those listed above), 24 for RNZAF, ten for Persian Air Force and five for SAAF. Pre-war deliveries from Hatfield included large batches to equip civilian-operated Elementary and Reserve Flying Training Schools; and total of 124 D.H.82As serving with seven of these schools impressed 1940-41 for RAF service (with serials in range BB672 to BB868) plus 41 miscellaneous privately-owned Tiger Moths. Production totals in UK were 114 D.H.82 and 1,950 D.H.82A at Hatfield and 3,432 D.H.82A by Morris Motors. For the Royal Norwegian Air Force, Haerens Flyvemaskinefabric built 17 D.H.82s and 20 D.H.82As. In New Zealand, the de Havilland Aircraft subsidiary built 181

D.H.82As against RNZAF contracts between 1940 and 1944. De Havilland Aircraft Pty Ltd in Australia built 1,085 D.H.82As between 1939 and 1945, of which 743 supplied to RAAF, 20 to RNZAF, 120 to South Africa, 94 to Southern Rhodesia and 128 to India. In Canada, de Havilland built 25 D.H.82As for RCAF to add to one British-built specimen and then went on to produce the D.H.82C variant noted below. Proposed production of 200 D.H.82As in Bombay cancelled but at least 120 previously civil Tiger Moths impressed for service in India 1940-42, of which a few converted as ambulances carrying one stretcher beneath hinged rear fuselage decking. Other impressments included 21 for the RAAF, 29 for the SAAF and 24 for the RNZAF, all from local sources.

D.H.82 Tiger Moth I: Initial production batch of 35 for RAF to Specification 23/31, deliveries starting 1932. Also two seaplanes to Specification 6/33 for evaluation in 1932.

D.H.82A Tiger Moth II: Major production version to Specifications 26/33 and 7/35. Two delivered as seaplanes in 1936. Rear fuselage strakes added retrospectively 1942 as anti-spinning precaution.

Equipped 28 Elementary Flying Training Schools in UK during World War II, and many exported to help equip RAF Empire Air Training Schools (in addition to Canadian production noted below). Adapted 1939-40 for use as emergency anti-invasion bomber carrying eight 20-lb (9.1 kg) bombs. *Max speed, 104 mph (167 km/h). Cruising speed, 90 mph (145 km/h). Initial climb, 635 ft/min (3.23 m/sec). Service ceiling, 14,000 ft (4,267 m). Range, 300 mls (393 km). Empty weight, 1,115 lb (506 kg). Gross weight, 1,825 lb (829 kg). Span, 29 ft 4 in (8.94 m). Length, 23 ft 11 in (7.29 m). Wing area, 239 sq ft (22.2 m²).*

D.H.82B Queen Bee: Refer to separate entry.

D.H.82C Tiger Moth: Canadian production version with enclosed and heated cockpits, revised undercarriage with main wheels moved forwards, wheelbrakes and different instrumentation. Production totalled 1,384

Below: The classic lines of the Tiger Moth, displayed by A17-565, one of the 1,085 D.H.82As built in Australia. Inset: The Tiger Moth BB704 was built as G-ADGF and impressed in 1940 for service with No 6 EFTS, subsequently acquiring the anti-spinning strakes on the rear fuselage (Mod 112) shown here in a 1949 photograph when it was serving with No 21 EFTS. Right upper: Ex-RAF, the Tiger Moth NZ859 acquired a coupe top in New Zealand and served with the Air Training Corps Touring Flight.

Above: One of the 136 Canadian-built Menasco Moths, 4923 is a Mk II version. The cockpit enclosure was standard on Tiger Moths used by the RCAF. Below: Camouflaged Queen Bee L5894 is prepared for catapult launch — apparently at RAE Farnborough — in the presence of the Prime Minister, Winston Churchill.

by late 1942, for RCAF and British Commonwealth Air Training Plan, including 200 funded by US through Lend-Lease and designated PT-24 for contract purposes, but retained in Canada. Also, 136 built with 132 hp Menasco Pirate D.4 engine in place of 145 hp Gipsy Major IC, delivered mid-1941 to RCAF and known locally as Menasco Moth, comprising ten pre-production D.H.82C-2 Menasco Moth I, 125 D.H.82C-4 Menasco Moth II with reduced fuel capacity and other minor changes, and one Menasco Moth III with Canadian radio.

DE HAVILLAND D.H.82B QUEEN BEE
This version of the D.H.82 Tiger Moth was designed to Specification 18/33 for a radio-controlled target aircraft, for anti-aircraft gunnery practice. Used D.H.60-type wooden fuselage in place of D.H.82 metal-and-fabric type, with 130 hp Gipsy Major I engine, larger fuel tank in centre section and radio control gear in rear cockpit. Alternative wheel or float undercarriage; normally launched from ship catapult as a seaplane for use at coastal ranges, landing on the sea afterwards for recovery. Prototype first flown (manually) on January 5, 1935; 320 built by DH at Hatfield to Specification 20/35, deliveries starting in 1935, and 60 by Scottish Aviation at Glasgow in 1943-44. Operated by Anti-Aircraft Co-operation Unit Flights in UK and overseas.
Max speed, 104 mph (167 km/h). Gross weight, 1,825 lb (829 kg). Span, 29 ft 4 in (8.94 m). Length, 23 ft 11 in (7.29 m).

DE HAVILLAND D.H.83 FOX MOTH
Four-seat light transport using D.H.82A mainplane, tail unit and undercarriage, designed in 1931 by A E Hagg and first

flown March 1932. Eleven civil examples, with 130 hp Gipsy Major engines, impressed in UK 1939-41 for communications duties, three similarly impressed in India and four in Australia for RAAF.
Max speed, 105 mph (169 km/h). Gross weight, 2,070 lb (940 kg). Span, 30 ft 10⁵/₈ in (9.40 m). Length, 25 ft 9 in (7.85 m).

DE HAVILLAND D.H.84 DRAGON
Seven-seat light transport designed in 1932 by A E Hagg with two 130 hp Gipsy Major Is and first flown November 24, 1932. Total of 115 built by DH at Hatfield for civil use, of which 25 served with NAC (National Air Communications) in civil guise in 1939, 17 being later impressed and used principally by Anti-Aircraft Co-operation Units for night flying. In Australia, the RAAF impressed 11 British-built civil D.H.84s and then acquired 87 built by de Havilland Aircraft Pty Ltd as radio/navigation trainers, the first of these flying on September 29, 1942.
Max speed, 134 mph (216 km/h). Gross weight, 4,500 lb (2,043 kg). Span, 47 ft 4 in (14.43 m). Length, 34 ft 6 in (10.51 m).

DE HAVILLAND D.H.85 LEOPARD MOTH
Three-seat lightplane designed to succeed Puss Moth in 1933 and first flown on May 27 that year, with 130 hp Gipsy Major. Production totalled 132 for civil use in UK and overseas. All 45 on UK register when war started impressed for Army Co-operation and communications duties. Seven impressed in India and at least three in South Africa.
Max speed, 137 mph (220 km/h). Gross weight, 2,225 lb (1,010 kg). Span, 37 ft 6 in (12.03 m). Length, 24 ft 6 in (11.12 m).

Above: The second of 87 Dragons built in Australia for use as radio/navigation trainers by the RAAF, known locally as Dragon Mk IIIs. Left: Fox Moth G-ACIY, impressed as DZ213, was used by No 781 Sqn at Lee in 1941/42. Below: Leopard Moth BD148, at Colerne in August 1945, was G-ACMA before impressment and was restored as such in 1946.

DE HAVILLAND D.H.86

The D.H.86 was designed in 1933 and first flew on January 14, 1934, as a ten-passenger four-engined airliner initially to meet Australian requirements. Production totalled 62 in D.H.86, D.H.86A and D.H.86B versions, with 200 hp Gipsy Six Srs I engines, of which four went to RAF — two as VIP transports for No 24 Squadron and two as wireless-operator trainers to Specification 28/37 for Radio School at Cranwell. Twenty-two D.H.86A/Bs assigned to National Air Communications September 1939 operating in civil guise; four remained civil for UK domestic services throughout war, eight others impressed for RAF and FAA use in UK, plus ten impressed in Middle East and India. Seven Australian civil D.H.86s impressed by RAAF 1939/41, including three in Middle East equipped as ambulances. Three D.H.86s in New Zealand impressed by RNZAF September 1939 and served to 1945 as radio/navigation trainers.

Max speed, 166 mph (267 km/h). Gross weight, 10,250 lb (4,654 kg). Span, 64 ft 6 in (19.66 m). Length, 46 ft 1 in (14.05 m).

Above: Serving in North Africa with No 1 Air Ambulance Unit of the RAAF, D.H.86 A31-7 was originally G-ADEA with Hillman Airways and later VR-SBC in Singapore before going to Australia as VH-UZX and subsequent impressment. Below: The D.H.86B (modified D.H.86A) G-ADUE at Heliopolis before its impressment as AX762 to serve with No 117 Sqn.

DE HAVILLAND D.H.87 HORNET MOTH

A side-by-side cabin biplane designed 1934 as replacement for D.H.60 Moth, first flown May 9, 1934. Production total, 165 in D.H.87A (pointed wing tips) and D.H.87B (blunt wing tips) versions, with 130 hp Gipsy Major 1 or 1F. Four delivered to RAF 1938 with twin Canadian Fairchild floats as seaplane trainers, converted to landplanes 1939 and used for communications by FAA. Sixty-four civil Hornet Moths impressed in UK (plus one escapee from Denmark in 1940) for RAF service, for communications and to equip six Coastal Patrol Flights in Coastal Command for off-shore radar calibration patrols in 1940. Three D.H.87B impressed for RAF in India, and at least 17 for SAAF in South Africa. A single ex-civil example served in the RCAF.

Max speed, 124 mph (200 km/h). Gross weight, 2,000 lb (908 kg). Span, 31 ft 11 in (9.73 m). Length, 24 ft 11½ in (7.59 m).

Below: The Hornet Moth W5830 was previously G-ADKE, impressed in October 1939 initially for the Station Flight at RAF Northolt. Above left: Inscribed 'RAF Transport Command North Bay', this Hornet Moth floatplane was reportedly CF-BFK before acquiring the apparently incorrect serial 5600, which properly belonged to a Canadian-built Hurricane XII.

DE HAVILLAND D.H.89 RAPIDE and DOMINIE

The D.H.89 was developed in 1933/34 as a light general purpose transport, the prototype flying on April 17, 1934. Total of 728 built, including 206 as D.H.89A Dragon Rapide up to 1939 and remainder as RAF Dominies, noted below, all with 200 hp Gipsy Queen III engines. Deliveries included two to RAF in 1938 for communications to Specification 21/38, three as R/T trainers to Specification T.29/38 and two as VIP transports, plus two to RAAF for communications. In 1939, 44 D.H.89As assigned to NAC in UK, of which 14 operated in civil guise for internal communications throughout war; 43 ex-civil examples impressed for RAF use, including ambulance duties, ATA ferry service and Anti-Aircraft Co-Operation Units. About eight D.H.89As impressed in India, plus four ex-RAF Dominies civil-registered for use by Air India and then also impressed. Seven civil D.H.89As impressed in Australia for RAAF as radio/navigation trainers until 1944; six impressed for RNZAF, several for SAAF. A number of Dragon Rapides was operated during the war by the Luftwaffe. They included two ex-Latvian and two ex-Lithuanian aircraft originally captured by the Soviet forces, and then by the Luftwaffe.

Max speed, 157 mph (253 km/h). Cruising speed, 132 mph (212 km/h). Initial climb, 867 ft/min (4.4 m/sec). Ceiling, 19,500 ft (5,944 m). Range, 578 mls (930 km). Empty weight, 3,276 lb (1,487 kg). Gross weight, 5,500 lb (2,497 kg). Span, 48 ft 0 in (14.63 m). Length, 34 ft 6 in (10.52 m). Wing area, 336 sq ft (31.2 m²).

D.H.89B Dominie: Production of D.H.89s from 1939 onwards for military purposes; name Dominie adopted 1941, with Mk I for navigation and W/T training and Mk II for communications with six passengers and two crew. Production totals, 186 by DH at Hatfield and 336 by Brush Coachworks at Loughborough, to 1945. Some transferred to USAAF in Europe; nine to RNZAF, 18 to SAAF and others to Allied air forces for communications duties.

DE HAVILLAND D.H.90 DRAGONFLY

The D.H.90 Dragonfly appeared in 1935 as a five-seat light twin for the private operator and small airline, with 130 hp Gipsy Major I engines. Impressments for communications duties included 15 in the UK, six in Canada, one in Australia and three in India. Also in Australia, Qantas Dragonflies were operated on charter to USAAF.

Above: Named 'Women of Britain' and 'Women of the Empire' respectively, Z7261 and Z7258 were among a batch of D.H.89As impressed for the RAF in July 1940. Originally G-AFMJ and G-AFMH, they served in the ambulance role with Hendon-based No 24 Sqn. Below left: A late production D.H.89B Dominie C Mk II, NR680 was built by Brush Coachworks and remained in the hands of de Havilland until sold in January 1948 to become G-AKSC. Below right: D.H.89A G-AFEP in late-1939 camouflage whilst serving with Air Commerce. It was impressed briefly in 1940 as X9388.

Max speed, 144 mph (232 km/h). Gross weight, 4,000 lb (1,816 kg). Span, 43 ft 0 in (13.11 m). Length, 31 ft 8 in (9.65 m).

DE HAVILLAND D.H.91 ALBATROSS

The D.H.91 was designed by A E Hagg during 1936 under Air Ministry contract as a long-range four-engined transport, covered by Specification 36/35. First aircraft flown May 20, 1937 and total of seven built 1938/39, with 525 hp Gipsy Twelve Srs I engines. Two impressed September 1940 for No 271 Sqn to operate UK-Iceland service; remainder operated by BOAC in civil guise

Above: The Dragonfly G-AECW, seen here in July 1940 in green/brown camouflage with yellow undersides, served de Havilland in the communications role until late 1944. Above right: Six Dragonflies were impressed to serve in the RCAF in 1940; this one is believed to be 7623, previously CF-BFF. Below: The second of two impressed D.H.91s, the Albatross G-AEVW 'Franklin' became AX904 in September 1940 to fly with No 271 Sqn.

until 1943.
Max speed, 225 mph (362 km/h). Gross weight, 29,500 lb (13,393 kg). Span, 104 ft 8 in (31.90 m). Length, 70 ft 0 in (21.34 m).

DE HAVILLAND D.H.93 DON

The D.H.93 Don was designed to Specification T.6/36 as an advanced trainer mounting a manually-operated dorsal turret in addition to accommodation for two pilots and a radio operator trainee. Prototype flown June 1937 with 525 hp Gipsy King I and 50 production aircraft built (20 as spare airframes without engines) in communications role without turrets after official requirements changed. Served with No 24 Sqn and numerous Station Flights throughout UK until early 1939, but all had been grounded for use as instructional airframes by the time the war began.
Max speed, 189 mph (304 km/h) at 8,750 ft (2,667 m). Gross weight, 6,530 lb (2,965 kg). Span, 47 ft 6 in (14.48 m). Length, 37 ft 4 in (11.38 m).

DE HAVILLAND D.H.94 MOTH MINOR

Two-seat open or coupé lightplane designed under direction of Capt Geoffrey de Havilland as a monoplane successor for the D.H.60 and first flown June 22, 1937, with 90 hp Gipsy Minor engine. Total of 73 completed at Hatfield by 1940, when jigs, tools and all stocks of completed components transferred to de Havilland Aircraft Pty Ltd at Bankstown, Australia. Total of 42 delivered to RAAF from Australian production for use as primary trainers. Thirty-two UK civil D.H.94s impressed for RAF service, of which 26 initially assigned (in October 1940) to Army Co-operation squadrons to give *ab initio* glider training; one impressed in Middle East assigned to USAAF; three impressed in India and one in Ceylon; one impressed for SAAF in South Africa. One used by de Havilland in 1940 with tricycle undercarriage and coupé rear cockpit.
Max speed, 118 mph (190 km/h). Gross weight, 1,550 lb (704 kg). Span, 36 ft 7 in (11.15 m). Length, 24 ft 5 in (7.44 m).

DE HAVILLAND D.H.95 FLAMINGO and HERTFORDSHIRE

The D.H.95 was designed by a team headed by R E Bishop as a twin-engined 12/17-passenger commercial transport, the prototype flying on December 28, 1938, with 890 hp

Above: D.H.94 Moth Minor G-AFTH in de Havilland's hands in 1940 after its evaluation as a prospective basic trainer at the A & AEE in December 1939. It later became HM585 for the Comm Flt at RAF Woodley. Below: Coupe Moth Minor G-AFOJ, which became E-0236 in 1942. Right: D.H.94 E-0226 with tricycle undercarriage in 1940.

Perseus XIIC engines. Two ordered as VIP transports for King's Flight to Specification 21/39, delivered September 1940, and one as communications aircraft for No 24 Sqn to Specification 20/39 delivered May 1940. One D.H.95 Hertfordshire military transport version built to Specification 19/39, with smaller cabin windows and other changes; production contract for 30 cancelled. Eleven production civil Flamingoes built of which three plus the prototype impressed for No 24 Sqn and FAA use; eight others with 930 hp Perseus XVI engines delivered to BOAC 1940/41 and based in Middle East throughout the war.
Max speed, 243 mph (391 km/h). Gross weight, 18,000 lb (8,172 kg). Span, 70 ft 0 in (21.34 m). Length, 51 ft 7 in (15.72 m).

Above right: The Flamingo R2766 was attached to the King's Flight in 1940 as G-AGCC when emergency evacuation of the Royal Family was a possibility, but later rejoined No 24 Sqn at Hendon as (below) 'Lady of Glamis'. Left: The sole example of the Hertfordshire I, R2510, which crashed after taking off from Hendon on October 23, 1940.

DE HAVILLAND D.H.98 MOSQUITO

The D.H.98 was developed in the course of 1938-39 by a design team headed by R E Bishop in accordance with an original concept for a high-speed two-seat unarmed bomber of wooden construction proposed by Capt Geoffrey de Havilland. Development proceeded during 1940 to Specification B.1/40, written round the DH proposal and covering a bomber/reconnaissance aircraft with provision for development of a fighter variant also, powered by 1,280 hp Merlin RM35M engines. Initial contract placed March 1, 1940, for 50 bomber/reconnaissance aircraft, including one prototype; amended July 1940 to include one fighter prototype and in January 1941 to include a reconnaissance prototype, with many subsequent amendments and additions to contracts which eventually covered production of 6,411 Mosquitoes in Britain, 1,134 in Canada and 212 in Australia, production continuing until 1950. In the UK, production shared between de Havilland at Hatfield, Leavesden and (post-war) Chester, Airspeed at Christchurch, Percival at Luton and Standard Motors at Coventry; Canadian and Australian production was by the de

Above: The third Mosquito, W4052, in night fighter finish and with AI Mk IV radar and early exhaust mufflers. Right: The same aircraft in day fighter finish, without radar, and with unshrowded, individual flame-damping exhausts. Never issued to a squadron, but used for a time by the Fighter Interception Unit, W4052 survived until 1946.

Havilland companies at Toronto and Sydney respectively. Mosquito prototype (W4050) with span of 52 ft 6 in (16.0 m), first flown at Hatfield November 25, 1940, with 1,460 hp Merlin 21 engines;

gross weight, 16,000 lb (7,264 kg) and speed of 392 mph (631 km/h) recorded in FS gear at full-throttle height of 22,000 ft (6,705 m), establishing Mosquito as world's fastest operational aircraft at that time, a distinction retained by subsequent Mosquito marks for next 2 1/2 years. Merlin 61s fitted in prototype and first flown June 20, 1942, when speed of 414 mph (666 km/h) recorded in MS gear at weight of 17,800 lb (8,081 kg). Merlin 77s fitted in October 1942 and span increased to 59 ft 2 in (18.03 m); speed of 437 mph (703 km/h) achieved at 29,000 ft (8,839 m) at 18,000 lb (8,172 kg) — the fastest of any Mosquito. Flown with dummy four-gun dorsal turret aft of cabin, July 1941.

Mosquito PR Mk I: Ten of initial production batch completed in photo-recce configuration, including one prototype, first flown June 10, 1941. Span 54

Above: Photographed on orthochromatic film which hides its overall yellow finish, the original Mosquito is seen here in November 1940, the month of its first flight, bearing the maker's serial E0234 (later to become W4050). Note the minimal provision for engine exhaust, short nacelles and absence of u/c doors. Below: The second Mosquito, W4051, in service with No 1 PRU at Benson, where it arrived in July 1941.

ft 2 in (16,51 m), as for all production aircraft; short nacelles for 1,300 hp Merlin 21 engines; three vertical and one oblique camera; gross weight 18,050 lb (8,195 kg). Two had extra fuel and higher weight; two modified for tropical service. Issued to No 1 PRU, Benson and flew first operational sortie September 17, 1941.

Mosquito F Mk II: Variant of basic D.H.98 design evolved to Specification F.21/40 as two-seat twin-engined day and night long-range fighter and intruder, with Merlin 21 or 23 engines in long nacelles, and four 20-mm cannon in the lower front fuselage plus four 0.303-in (7.7-mm) Brownings in the nose. Prototype (from initial Mosquito production batch) first flown May 15, 1941. Production aircraft carried AI Mk IV or Mk V (with arrow-head aerials), and used primarily as UK-based night fighters, in

Built by Standard Motors at its Coventry works early in 1945, Mosquito FB Mk VI RF610, with underwing armament of four RPs (two each side), served with No 248 Sqn on coastal strike duties. It was among a batch of ex-RAF Mosquitos transferred to Yugoslavia in September 1952.

overall black finish, often referred to as NF Mk IIs. Total 589 built (including 199 converted to NF Mk XII & XVII), initial deliveries to No 157 Sqn, March 1942. Twenty-five modified as Special Intruders for No 23 Sqn, without AI and

Above: Still in day fighter finish but carrying AI Mk IV radar for night fighting, the Mk II W4092 came from the initial Mosquito production batch and is here serving with No 157 Sqn. Below: G-AGGD (ex-HJ681) was one of six unarmed Mk VIs supplied to BOAC in April/May 1943 for the strategic run to Sweden.

Left: One of the ten bomber Mosquitos from the original production batch, W4072 was a B Mk IV Srs 1, distinguished by the short-tailed nacelles. Below: In February 1944, No 692 Sqn began operating the B Mk IV (Special), featuring a bulged bomb-bay to carry a 4,000 lb (1,816 kg) bomb.

with extra fuel. Two flown with dorsal four-gun turrets, on September 14 and December 5, 1941, respectively, but not further developed. One fitted with Turbinlite airborne searchlight in nose for trials with Nos 151, 532 and 85 Sqns in 1943. One to RAAF in Australia as pattern for FB Mk 40.

Max speed, 370 mph (595 km/h) at 22,000 ft (6,706 m). Initial climb, 3,000 ft/min (15.2 m/sec). Ceiling, 36,000 ft (10,973 m). Max range, 1,705 mls (2,743 km). Empty weight, 13,431 lb (6,098 kg). Gross weight, 18,547 lb (8,420 kg). Span, 54 ft 2 in (16.51 m). Length, 40 ft 6 in (12.34 m).

Mosquito T Mk III: Dual control unarmed training version, initially with Merlin 21 and later with Merlin 23 and 25. Five of initial production batch completed as Mk IIs with dual controls, the first of these being one of the two examples with dorsal turrets, flown on December 5, 1941. 200 built at Leavesden up to July 1945, 164 more post-war at Leavesden and Hatfield. Fourteen to RAAF and 24 to RCAF.

Mosquito B Mk IV: Initial day and night bomber variant. Ten aircraft in initial production batch started as PR Mk I airframes but completed as bombers, known initially as PR/Bomber Conversion Type but redesignated B Mk IV Series 1 before service, including the bomber prototype first flown mid-September 1941, also considered as prototype for B Mk V. B Mk IV Srs 1s had Merlin 21s, short nacelles and bomb load of 2,000 lb (908 kg) in two or four bombs. Deliveries to No 105 Sqn began November 1941 but large-scale operations awaited arrival of B Mk IV Srs 2, the first example of which flew March 1942, this having long-tail nacelles, Merlin 21 or 23 engines and provision for 50-Imp gal (227-1) wing drop tanks. First operation (four aircraft to Cologne) on May 31, 1942. Production of 300 B Mk IV Srs 2, less nine converted to other versions in production. Post-delivery modifications of 27 to PR Mk IV, with cameras as PR Mk I; 20 to carry one 4,000-lb (1,816-kg) bomb each in bulged bomb-bay, with gross weight of 21,500 lb (9,760 kg), commenced operations with Nos 627 and 692 Sqns February 23, 1944; 36 aircraft modified 1943 to carry *Highball* anti-shipping spinning bomb for operations with No 618 Sqn, 24 of these later having arrester gear, Merlin 25s and other mods for carrier-based operations in Pacific, but no operations undertaken. Data for standard B Mk IV Srs 2:
Max speed, 380 mph (611 km/h). Cruising

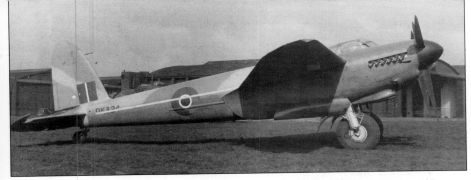

Above: Five Mosquito B Mk IVs fitted with two-stage Merlin 61 engines and cameras became PR Mk VIIIs for interim use by No 540 Sqn in 1943; DK324 was the first, here seen at the A & AEE. Left: Essentially a B Mk IV with Merlin engines, this B Mk IX was at the A & AEE in mid-1943 for SCI (smoke-curtain installation) trials.

speed, 265 mph (426 km/h). Rate of climb, 2,500 ft/min (12.71 m/sec). Ceiling, 34,000 ft (10,363 m). Max range, 2,040 mls (3,282 km). Empty weight, 13,400 lb (6,084 kg). Gross weight, 21,462 lb (9,744 kg).

Mosquito PR Mk IV: Twenty-seven B Mk IV Srs 2 converted, April 1942 onwards, to have cameras as PR Mk I.

Mosquito B Mk V: Proposed version of B Mk IV with provision for two 1,000-lb (454-kg) internal and two 500-lb (227-kg) underwing bombs. Tests on B Mk IV prototype; no production.

Mosquito PR Mk V: Projected photo-recce version with same wing as B Mk V and extra fuel capacity. Not built.

Mosquito FB Mk VI: Day and night fighter-bomber/intruder, armed with four machine guns and four cannon as F Mk II, plus two 250-lb (113-kg) bombs in rear of bomb-bay and one 250-lb (113-kg) under each wing; (increased to 500-lb/227-kg bombs in Srs 2 aircraft); alternative wing loads included SCI, mine, depth charge, four 60-lb (27-kg) rockets each side or 50- or 100-Imp gal (227- or 455-1) drop tank. Prototype first flew June 1, 1942; total of 2,305 built. Merlin 21, 23 or 25, and some aircraft with AI Mk IV, V or XV radar. First deliveries to No 418 Squadron May 1943. Nine Mk VI aircraft (plus one Mk IV and three Mk III) modified for use by BOAC, in civil markings, on courier service between Scotland and Sweden, making 520 round trips between February 1943 and May 1945. Thirty-eight supplied to RAAF.

Mosquito NF Mk VI: Projected night-fighter in parallel with FB Mk VI, not built.

Mosquito B Mk VII: Initial Canadian production version, based on B Mk V design and powered by 1,460 hp Packard-built Merlin 31s. Twenty-five built, first flight September 24, 1942. All retained in Canada; six transferred to USAAF as F-8 with cameras for PR duties.

Mosquito PR Mk VIII: Similar to PR Mk IV but fitted with Merlin 61s with two-speed two-stage superchargers. One B Mk IV converted to prototype and flown October 20, 1942, and four others converted from B Mk IVs in production.

Mosquito PR Mk IX: As PR Mk VIII but powered by 1,680 hp Merlin 72 engines. First of 90 production examples flown April 1943. Service introduction

June 1943 by No 540 Sqn; also flown by No 60 Sqn, SAAF, 1944-45. At least eight modified to have 1,710 hp Merlin 76/77 engines with paddle blade propellers, and one with 1,705 hp Merlin 67s (RM10SM).

Mosquito B Mk IX: As B Mk IV but powered by 1,680 hp Merlin 72 engines. First of 54 production examples flown March 24, 1943; provision for four 500-lb (227-kg) bombs internal and one under each wing. Normal gross weight 22,823 lb (10,360 kg), or 24,753 lb (11,238 kg) with 100-Imp gal (454-1) drop tanks. Some modified to carry 4,000-lb (1,816-kg) bomb in bulged bomb-bay and *Oboe* in nose; a few fitted with H2S Mk VI.

Mosquito NF Mk X: Proposed night fighter, similar to NF Mk II with Merlin 61 engines. Not built.

Mosquito FB Mk X: Proposed fighter-bomber, similar to FB Mk VI with Merlin 101 engines. Not built.

Mosquito FB Mk XI: Proposed fighter-bomber, similar to FB Mk VI with Merlin 61 engines. Not built.

Mosquito NF Mk XII: Night fighter derivative of Mk II with AI Mk VIII radar in 'thimble' nose replacing nose machine guns. Two prototype Mk II conversions at Hatfield mid-1942 followed by 97 by Marshalls at Cambridge, 1943. Initial deliveries to No 85 Sqn, February 28, 1943.

Mosquito NF Mk XIII: As Mk XII but based on FB Mk VI, with provision for wing drop tanks, and Merlin 21 or 23 engines. Total of 270 built, delivered February 1944 onwards.

Mosquito NF Mk XIV: Proposed production night fighter, as Mk XIII with Merlin 72/73 engines. Not built.

Mosquito NF Mk XV: Specialised high-altitude night fighter, with pressure cabin, Merlin 61, 73 or 77 engines and span extended to 59 ft 0 in (17.98m). Prototype flown September 14, 1942, with guns in nose as single-seater and in November as two-seater with AI Mk VIII in nose and four guns in ventral pack, followed by four similar production conversions of Mk II airframes in 1942-43. Issued to No 85 Sqn March 1943, operated at altitudes up to 44,600 ft (13,594 m).

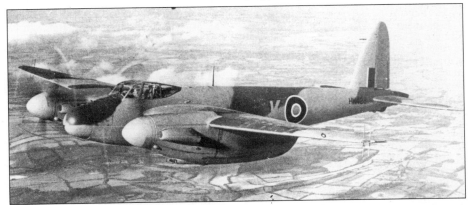

Above: Serving with No 29 Sqn, HK428 is an NF Mk XIII with the small 'thimble' radome first used for the AI Mk VIII. Right: A later Mk XIII, MM478, with the bulbous 'universal' radome. Below: One of four Mk II conversions to NF Mk XV, DZ385 displays its ventral gun pack and extended wing tips.

Mosquito PR Mk XVI: Similar to PR Mk IX, but with pressurised cockpit. Pressure cabin prototype flown August 8, 1942, and first pressurised PR Mosquito (a converted B MK IV) in July 1943. Production deliveries began November 1943; first operational use by No 140 Sqn, February 1944. Total of 433 built of which 79 supplied to USAAF units in UK including six trials aircraft with H2X in nose. Twenty-three to RAAF and also used by No 60 Sqn, SAAF, in Italy, 1944-45.

Mosquito B Mk XVI: Similar to B Mk IX with pressure cabin, based on prototype development (see PR Mk XVI). First production B Mk XVI flown October 1943; 80 built with Merlin 72/73 and 320 with Merlin 76/77; all but first 12 with bulged bomb-bay for 4,000-lb (1,816-kg) bomb. Some fitted with *Oboe* H2S and other bombing navaids. Initial deliveries to Nos 109 and 139 Sqns, end-1943.

Max speed (with 4,000-lb/1,816-kg bomb), 408 mph (656 km/h) at 28,500 ft (8,687 m) and 329 mph (529 km/h) at sea level. Intitial operating ceiling, 28,500 ft (8,687 m). Operational range, 1,100 mls (1,770 km) with 597 Imp gal (2,714 l) including two 100-Imp gal (454-l) drop tanks. Empty weight, 14,901 lb (6,765 kg). Gross weight, 25,200 lb (11,440 kg). Span, 54 ft 2 in (15.51 m). Length, 40 ft 6 in (12.34 m).

Mosquito NF Mk XVII: Similar to NF Mk XII but fitted with American SCR 720 (AI Mk X). First flown March 1943, and total of 99 converted from F Mk IIs by Marshalls of Cambridge in 1943 after one prototype at Hatfield.

Mosquito FB Mk XVIII: As FB Mk VI with 57-mm, 6-lb (2.7-kg) Molins gun in fuselage replacing four 20-mm cannon; also armed with four 0.303-in (7.7-mm) machine guns and two 500-lb (227-kg) bombs or eight 60-lb (27-kg) RPs under wings. Total of 27 converted from FB Mk VIs; first flown June 8, 1943; initial operations October 24, 1943, with No 248 Sqn, Coastal Command. Sometimes referred to as the 'Tse-tse'.

Mosquito NF Mk XIX: Similar to NF Mk XIII but fitted with American SCR 720 (AI Mk X) radar in 'bull nose' fairing able to accommodate either US or British equipment, and Merlin 25s. First flown April 1, 1944; 280 built.

Mosquito B Mk XX: Principal Canadian production version, similar to B Mk VII with 1,460 hp Packard-built

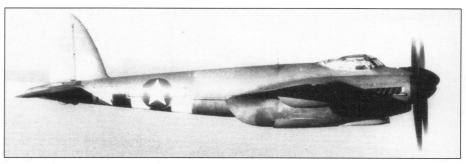

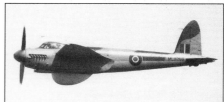

Above: NS635 was one of the Mosquito PR Mk XVIs operated by the USAAF, here seen flying from BAD 2 at Warton in July 1944. Right: The B Mk XVI ML926/G with an experimental H2S bombing aid installation in June 1944. Below: A standard B Mk XVI, ML963 was lost on a mission to Berlin on April 10, 1945, flying with No 571 Sqn.

Merlin 31 or 33 engines and North American equipment. Two-hundred-and-forty-five built, 1943-June 1944, of which 98 to RCAF, 34 to USAAF as F-8 with cameras for PR duties and balance to RAF in UK, August 1943 onwards.

Mosquito FB Mk 21: Canadian production equivalent of FB Mk VI, built in 1943. Two with Merlin 31s and one with Merlins 33s.

Mosquito T Mk 22: Canadian production equivalent of T Mk III, with Merlin 33s. Six built in 1943.

Mosquito B Mk 23: Projected Canadian production equivalent of B Mk IX with Packard Merlin 69s or 76s. Not built.

Mosquito FB Mk 24: Similar to FB Mk 21 with Packard Merlin 301 engines. Two commenced 1943, only one completed, cancelled before flight February 1944.

Mosquito B Mk 25: Canadian production version to succeed B Mk XX,

with 1,620 hp Packard Merlin 225 engines. Total 400 built, June 1944 onwards, of which 51 to RCAF and balance to RAF in UK. Few modified to carry 4,000-lb (1,816-kg) bomb in deepened bay. One converted to have two-stage modified Merlin 68s by Marshalls of Cambridge, January 1945.

Mosquito FB Mk 26: Similar to FB Mk 21 with Packard Merlin 225 engines. Production totalled 337, October 1944 onwards; 197 to RCAF, balance to RAF, used principally in Middle East.

Mosquito T Mk 27: Similar to T Mk 22 with Packard Merlin 225 engines. Forty-nine built, 1945, of which 19 to RCAF.

Mosquito 28: Unused mark number for Canadian production.

Mosquito T Mk 29: Dual control conversions of FB Mk 26; 39 completed 1945.

Mosquito NF Mk 30: As NF Mk XIX with two-stage 1,680 hp Merlin 72s; later

Below left: An FB Mk XVIII conversion from an FB Mk VI, MM424 served with Nos 248 and 254 Sqns, and survived the war.
Below right: A production NF Mk XIX, MM652 served with Nos 157 and 169 Sqns before being sold to Sweden in 1948.

Above: Of 40 Mosquito B Mk XXs transferred to USAAF as F-8s for photo-recce, only 16 came to Britain; this one, 43-34928, stayed in the US. Left: The T Mk 29 KA117 in the UK in late 1945; a converted FB Mk 26, it was on RCAF charge for only a month earlier that year.

1,710 hp Merlin 76 and finally 1,690 hp Merlin 113 engines. First flown March 1944; 530 built and operational service began June 13, 1944, with No 219 Sqn. *Max speed, 338 mph (544 km/h) at sea level and 424 mph (682 km/h) at 26,500 ft (8,077 m). Initial rate of climb, 2,250 ft/min (11.4 m/sec). Operational ceiling, 35,000 ft (10,668 m). Cruising speed, 288 mph (463 km/h) at sea level and 380 mph (611 km/h) at 30,500 ft (9,296 m). Cruising range, 1,180 mls (1,900 km). Empty weight, 15,156 lb (6,880 kg). Gross weight, 21,105 lb (33,958 kg). Span, 54 ft 2 in (16.51 m). Length, 41 ft 4 in (12.59 m).*

Mosquito NF Mk 31: Proposed variant of NF Mk 30 with Packard-built Merlin 69s. Not built.

Mosquito PR Mk 32: Lightened version of PR Mk 16 with extended wingtips for very high altitude operation. Five built, first flown August 1944, operational from December with No 540 Sqn.

Sea Mosquito TR Mk 33: Variant of FB Mk VI evolved to Specification N.15/44 for a carrier-borne torpedo-reconnaissance fighter/bomber. Converted Mk VI with arrester gear made first deck landings on *HMS Indefatigable*, March 25, 1944. Second converted Mk VI in August 1945 had folding wing and two Sea Mosquito prototypes with fixed wings flown in 1945 followed by first production TR Mk 33 on November 10, 1945, with Merlin 25 engines, folding wings, four-bladed propellers, JATO provision, four 20-mm cannon, underwing bombs as FB Mk VI and provision for

two 500-lb (227-kg) bombs in rear bomb-bay in lieu of a 2,000-lb (908-lb) torpedo, bomb or mine externally under fuselage. Length increased to 42 ft 3 in (12.88 m) by ASH radar in nose.

Mosquito PR Mk 34: Very-long-range reconnaissance version with extra fuel in deepened fuselage and two 200-Imp gal (909-l) wing drop tanks. Total fuel capacity 1,269 Imp gal (5,769 l) giving cruising range of 3,600 mls (5,792 km) at 300 mph (483 km/h) at 25,000 ft (7,620 m), on Merlin 113/114 engines and gross weight of 25,500 lb (11,577 kg). Four F.52 vertical and one F.24 oblique cameras. First flown December 4, 1944, and 231 built. Service principally post-war.

Mosquito B Mk 35: Final Mosquito bomber variant. Similar to B Mk XVI with 1,690 hp Merlin 113/114 engines. First flown March 12, 1945, and 276

built, completed early 1948. Some post-war conversions to TT Mk 35.

Mosquito NF Mk 36: As NF Mk 30 with Merlin 113 engines and British AI Mk IX radar. First flown May 1945 and 163 built for post-war service.

Sea Mosquito TR Mk 37, Mosquito NF Mk 38 and TT Mk 39: Post-war production and conversion programmes.

Mosquito FB Mk 40: Australian production version, by de Havilland at Bankstown, Sydney, based on FB Mk VI. Prototype converted from British-built Mk II with Packard Merlin 31s and flown on July 23, 1943. Production totalled 100 with Merlin 31s and 112 with Merlin 33s and paddle-blade propellers, first flown July, 23, 1943, and deliveries to RAAF commencing March 4, 1944, and continuing post-war. Service with No 1 Sqn against Japanese targets, and with Nos 87 and 94 Sqns.

Mosquito PR Mk 40: Six FB Mk 40 converted for PR role, May-October 1944, with increased internal fuel, drop tanks and three vertical and two oblique cameras.

Mosquito PR Mk 41: Twenty-eight FB Mk 40 converted for PR role, 1947-48, with Merlin 69s.

Mosquito FB Mk 42: One FB Mk 40 converted with Merlin 69 engines.

Mosquito T Mk 43: Twenty-two converted FB Mk 40s as dual control trainers with Merlin 33s, June 1944 onwards.

DE HAVILLAND D.H.100 VAMPIRE

The D.H.100 was Britain's second jet fighter, designed during 1942 to Specification E.6/41 around a single 2,700 lb st (1,226 kgp) H-1 Goblin turbojet, with an armament of four 20-mm Hispano cannon. First of three prototypes flown September 20, 1943, under codename 'Spider Crab'. Production contracts

Below: A Mosquito NF Mk 30 night fighter, NT484, serving with No 85 Sqn in April 1945 at Castle Camps. Above right: The Hooked Mosquito Mk VI LR359, unarmed and with four-bladed props, in 1944 and (below right) the first landing on HMS Indefatigable on March 25, 1944.

Above: Australian production of the Mosquito was supplemented early-1945 by the delivery of 38 FB Mk VIs from the RAF, for use by No 1 Sqn RAAF on Labuan Island; this was the last-but-one, A52-526. Left: A52-300, converted from the FB Mk 40 A52-90, was in effect the prototype PR Mk 41.

too late for combat use.

Max speed, 472 mph (759 km/h) at 22,000 ft (6,706 m) and 438 mph (705 km/h) at 10,000 ft (3,050 m). Max climb, 4,000 ft/min (20.32 m/sec). Service ceiling, 37,500 ft (11,430 m). Range (with 100-Imp gal/455-1 drop tanks), 1,500 mls (2,414 km). Range (with 200-Imp gal/910-l) drop tanks) 2,500 mls (4,023 km) at 340 mph (547 km/h) at 30,000 ft (9,150 m). Empty weight, 12,820 lb (5,820 kg). Gross weight, 17,700 lb (8,036 kg). Span, 45 ft 0 in (13.72 m). Length, 36 ft 8 in (11.17 m). Wing area, 361 sq ft (33.54 m²).

Sea Hornet: Two Hornet Is converted during 1944-45 to Specification N.5/44 as carrier-based long-range fighter prototypes for FAA use. First flown April 19, 1945. Third prototype, flown post-war, followed by production Sea Hornet F Mk 20s and NF Mk 21s.

Above: First of the Vampires, LZ548/G, at Hatfield in 1944, showing the original tall fins and rudders. Below: The fifth production Vampire F Mk I, by English Electric Co, showing the definitive 'square-topped' fins and rudders.

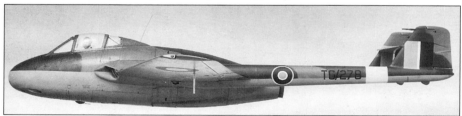

DESOUTTER MK I AND MK II
The Desoutter monoplane was a British license-built version of the Koolhoven F.K.41, a three-seat lightplane that originated in the 'twenties. Impressments for RAF communications duties totalled three Mk I with 115 hp Hermes II and one Mk II with 120 hp Gipsy III.
Max speed, 115 mph (185 km/h). Gross weight, 1,900 lb (863 kg). Span, 36 ft 0 in (10.97 m). Length, 27 ft 0 in (8.23 m).

placed with English Electric Co at Preston, for 120 on May 13, 1944, and 180 more on May 7, 1945; first production Vampire F Mk I flown at Salmsbury April 20, 1945. Deliveries, initially to equip No 247 Sqn, began after end of war.
Max speed, 531 mph (854 km/h) at 17,500 ft (5,334 m). Initial climb, 4,200 ft/min (21.34 m/sec). Range, 730 mls (1,175 km) at 380 mph (611 km/h) at 30,000 ft (9,150 m). Empty weight, 6,372 lb (2,893 kg). Gross weight, 10,480 lb (4,758 kg). Span, 40 ft 0 in (12.20 m). Length, 30 ft 9 in (9.37 m). Wing area, 266 sq ft (24.71m²)

engines and armed with four 20-mm cannon. First of two prototypes (unarmed) flown July 28, 1944 (initially with two Merlin 130s); second prototype carried armament and 200-Imp gal (910-l) underwing drop tanks. Initial production flight February 1, 1945, but quantity deliveries (to equip No 64 Sqn initially)

DE HAVILLAND D.H.103 HORNET
Design of the D.H.103 single-seat twin-engined fighter was undertaken at Hatfield as a private venture during 1942 and prototypes were ordered in June 1943 to Specification F.12/43. Intended for very long range operation in the South Pacific area, the D.H.103 was powered by 2,030 hp Merlin 130/131 (handed)

Below: The first production Hornet at Hatfield, PX210 displays the two-tone blue camouflage adopted for this fighter in 1945. Above right: Desoutter Mk II HM507, ex-G-AAZI, at Twinwood Farm in July 1944, where it deteriorated and did not fly again. It was from Twinwood, near Bedford, that Glenn Miller went missing on December 15, 1944 – but not in a Desoutter!

FAIREY FIREFLY II (BIPLANE)

The Firefly single-seat fighting biplane was designed by Marcel Lobelle in 1924, in the first place around the Curtiss D-12 engine. First flown on November 9, 1925, the Firefly was tested, but never adopted, by the RAF. Total of 87 Firefly IIM, with 480 hp Rolls-Royce F.XIS engines, metal construction and armed with two Vickers (later, FN) 0.303-in (7.7-mm) machine guns, acquired by *Aéronautique Militaire Belge*, 1931-33, of which 62 built by Avions Fairey at Gosselies. About 30 still serving 1940, some as advanced trainers and others equipping two *escadrilles* of IIe *Groupe de Chasse*. Briefly operational in May 1940 over Belgium and 14 then evacuated to France, flying in defence of Chartres area until June 16.

Max speed, 175 mph (292 km/h) at sea level and 223 mph (359 km/h) at 13,120 ft (4,000 m). Time to 19,685 ft (6,000 m), 10 min 55 sec. Ceiling, 30,840 ft (9,400 m). Empty weight, 2,387 lb (1,083 kg). Gross weight, 3,285 lb (1,490 kg). Span, 31 ft 6 in (9.6 m). Length, 24 ft 8 in (7.52 m).

FAIREY FOX

The original Fox two-seat high-speed bomber was designed around the 450 hp Curtiss D-12 engine by Marcel Lobelle in 1924, first flight being on January 3, 1925. Production of later versions included 201 for the *Aéronautique Militaire Belge*, of which the following were in service in 1940, some 65 operational sorties being made in May and about 17 Foxes then evacuated to France, where they survived, unflown, until 1944.

Fox II: Open-cockpit two-seat reconnaissance-fighter powered by 480 hp Kestrel IIS, with one fixed forward-firing FN 0.30-in (7.62-mm) and one similar gun on Fairey high-speed mount in rear cockpit, and eight 22-lb (10-kg) bombs under wings. Twelve Fairey-built and 26 from Avions Fairey in Belgium delivered 1931-1934; in service 1940 with three *escadrilles* of I, II and III observation *Groupes*, after modification to add cockpit canopies.

Fox III: As Mk II with two forward-firing machine guns. Fifteen built with open cockpits and 46 IIIC with enclosed

Above: A pre-war photograph of one of the Greek Fairey IIIFs in floatplane configuration, as operated by 11 Mira in 1940 when Italian forces invaded Greece.

cockpits, plus six IIIS dual control trainers. In service 1940 with five *escadrilles* of I, II and III *Groupes*.

Fox VI: Reconnaissance-fighter similar to Fox II with 860 hp Hispano-Suiza 12 Vdrs engine. Twenty-five VIR and 57 VIC, respectively with reconnaissance and combat equipment, built for AeMB; in service 1940 with three *escadrilles* of III *Groupe*.

Max speed, 227 mph (365 km/h) at 13,120 ft (4,000 m). Time to 16,400 ft (5,000 m), 6.5 min. Ceiling, 36,090 ft (11,000 m). Endurance, 2 hr 45 min. Empty weight, 3,680 lb (1,670 kg). Gross weight, 5,396 lb (2,450 kg). Span, 38 ft 0 in (11.58 m). Length, 28 ft 8 in (9.04 m).

Fox VIII: Final production version, as Fox VI with three-blade Ratier propeller and other improvements. Twelve delivered 1938-39 and in service 1940 with one *escadrille* of III *Groupe*.

FAIREY IIIF

Ending a long line of Fairey Series III types, the IIIF first flew on March 19, 1926, and was produced in a number of variants for FAA and RAF use, and for export. Among the latter, ten IIIF Mk IIIBs went to Greece in 1931 (as did four ex-FAA Mk IIIMs) and provided the equipment of 11 *Mira* of the Royal

Hellenic Air Force at the time of the Italian invasion of Greece in 1940. Any continuing use was ended by the German intervention in April 1941. The two/three-seat IIIF Mk IIIB was powered by a 530 hp Lion XIA and armed with one fixed Vickers and one flexible Lewis gun.

Max speed, 136 mph (219 km/h). Gross weight, 5,874 lb (2,664 kg). Span, 45 ft 9 in (13.94m). Length, 34 ft 0 in (10.36 m).

FAIREY GORDON

The Gordon was a general-purpose aircraft and day bomber developed for RAF use from the Fairey IIIF, first flown on March 3, 1931, and featuring an uncowled 605 hp Panther IIA radial, one aft-mounted Lewis 0.303-in (7.7-mm) gun on Fairey high-speed mount, a fixed forward-firing Vickers gun and up to 500 lb (227 kg) of bombs. Production for RAF totalled 154 Mk I (plus about 80 earlier IIIFs converted) and 24 Mk II with taller, more rounded fin-and-rudder and other changes; some served as floatplanes. Up to 30 still serving in Middle East (Nos 6, 45 and 47 Squadrons) in 1939 and a few in UK as target tugs at air armament schools. Six transferred to Royal Egyptian Air Force and, in April-August 1939, 49 Mk Is and IIs to RNZAF of which 30 in service when

Below left: A Fairey Firefly IIM, one of 87 acquired by the Aéronautique Militaire Belge serving with the 3ᵉ escadrille, IIᵉ Groupe. Below right: Fox IIs of the Aéronautique Militaire Belge in service early 1940.

Above: Fairey Gordon II K3994, which was operated by the TT Flight at Helwan until written off in a taxying accident in April 1941. Below: Ex-RAF Gordon I NZ616 as used at the RNZAF's Flying Training School at Wigram in 1940. Below right: Seal K4788, seen here before the war, was one of the four that served with No 273 Sqn, RAF, at China Bay in Ceylon until 1942.

Pacific War opened in December 1941.
Max speed, 145 mph (233 km/h) at 3,000 ft (914 m). Gross weight, 5,906 lb (2,679 kg). Span, 45 ft 9 in (13.95 m). Length, 36 ft 9 in (11.20 m).

FAIREY SEAL

Derived, like the Gordon, from the Fairey IIIF, the Seal first flew on September 11, 1930, and 91 were built for FAA service. Retired from the latter's front-line squadrons by 1938, a dozen Seals were with the RAF's No 10 Bombing and Gunnery School as target-tugs until mid-1940. Four others flew with No 273 Sqn, RAF, in Ceylon until May 1942, some as floatplanes, on coastal patrols. The three-seat Seal was powered by a 605 hp AS Panther IIA and armed as the Gordon.
Max speed, 138 mph (222 km/h). Gross weight, 6,000 lb (2,722 kg). Span, 45 ft 9 in (13.94 m) Length, 33 ft 8 in (10.26 m).

FAIREY SWORDFISH

The prototype of the Swordfish torpedo-spotter-reconnaissance aircraft for the Fleet Air Arm was developed under the direction of Marcel Lobelle to meet the requirements of Specification S.15/33. Known as the Fairey TSR.II, it was a derivative of the earlier TSR.I and, first flown on April 17, 1934, was powered by a 690 hp Pegasus IIIM3. Three development aircraft were ordered in May 1935 to Specification S.38/34 and production was authorised at the same time. The Swordfish carried three crew for recon-

naissance or two for torpedo duties, could operate as a floatplane and carried one 18-in (46-cm), 1,610-lb (731-kg) torpedo or 1,500-lb (681-kg) mine under the fuselage or up to 1,500-lb (681-kg) of assorted bombs under fuselage and wings; other armament comprised one forward-firing and one free-mounted aft 0.303-in (7.7-mm) gun. First flight of a development aircraft was on December 31, 1935, the other two following in 1936, one on floats.

Swordfish I: Initial production contract placed April 1935 for 86 aircraft, increased by subsequent contracts to 989 of which 300 were built by Blackburn at Sherburn-in-Elmet (sometimes known colloquially as 'Blackfish') and the remainder by Fairey. Deliveries began mid-1936 to No 825 Squadron, and 12 more squadrons equipped by September 1939; 13 more front-line FAA units were

equipped by June 1943, and more than 20 second-line units used Swordfish for training and other duties. Operational use included gun-spotting, mine-laying and torpedo attacks (notably at Taranto, when a complete Italian fleet was virtually eliminated, and on the battleships *Scharnhorst*, *Gneisenau* and *Prinz Eugen* in the English Channel).
Max speed, 139 mph (224 km/h) at 4,750 ft (1,448 m). Cruising speed, 104 mph (167 km/h) at 5,000 ft (1,525 m). Time to 5,000 ft (1,525 m), 10 mins. Service ceiling, 10,700 ft (3,260 m). Range, 546 mls (879 km) with torpedo, 1,030 mls (1,657 km) for reconnaissance. Empty weight, 5,200 lb (2,361 kg). Gross weight, 9,250 lb (4,200 kg). Span, 45 ft 6 in (13.87 m). Length, 36 ft 4 in (11.07 m). Wing area, 607 sq ft (56.39 m²).

Swordfish II: Improved version of Mk I with Pegasus IIIM3 or 775 hp Pegasus 30 engine, introduced 1943, with metal covered undersurfaces of lower wings to permit carriage and launching of eight 60-lb (27-kg) rocket projectiles. 1,080 built by Blackburn, of which 99 to Canada (some post-war) for RCAF and RCN. First successful operational use of

Below: Swordfish I K8871 flying with No 785 Sqn, formed at Crail in November 1940 to serve as a Torpedo Bomber Reconnaissance Training squadron. Above right: Swordfish II HS158, with underwing rocket launchers, seen on test from the Blackburn facility at Sherburn-in-Elmet on June 28, 1942.

Above: Swordfish III NF374 of No 119 Sqn, RAF, which flew these aircraft, plus Albacores, from Belgium bases against maritime targets in the final months of the war. Right: Trials Swordfish HS553, with covered canopy for Canadian use on test in the UK.

RPs from Swordfish on May 23, 1943, by No 819 Sqn, sinking a U-boat. Also used by two RAF squadrons until May 1945.

Swordfish III: As Mk II with ASV Mk X air-to-surface-vessel radar in large radome between undercarriage legs. 320 built by Blackburn, final delivery August 18, 1944. Operational, alongside Swordfish IIs, with several FAA front-line squadrons up to May 1945, aboard merchant aircraft carriers, escort carriers and from shore bases.

Swordfish IV: Some Swordfish IIs converted in Canada to have enclosed and heated cockpits. The designation was not officially confirmed.

FAIREY FANTOME

The Fantome, designed by Marcel Lobelle in 1934 and first flown on June 6, 1935, was intended to meet Belgian requirements for a successor to the Firefly II. Three more (called Feroce) were assembled by Avions Fairey in Belgium of which two were sold to Soviet Union and eventually served with Republican forces in Spain; the third was evaluated in UK by RAF during 1938 and 1939 (as L7045) and was on the strength of a gas contamination practice unit at Rollestone in 1940/41. The engine was a 925 hp Hispano-Suiza 12 Ycrs with a 20-mm Oerlikon motor-cannon.

Max speed, 270 mph (435 km/h) at 13,120 ft (4,000 m). Gross speed, 4,120 lb (2,060 kg). Span, 34 ft 6 in (10.52 m). Length, 27 ft 7 in (8.40 m).

FAIREY BATTLE

The Battle single-engined day bomber

monoplane was designed by a team headed by Marcel Lobelle during 1932-3 to the requirements of Specification P.27/32, and ordered for prototype construction on June 11, 1934. Powered by an 890 hp Merlin C, the prototype flew on March 10, 1936, and was intended as a two-seater (pilot and observer); provision for a radio operator/air gunner was made later, to man a Vickers 'K' 0.303-in (7.7-mm) dorsal gun. One Browing gun of similar calibre was carried in the starboard wing and a 1,000-lb (454-kg) bomb-load accommodated in wing cells could be supplemented by external wing bomb-racks.

Battle I: Initial production orders placed 1935 for 655 aircraft to Specification 23/35, built by Fairey at Stockport and the first of which flew early 1937. Subsequent production orders to Specification 14/36 brought total built to 2,184 including 1,029 by Austin Motors Shadow Factory at Longbridge to Specification 32/36, and including target-tug and training versions noted below. Production Battles were fitted with 1,030 hp Merlin I, II, III or V, and were often referred to as Battle I, II, III or V respectively to facilitate spares backing and maintenance. Entered service May 1937 with No 63 Sqn, and about 15 squadrons operational by September 1939. Operated with AASF in France but little used as day bomber after 1940. One RAF squadron operational in Iceland until July 1941. One Battle I supplied, ex-RAF, to SAAF in April 1939 was followed by about 160 more in 1940, used by squadrons in Western Desert and East Africa until 1942. Twenty-eight transferred to Turkey, September 1939, and 12 to Greece, also in 1939; one earmarked for Poland not delivered. Several Battles used as engine test beds during war, with Fairey P.24 and Prince, Napier Dagger VIII and Sabre, Bristol Taurus and Hercules and Rolls Royce Exe and Merlin XII.

Max speed at sea level, 257 mph (414 km/h) at 15,000 ft (4,572m), 215 mph (346 km/h) at 25,000 ft (7,620 m). Cruising speed, 200 mph (322 km/h) at 16,000 ft (4,877 m). Time to 15,000 ft (4,572 m), 13 min 36 sec. Range, 1,100 mls (1,770 km) at 16,000 ft (4,877 m). Empty weight, 6,647 lb (3,018 kg). Gross weight, 10,792 lb (4,900 kg). Span, 54 ft 0 in (16.46 m). Length, 42 ft 4 in (12.90 m). Wing area, 422 sq ft (39.20 m²).

Above: The last of the Fantôme fighters built by Avions Fairey, L7045 was tested at the A&AEE in 1938 and used for a variety of trials into 1939. Left: One of the Greek Battles, diverted from RAF stocks in 1939. Below left: Battle I K9264, with No 103 Sqn, was lost on May 10, 1940, when bombing German troops in Luxembourg. Below right: Battle Is of No 35 Sqn; aircraft 'G' and 'X' were also lost in France in May 1940, but 'O' survived for training use at 4BGS.

Above: A pair of Battle Is serving in the training role with the RCAF at 8 Bombing & Gunnery School, Lethbridge, Alberta. Nos 2054 (nearest camera) and 2056 were originally K9288 and L4957 respectively. Right: Still bearing its RAF serial, Battle IIT R7439 was fitted with a Wright Cyclone in Canada in May 1943.

Left: The Battle K9240 was one of a number used as engine test-beds, and seen here with a Napier Dagger VIII vertically-opposed 24-cylinder upright H-shaped engine. Below: A Battle target-tug, L5664, serving with No 2 Anti-Aircraft Co-operation Unit at Gosport; the ventral fairing provided stowage for the target drogues.

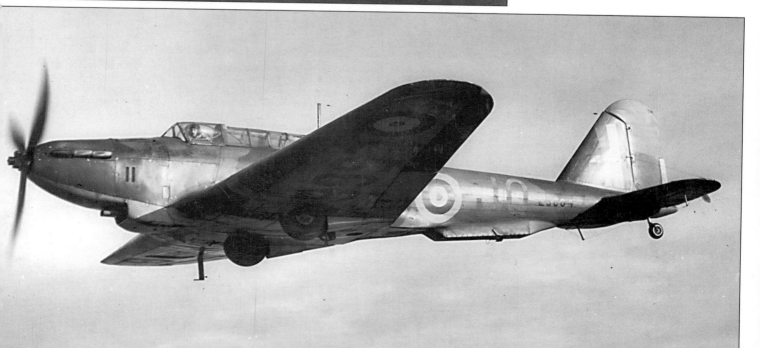

Battle T: After the Battle was retired from front-line service, several units used the type, basically unmodified, for training. A special dual-control trainer evolved in 1939 had separate, similar cockpits in tandem; after prototype testing, 200 built by Fairey and 66 by Austin. Total of 740 Battles shipped to Canada, August 1939 onwards, for training school use, included 70 twin-cockpit Battle Ts and some Battle TT target tugs (see below); similarly, 364 ex-RAF Battles shipped to Australia, 1940 onwards, for training and target towing. For gunnery training, some Battles carried Bristol Type I single-gun dorsal turret in place of rear cockpit; two prototypes tested in UK and 204 similarly converted in Canada, 1942/43, as Battle IT, plus one turret trainer with R-1820-G3B Cyclone radial as Battle IIT.

Battle TT: Variant for use as target tug, with wind-driven winch on port side of fuselage and drogue stowage box below rear fuselage. 200 built by Austin, starting February 1940, plus conversions of Battle bombers in UK and Canada.

Belgian Battle: Sixteen Battles ordered for *Aéronautique Militaire Belge* in 1938, assembled by Avions Fairey at Gosselies from Stockport-built components. Radiator farther forward than British version; Merlin III engine. In service with 5e *escadrille*, III *Groupe*, in May 1940 and used for a single mission against bridges over the Albert Canal.

FAIREY SEAFOX

The Seafox was designed to Specification S.11/32 for a two-seat reconnaissance floatplane to be carried on RN light cruisers. Powered by a 365 hp Rapier VI, the first of two prototypes was flown on May 27, 1936, and followed by 64 production Seafox Is delivered from April 1937 onwards. One prototype and one production Seafox were flown as landplanes, all others being floatplanes for catapult launching and subsequent landing alongside their parent ships for recovery. Equipped five catapult flights (which merged to form No 700 Squadron in January 1940) and operated during Battle of the River Plate to spot for the guns of HMS *Ajax*, *Achilles* and *Exeter*.
Max speed, 124 mph (200 km/h) at 5,860 ft (1,786 m); Gross weight, 5,420 lb (2,559 kg). Span, 40 ft 0 in (12.19 m). Length, 33 ft 5 in (10.20 m).

Above: A Battle T trainer, P6723, in service with Polish-manned No 304 Sqn in 1940 alongside Battle bombers.
Right: Battle TT, RCAF serial 1650, in target-tow colours, was ex-RAF L5608, delivered direct to Canada for service at No 4 B&G School. Below: Battle IT 1966 was ex-RAF L5421, delivered to Canada in June 1941 and fitted with a dorsal turret in April 1943.

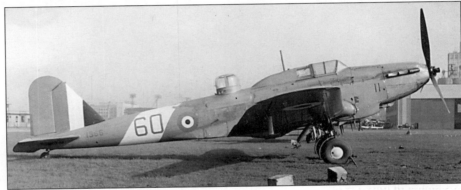

FAIREY P.4/34

Two prototypes (K5099 and K7555) of a two-seat dive bomber designed by Marcel Lobelle to Specification P.4/34 for the RAF were built, making their first flights on January 13 and April 19, 1937, respectively. Power plant was a 1,030 hp

Merlin I in the first and a 1,030 hp Merlin II in the second, and 500 lb (227 kg) of bombs were carried externally. The first prototype served at RAE Farnborough and the second became a prototype for the Fulmar, later testing the Fairey-Youngman flaps and four-cannon installation for the Firefly. The Danish Naval Workshops (*Orlogsvaerftet*) obtained a licence for P.4/34 production but none had been completed by the time of German occupation in 1940.
Max speed, 283 mph (453 km/h) at 15,000 ft (4,575 m). Gross weight, 8,787 lb (2,986 kg). Span, 47 ft 4¹/₂ in (14.44 m). Length, 40 ft (12.2 m).

FAIREY FULMAR

The Fulmar emerged in 1938 as an adaption to Specification O.8/38 for a two-seat Naval fighter, of the P.4/34 day bomber. Differences included a small reduction in wing span, folding wings, deck-arrester gear, catapult points, modified cockpit canopy, Naval equipment and use of a 1,275 hp Merlin VIII. Armament comprised eight Browning 0.303-in (7.7-mm) guns in the wings and provision for a similar Vickers K gun in the rear cockpit. One P.4/34 prototype was converted to test features of Fulmar in March 1938.

Fulmar I: Total of 250 built for FAA, first flight being on January 4, 1940, with Merlin VIII engine. Entered service June 1940 with No 808 Sqn, and first operations Sept/Oct 1940 on Malta convoys. Equipped 14 front-line squadrons by end-1942 including one in Egypt and one

Above right: The second of two Fairey P.4/34s, K7555 was used in the early war years to flight-test Fairey Youngman flaps and, later, pneumatically-operated bellows-type airbrakes. Below: Seafox I of No 765 Sqn at Sandbanks in 1942.

began operations in June, joined by three more during 1940, all engaged in land-based anti-submarine patrols and night-bombing attacks on Channel targets. First major operation by carrier-based Albacores was Battle of Cape Matapan in March 1941. One squadron operated from Malta and several in North Africa; one UK-based RCAF Squadron, No 415, flew Albacores in 1943/44, and as No 119 Sqn continued into 1945.

Max speed, 161 mph (257 km/h) at 4,500 ft (1,370 m). Cruising speed, 116 mph (186 km/h). Time to 6,000 ft (1,830 m), 8 min. Service ceiling, 20,700 ft (6,310 m). Range, 710 mls (1,143 km), with 2,000-lb (907-kg) warload. Empty weight, 7,250 lb (3,292 kg). Gross weight, 10,460 lb (4,749 kg). Span, 50 ft 0 in (15.25 m). Length, 39 ft 10 in (12.14 m). Wing area, 623 sq ft (57.9 m²).

FAIREY BARRACUDA

The Barracuda torpedo/dive-bomber was evolved to meet Specification S.24/37 under the direction of Marcel Lobelle during 1938, initially to be powered by a 1,150 hp Exe but eventually based on the 1,300 hp Merlin 30. Two prototypes ordered January 30, 1939, of which the first was flown on December 7, 1940, initially with low-set tailplane. Second prototype, with definitive high tailplane, flown June 29, 1941, and first prototype flown in Mk II configuration with Merlin 32 on August 17, 1942. With crew of three, the Barracuda had armament of two 0.303-in (7.7-mm) Vickers 'K' guns in rear cockpit and carried one torpedo or 1,500-lb (681-kg) mine under fuselage or four 500-lb (227-kg) or six 250-lb (114-kg) bombs under wings.

Barracuda I: Initial production batch of 25 by Fairey and five by Westland; first flown May 18, 1942. Merlin 30 engine and 13,500 lb (6,129 kg) gross weight.

Barracuda II: Principal production version, with 1,640 hp Merlin 32 engine and 14,100 lb (6,401 kg) gross weight. ASV Mk IIN radar fitted. Production

Above: A pair of Fulmar IIs in service with No 803 Sqn in 1942. Below: Albacore I X8980 of No 826 Sqn, bearing codes S4K and black undersurfaces for night intruder missions, in Egypt in 1942.

in India; also operated as night-intruder from shore bases, including Malta, and as night-fighter with No 813 Sqn on Russian convoys. One captured and operated by Vichy French forces at Dakar in 1941.

Max speed, 280 mph (451 km/h). Cruising speed, 235 mph (375 km/h). Initial rate of climb, 1,200 ft/min (6.1 m/sec). Service ceiling, 26,000 ft (7,925 m). Max range, 800 mls (1,287 km). Empty weight, 6,915 lb (3,137 kg). Gross weight, 9,800 lb (4,445 kg). Span, 46 ft 4½ in (14.14 m). Length, 40 ft 3 in (12.2 m).

Fulmar II: As Fulmar I but fitted with 1,300 hp Merlin 30, Rotol propeller and tropical filters. One Mk I converted, first flown January 20, 1941, and 350 production aircraft delivered, ending February 1943.

FAIREY ALBACORE

The Albacore torpedo-bomber-reconnaissance biplane was designed by Marcel Lobelle to meet the requirements of Specification S.41/36 and a prototype flew on December 12, 1938. Power plant was a 1,065 hp Taurus II and armament

comprised a fixed forward-firing 0.303-in (7.7-mm) gun and one or two similar guns in the rear cockpit, with one 18-in (46-cm), 1,600-lb (727-kg) torpedo under fuselage or four 500-lb (227-kg) bombs under wings. Production totalled 800 (including prototypes), completed in 1943, later aircraft having the 985 hp Taurus XII engine. Service deliveries began March 1940 to No 826 Sqn, which

Below left: Barracuda II DN633 serving in 1943 with No 736 Sqn, the FAA School of Air Combat at Yeovilton. Below right: Barracuda II MX613 trials aircraft carrying an ASR lifeboat. Above right: The third Barracuda TR Mk V prototype, LS479.

Above: Firefly F Mk I, with underwing bombs. Below left: Firefly NF Mk 1 MB590 in service with No 1791 Sqn in mid-1945. Below right: Firefly NF Mk II Z1875, with lengthened forward fuselage and wing-root radomes.

total, 675 by Fairey, 700 by Blackburn, 300 by Boulton Paul and 13 by Westland. Initial deliveries to No 827 Sqn, January 1943, and 12 squadrons operational by January 1944; first actions September 1943. One Mk II flown with airborne lifeboat carried under fuselage and another tested with underwing containers each to carry two parachute-equipped occupants.

Max speed, 228 mph (367 km/h) at 1,750 ft (533 m). Cruising speed, 172-193 mph (277-311 km/h) at 5,000 ft (1,524 m). Time to 5,000 ft (1,524 m), 6 min. Service ceiling, 16,600 ft (5,060 m). Range, 524 mls (843 km) with 1,800 lb (816 kg) bombs, 1,150 mls (1,850 km) with max fuel. Empty weight, 9,350 lb (4,241 kg). Gross weight, 14,100 lb (6,396 kg). Span, 49 ft 2 in (14.99 m). Length, 39 ft 9 in (12.12 m). Wing area, 405 sq ft (37.62 m).

Barracuda III: As Mk II with ASV Mk X scanner in ventral radome, for anti-submarine duties. Deliveries began 1943; 460 built by Fairey and 392 by Boulton Paul.

Barracuda IV: One Mk II converted to have 1,850 hp Griffon VIII and flown November 16, 1944. Span increased to 53 ft 0½ in (16.17 m) and crew reduced to two.

Barracuda V: Production form of Mk IV with 1,960 hp Griffon 37 and revised cowling. No rear defensive armament but one forward-firing Browning in wing. Max external bomb load 2,000 lb (907 kg). Some Mk IIs converted to Mk V during production in 1945; first genuine production Mk V flown post-war.

FAIREY FIREFLY

The Firefly was developed by a design team headed by H E Chaplin to meet FAA requirements for a carrier-borne fighter-reconnaissance aircraft as defined at first by Specifications N.8/39 and N.9/39 and subsequently revised in Specification N.5/40 in the light of Fairey's initial proposals. An initial production contract was placed in 1940, the first three aircraft to serve as prototypes and the next ten as pre-production aircraft. The all-metal Firefly was powered by a 1,735 hp Griffon IIB or 1,815 hp Griffon XII, armed with four 20-mm cannon in the wings and seated pilot and observer in tandem. First flight was made on December 22, 1941, second prototype on June 4, 1942, and third on August 26, 1942.

Firefly F Mk I: Initial production contract for 200 in June 1940, 100 more in September 1941, 300 more in June 1942 and 200 more in August 1943, of which total 770 were built, including variants noted below and diversions to Mk IV. Power plant and armament as prototypes; provision for two 1,000-lb (454-kg) bombs under wings. First unit, No 1770 Sqn, equipped February 1944; first operation, July 1944 against the *Tirpitz*. Four Firefly squadrons operational with British Pacific Fleet by July 1945. Production total of F Mk I, 297 plus 132 by General Aircraft Ltd.

Max speed (clean), 319 mph (513 km/h) at 17,000 ft (5,180 m). Service ceiling, 29,000 ft (8,840 m). Range (with 90 Imp gal/409 1 drop tanks), 1,364 mls (2,195 km) at 204 mph (328 km/h). Empty weight, 8,925 lb (4,048 kg). Gross weight (clean), 12,250 lb

(5,556 kg). Gross weight (with bombs), 14,288 lb (6,481 kg). Span, 44 ft 6 in (13.56 m). Length, 37 ft 7 in (11.45 m). Wing area, 328 sq ft (30.47 m).

Firefly FR Mk I: Fighter reconnaissance version similar to F Mk I with ASH radar in canister beneath forward fuselage. First deliveries late 1944. 273 built, plus some F Mk Is converted to same standard as F Mk IA.

Firefly NF Mk I: Similar to FR Mk I, with same ASH radar, dedicated to night fighting role (with shrouded exhausts) and adopted after failure of NF Mk II programme. Total of 140 completed by diversions from F Mk I contracts. Entered service (usually known as Firefly INF) with No 746 Sqn mid-1944 and No 1740 Sqn January, 1945.

Firefly NF Mk II: Night fighter version of F Mk I, carrying AI Mk X radar with small radomes on each wing leading edge, and 15 in (38 cm) extra length in fuselage. Prototype conversion completed March 1943 and 37 completed as production-line conversions of Mk Is, later being converted back to Mk I standard.

Firefly F Mk III: As F Mk I with 1,540 hp two-stage Griffon 61 and annular-type chin radiator. Prototype conversion of Mk I flown April 18, 1943; no production.

Firefly IV: Succeeded F Mk III proposal, based on Griffon 70 series using wing root radiators and changed wing planform. Radome on starboard wing and flush-fitting fuel tank on port wing. Firefly III prototype (with Griffon 72) and three modified Mk Is with 2,245 hp Griffon 74s tested 1944-45 and first production Mk IV flown May 25, 1945. Subsequent variants, production and service were post-war.

Firefly IV prototype MB649, one of four Mk I airframes converted to have wing-root radiators and Griffon 72 or 74 engines.

FAIREY SPEARFISH

Designed to Specification O.5/43 as a successor for the Barracuda, the Spearfish was a two-seat torpedo/dive-bomber, powered by a 2,470 hp Centaurus 58. The first prototype (RA356) flew on July 5, 1945, and one other prototype and two production aircraft flew after the war against Japan had ended, further production then being cancelled. The Spearfish was the largest and heaviest single-engined aircraft built in Britain at the time of its completion.

Max speed, 292 mph (470 km/h) at 14,000 ft (4,267 m). Gross weight, 22,083 lb (10,017 kg). Span 60 ft 3 in (18.4 m). Length, 44 ft 7 in (13.6 m).

FANE F.1/40

Two-seat air observation post monoplane developed by Capt Gerard Fane from incomplete Comper CF-1 Scamp (with serial T1788) with 80 hp Continental A-80 engine and pusher propeller, to meet requirements of School of Army Co-operation. Single example built 1940, tested briefly at Heston in March 1941 after acquiring civil registration G-AGDJ.

Gross weight, 1,500 lb (681 kg). Span, 37 ft 0 in (11.28 m). Length, 23 ft 5 in (7.14 m).

FOLLAND FO.108

The FO.108 was designed under the direction of H P Folland to the requirements of Specification 43/37 for a large flying testbed in which to develop high-powered aero-engines. Twelve were built (P1774-P1785) during 1940, each accommodating pilot and two observers, and up to 1945 they flew with a variety of engines including Sabre I, II, V and VII, Hercules VIII and XI, Centaurus IV and various Griffons. Performance varied with engine, typical max speeds being 266 mph (428 km/h) at 15,600 ft (4,755 m) with the Napier Sabre I and 292 mph (470 km/h) at 15,000 ft (4,572 m)

Above: Fairey Spearfish RA356 (identified in AP 1480X as Experimental Aeroplane 244) was the only example of this heavyweight to fly before War's end. Below: The Fane F1/40 (not an Air Ministry Specification number) derived from a pre-war design by Nick Comper.

with Centaurus I. Typical gross weight was 15,000 lb (6,810 kg).

Span, 58 ft 0 in (17.68 m). Length, about 43 ft 6 in (13.26 m).

FOSTER WIKNER G.M.1 WICKO AND WARFERRY

Two-seat high-wing monoplane designed by G N Wikner and first flown in September 1936. Eleven built by 1939, of which eight impressed for RAF communications duty, with Service name Warferry. One other was impressed in New Zealand to serve with the Central Communications Fleet until November 1942. One 130 hp

Gipsy Major engine.

Max speed, 140 mph (225 km/h). Gross weight, 2,000 lb (908 kg). Span, 34 ft 6 in (10.52 m). Length, 23 ft 3 in (7.09 m).

GENERAL AIRCRAFT MONOSPAR ST-4, ST-6, ST-10 AND ST-12

The Monospar series of lightplanes was developed from 1931 onwards to exploit a system of construction evolved by H J Stieger, for which purpose General Aircraft Ltd was founded. First in a family of related twin-engined light transports using Monospar wing construction, the prototype ST-4 flew in May 1932. Three four-seat ST-4s with 85 hp Pobjoy R engines, impressed for service with Anti-Aircraft Co-operation Units, of which one modified in 1941 to have retractable undercarriage. One ST-4 impressed by SAAF. One five-seat ST-6, with retractable gear and Pobjoy Rs, and one similar ST-10 with 90 hp Niagara IIs and fixed gear, powered by two 130 hp Gipsy Majors; two impressed for AACU use in 1940. Data for ST-4; other variants a little heavier and faster.

Max speed, 130 mph (209 km/h). Gross weight, 2,550 lb (1,158 kg). Span, 40 ft 2 in (12.25 m). Length, 26 ft 4 in (8.03 m).

GENERAL AIRCRAFT MONOSPAR ST-25

Improved Monospar twin evolved in 1935 and known as the Jubilee model, with 90 hp Niagara II engines, fixed undercarriage and five-six seats. Two sold to RAF for radio

Above: The Foster Wikner Wicko exported to New Zealand as ZK-AGN was impressed as NZ580 and used by the RNZAF for communications until November 1942. Below: Folland FO.108s were used principally by Napier and Bristol, and included (left) P1774 (Experimental Aeroplane 103) with a Sabre and P1775 (Ex Ae 123) with Centaurus IV.

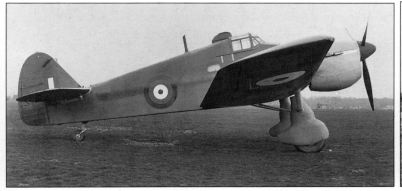

Right: The G.A.L.41 was built for early research into pressure cabins, flying first as T45 and then in Class B marks as T-0222 until grounded in 1941. Below: Completed in May 1938, this ST-25 was used, as N1531, to give RAF crews handling experience with tricycle undercarriages.

Above: The Monospar ST-25 G-AGDN, used for much of the war as a runabout by General Aircraft Ltd. Left: The ST-12 G-ADBN was one of two of this type impressed, serving as BD150 until April 1942.

FOP (Flying Observation Post) trainer by School of Army Co-operation February-June 1940 (as W7646) and later used for sundry experiments.
Cruising speed, 100 mph (161 km/h). Gross weight, 1,350 lb (613 kg). Span, 33 ft 0 in (10.06 m). Length, 33 ft 9 in (6.93 m).

GENERAL AIRCRAFT G.A.L.38
The G.A.L.38 was designed (in common with the Airspeed AS.39) to Specification S.23/37 for a carrier-based slow-flying reconnaissance aircraft with a long duration to serve in the 'fleet shadowing' role. Powered by four 130 hp Niagara V engines, the prototype (P1758) flew in 1940, initially with triple tail unit and later with large single fin and rudder. The advent of airborne radar rendered the 'fleet shadowing' role obsolete, and construction of a second prototype was abandoned.
Max speed, 115 mph (185 km/h). Gross weight, 9,585 (4,348 kg). Span, 55 ft 10 in (17.02 m). Length, 36 ft 1 in (10.99 m).

GENERAL AIRCRAFT G.A.L.41
Single prototype based on ST-25 Universal with a new fuselage incorporating a pressure vessel containing two seats, built to investigate pressurisation systems for proposed G.A.L.40 airliner. Powered by two 95 hp Pobjoy Niagara III radials and first flown (as T45) on May 11, 1939. Testing continued into 1941 and aircraft marked T-0222 before being grounded.
Cruising speed, 110 mph (177 km/h). Endurance, 3.5 hrs. Span 40 ft 2 in (12.2 m). Length, 26 ft 4 in (8.03 m).

GENERAL AIRCRAFT G.A.L.42 CYGNET
The Cygnet was a side-by-side two-seat light plane developed (originally by C W

equipment trials at RAE, continued in wartime service with four civil examples impressed for AACU use. ST-25 Universal appeared 1937 with twin fins and rudders; nine examples impressed, plus two (L4671, L4672) purchased by RAF in 1937 for communications duties and one in 1938 (N1531) with experimental tricycle undercarriage, surviving until mid-1941. Data for ST-25 Universal.

Max speed, 131 mph (211 km/h). Gross weight, 2,875 lb (1,305 kg). Span, 40 ft 2 in (12.25 m). Length, 25 ft 4 in (7.72 m).

GENERAL AIRCRAFT G.A.L.33 CAGNET
Prototype light trainer with side-by-side open cockpits and twin boom layout, powered by 90 hp Cirrus Minor pusher engine, first flown 1939, marked T46. Tested as

Below: The G.A.L.38 conformed to Specification S.23/37 for a slow-flying, long endurance aircraft for the 'fleet-shadowing' role. The prototype P1758 (Ex Ae 107) first flew with the triple tail unit shown here and later had a single tall fin and rudder. Above right: The G.A.L.33 Cagnet on test in 1940, probably at Old Sarum. The name derived from its originally intended role as a trainer for the Civil Air Guard (CAG).

Above: G.A.L.42 Cygnet G-AGBN was completed in 1941 and quickly impressed as ES915 for use – with others of the type – to give tricycle undercarriage handling familiarisation. Left: Based on the Cygnet, the single Owlet was impressed as DP240. Below: The G.A.L.47 was never taken on RAF charge, but was identified as Ex Aero 109 for recognition purposes.

GENERAL AIRCRAFT G.A.L.48 HOTSPUR

The G.A.L.48 was designed by a team headed by F F Crocombe as Britain's first assault transport glider, to Specification X.10/40, to carry pilot and seven troops. Prototype flown on November 5, 1940, four months after design started.

Hotspur I: Initial production version, designed for launch at high altitude and some distance from landing zone to permit silent approach. Jettisonable main undercarriage and 'lid' type fuselage to permit simultaneous exit of all troops. Range, 83 mls (134 km) from 20,000 ft (6,100 m) launch. Ten built by GAL, eight by Slingsby.
Gliding speed, 70 mph (113 km/h). Gross weight, 3,450 lb (1,565 kg). Span, 61 ft 10¾ in (18.87 m). Length, 39 ft 3½ in (11.98 m).

Hotspur II: Revised design for low-altitude launch close to landing zone. Modified fuselage with doors each side for troop exit, and reduced wing span. Production to Specifications X.22/40 and X.23/40; total of 996 built by Harris Lebus and one by Airspeed but no operational use and issued instead to Glider Training Schools, for use with Audax, Hector and Master tugs. Twenty-two to Canada 1942, of which six later to USN and one to USAAF.
Gliding speed, 80-90 mph (129-145 km/h). Gross weight, 3,598 lb (1,633 kg). Span, 45 ft 10¾ in (13.99 m). Length, 39 ft 3½ in (11.98 m).

Hotspur III: Fifty Hotspur IIs modified to have dual controls for training use.

Twin Hotspur: One G.A.L.48B prototype (MP486) tested August 1942 behind a Whitley tug, comprising two Hotspur II fuselages joined by a 12 ft (3.66 m) centre section, with standard outer wings, to carry 15 troops.
Span 57 ft 11 in (17.65 m). Gross weight, 6,450 lb (2,926 kg).

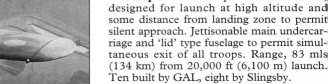

Aircraft) in 1936 and redesigned by General Aircraft to feature a tricycle undercarriage and twin tail unit as the Cygnet II. With a 150 hp Cirrus Major II, production aircraft were delivered in 1939/41, five being impressed for RAF service that included training in tricycle undercarriage techniques and two others used in civil guise by the makers for communications.
Max speed, 135 mph (217 km/h). Gross weight, 2,200 lb (999 kg). Span, 34 ft 6 in (10.52 m). Length, 23 ft 3 in (7.09 m).

GENERAL AIRCRAFT G.A.L. 45 OWLET

The G.A.L.45 was a two-seat open cockpit trainer developed from the Cygnet, powered by a 150 hp Cirrus Major 1 and first flown as G-AGBK on September 5, 1940. After impressment in July 1941 as DP240 the single prototype was used by No 23 Squadron, No 51 OTU and No 605 Sqn to train pilots in tricycle undercarriage techniques, until written-off on August 30, 1942.
Cruising speed, 110 mph (177 km/h). Gross weight, 2,300 lb (1,044 kg). Span, 32 ft 5 in (9.88 m). Length, 24 ft 7 in (7.49 m).

GENERAL AIRCRAFT G.A.L.47

The G.A.L.47 was a prototype FOP (Flying Observation Post) two-seat pusher highwing monoplane, with 90 hp Cirrus Minor, flown as T47 in 1940 and remarked as T-0224 before being written-off in April 1942.
Cruising speed, 75 mph (121 km/h). Gross weight, 1,615 lb (733 kg). Span, 37 ft 10 in (11.53 m). Length, 25 ft 9 in (7.85 m).

Above, upper: Slingsby-built Hotspur I BV136 in March 1941, compared with (above) a Hotspur II BT739 at the Glider Pilot's Exercise Unit in December 1942. Right: A Hotspur II engaged in rocket-assisted take-off trials, late 1942. Below: The sole Twin Hotspur, MP486, which completed only 3 hr 5 min flying.

GENERAL AIRCRAFT G.A.L.49 HAMILCAR

The G.A.L.49 was designed to Specification X.27/40 as a tank-carrying heavy glider. Half-scale model tested as G.A.L.50 (T-0227; serial DP226 not carried) in 1941 and prototype Hamilcar I (DP206) flown March 27, 1942. Production aircraft able to carry Tetrarch Mk IV or Locust tank, two Bren gun universal carriers, self-propelled Bofors gun, two armoured scout cars or freight loads up to 17,500 lb (7,945 kg). Operational in D-Day landings, June 1944, onwards. Twenty-two built by G.A.L. and 390 by various sub-contractors.

Max towing speed, 150 mph (241 km/h). Gross weight, 37,000 lb (16,798 kg). Span, 110 ft 0 in (33.53 m). Length, 68 ft 0 in (20.73 m).

Hamilcar X: Powered version of Hamilcar I designed to Specification X.4/44 for operations in the Pacific area. First of two prototypes (LA704) flown February 1945; 20 built with 965hp Mercury 31 engines, by conversion of Hamilcar I airframes. Towed take-off still necessary at max weight; capable of return flight, lightly loaded, under own power.

Max speed, 145 mph (233 km/h). Gross weight, 45,500 lb (20,657 kg). Dimensions as Hamilcar I.

GENERAL AIRCRAFT G.A.L.55

Two-seat (side-by-side) training glider designed and built during 1943 to Specification TX.3/43, with steel tube, wood and fabric fuselage and wooden wings. Two prototypes (NP671, NP674) tested from late-1943 on, behind a Lysander.

Max towing speed, 175 mph (282 km/h). Gross weight, 2,407 lb (1,022 kg). Span, 35 ft 1 1/2 in (10.71 m). Length, 25 ft 6 1/2 in (7.79 m).

The first of two prototypes of the G.A.L.55 training glider, NP671 is seen here in April 1944 at the manufacturer's Feltham airfield. It was identified as Experimental Aeroplane 210 in AP.1480X.

GENERAL AIRCRAFT G.A.L.56

Starting in 1943, GAL designed and built a series of four tailless research gliders, featuring differing planforms. Three were covered by the designation G.A.L.56 and the last, completed post-war but not flown, was G.A.L.61. First to fly, starting mid-November 1944, was the G.A.L.56 Medium-V (TS507), with constant sweepback on leading and trailing edges, span of 45 ft 4 in (13.82 m) and gross weight of 4,400 lb (2,000 kg). Flight trials were made behind a Whitley, Halifax and, eventually, Spitfire IX. The second G.A.L.56 was the Medium-U (TS510), with a parallel-chord centre section, and the third, also completed post-war, was the Maximum-V (TS513), with sweepback on quarter-chord line increased from 28.4 to 36.4 deg.

GLIDERS

Starting in mid-1940, some 32 assorted gliders were impressed for military use in Britain. They were not issued with serial numbers but retained the numbers issued by the British Gliding Association (BGA) or displayed their c/ns or single letter codes. A few of these gliders were used by the Special Duty Flight at Christchurch to study the effectiveness of radar in detecting wooden aircraft approaching the southern British coast. Larger numbers were assembled at Ringway for use by the Central Landing School and the Glider Training Squadron/School, for the training of Army glider pilots.

In 1942, with growing use of gliders to give preliminary flying experience to ATC cadets, 67 gliders were impressed with serial numbers in the HM range and three with NF serials. Most, if not all, of these were in addition to those impressed earlier, although some of the latter were transferred to the ATC before the war ended. In April 1943, a further allocation was made of 300 serials, in the PD range, for use on gliders made up by ATC units from spares and components. Only the first 57 of the allotted serials appear to have been used in this way.

Another allocation of 60 serials, in the VD

Above: Before construction of the Hamilcar was completed, the configuration was tested with this half-scale version, marked T-0227 (Ex Aero 153). Below: The Hamilcar I prototype DP206 engaged in RATO trials at Hartford Bridge in late 1942.

Above: The Hamilcar Mk X LA728, one of the two prototype conversions (Ex Aero 239) of Mk I gliders. Below: An early production Hamilcar awaiting delivery from Feltham.

Above: First of the two G.A.L.56 tailless research gliders, TS507 was in the 'Medium-V' configuration. Below: Serial TS467 was issued in October 1944 for this Dagling-type primary glider, used at the No 1 STT Gliding Club at Halton. Although recorded as an RFD type, it may have been built or assembled by Ottley Motors (a Slingsby sub-contractor) in 1944/45. (Photo, Chris Ashworth).

range, was made in March 1945, for use by the (then re-constituted) ATC on its surviving gliders. Some of the aircraft given serials in this series had previously flown with HM and/or PD serials.

The great majority of the gliders involved in all of these transactions were of Slingsby origin, and are described more fully in proper sequence later in this volume. The other British gliders and sailplanes known to have seen military service included the following:

BAC (British Aircraft Co): Impressments included several BAC I and BAC II Primaries, and one BAC VII two-seater.

Dart Totternhoe: One, perhaps two, of these secondary sailplanes were impressed, from four built before the war.

RFD Dagling: Several of these British-built versions of the German Zogling primary glider were impressed, from some 26 made by RFD, a company run by RF Dagnell (hence the name, from *Dag*nell Zog*ling*). The same type was later produced by Slingsby as the Type 2, and it is difficult to distinguish RFD from Slingsby primary types in surviving records of impressments.

Scott Primary: Four, at least, primary gliders (some with nacelles) were impressed, from eight built by Zander and Scott, or Scott Light Aircraft, at Dunstable.

GLOSTER GAMECOCK

Two British-built Gamecock IIs were purchased by the Finnish Air Force (*Ilmavoimat*) in 1928 and 15 more built by the National Aircraft Factory in Helsinki were delivered 1929/1930, with 420 hp Gnome-Rhône Jupiter IV9Ab or IV9Hk, or 450 hp IV9Ag, engines, and armament of two fixed forward-firing 0.303 in (7.7 mm) machine guns. With the local name Kukko, the Gamecocks were still in service as fighter trainers when the Winter War began in 1939 and the last was not retired until 1944.
Max speed, 157 mph (252 km/h) at 5,000 ft (1,525 m). Gross weight, 3,082 lb (1,398 kg). Span, 30 ft 1 in (9.16 m). Length, 19 ft 10¹/₂ in (6.04 m).

GLOSTER AS.31

Of the two examples of this aerial survey biplane designed by HP Folland and built in 1929, one (G-AADO) passed into service with

the SAAF in 1935 and was used by that Service (with serial 250) for aerial photography until 1942. The two engines were 500 hp Jupiter XIFs.
Max speed, 131 mph (210 km/h) at 1,000 ft (305 m). Gross weight, 8,570 lb (3,886 kg). Span, 61 ft 0 in (18.9 m). Length, 48 ft 6 in (14.7 m).

GLOSTER GAUNTLET

The Gauntlet was designed by H P Folland to meet RAF requirements for a new day-and-night single-seat fighter during 1927 and entered production in 1934 to Specification 24/33. A total of 24 Gauntlet Is and 204 Gauntlet IIs was built for the RAF, with 605 hp Mercury VIS engines and two fixed forward-firing 0.303 in (7.7 mm) machine guns. A handful remained in service with No 616 Squadron in September 1939 but were soon retired from front-line squadrons, continuing to fly in the UK as station hacks and for meteorological duties. A few others equipped 'D' Flight of 47 Squadron (later No 430 Flight) in the Sudan and saw combat in 1940, against Italian forces; ex-RAF Gauntlets also operated briefly in North Africa with RAAF squadrons and in East Africa with the SAAF. 24 ex-RAF Gauntlets supplied to Finland in 1940 served as fighter trainers until 1945, some on skis. Seventeen Gauntlet IIs were built in Denmark in 1936/38 by the *Haerens Flyvertroppers Vaerksteder* and equipped 1 *Eskadrille* of Danish Army Aviation at the time of the German invasion in April 1940.
Max speed, 230 mph (370 km/h) at 15,800 ft (4,815 m). Time to climb to 20,000 ft (6,100 m), 9 min. Service ceiling, 33,500 ft (10,210 m). Empty weight, 2,770 lb (1,255 kg). Gross weight, 3,970 lb (1,800 kg). Span, 32 ft 10 in (9.99 m). Length, 26 ft 2 in (8.0 m).

GLOSTER GLADIATOR

The Gloster SS.37 single-seat four-gun fighter biplane was designed by H P Folland's team during 1933 as a Gauntlet derivative to Specification F.7/30. A prototype, powered initially by a 485 hp Mercury IV and with open cockpit, was flown on September 12, 1934. Armament comprised two 0.303 in (7.7 mm) Vickers guns in forward fuselage and two similar calibre Lewis guns under the lower wings.

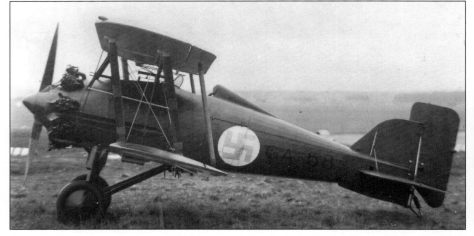

Above: GA-58 was the last of 15 Gamecock IIs built in Finland in 1930 by the State Aircraft Factory. It was serving with Llv 29 in 1939/40, when this photo was taken. Below: First flown as G-AADO, this Gloster AS.31 served in the SAAF with the serial 250, until 1942.

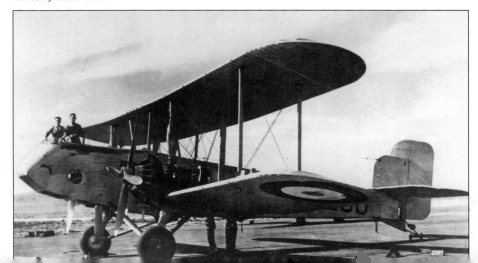

Left: Gauntlet GT-408 was one of 24 ex-RAF Mk IIs purchased by South Africa and shipped to Finland in 1940. Here seen on skis, it totalled 455 hrs in Finnish service by November 1944. Above: One of the 17 Gauntlets built in Denmark in 1937.

Gladiator I: Initial production batch of 23 ordered to Specification F.14/35 in June 1935 and subsequent RAF contracts for 203, first flown January 1937 and deliveries February 1937 to late 1938. Fully enclosed cockpit, 825 hp Mercury IX with Watts two-blade wooden propeller and four 0.303 in (7.7 mm) Browning guns (early aircraft had Lewis or Vickers Mk V underwing guns). Entered service with No 72 Squadron, February 1937. Some converted to Gladiator II standard, and operational details as noted under Gladiator II. During 1937, 26 Gladiator Is supplied to Latvia and 14 to Lithuania, some of these subsequently flying in Soviet markings after those countries had been sequestered in 1940. Fifteen of these Gladiators fell into German hands in 1941, and most of them were then adapted to serve as tugs at the *Erganzungsgruppe (S) 1* glider pilot training school as Langendiebach during 1942 and 1943, towing DFS 230 gliders. Norway acquired six Gladiator Is with 0.30 in (7.62 mm) Colt guns in 1938 and these were operational against German forces in 1940. The Belgian *Aeronautique Militaire* acquired 22 Gladiator Is in 1937/38, these equipping the lere *Escadrille de Chasse* at the time of the German invasion in May 1940. Fifteen Gladiator Is went to the Iraqi Air Force in 1937-38, some being operational in the Iraqi uprising in 1941. Up to 29 ex-RAF Gladiator Is and IIs went to Iraq in 1942-44.

Max speed, 253 mph (407 km/h) at 14,500 ft (4,420 m). Time to 10,000 ft (3,050 m), 4.75 min. Service ceiling, 32,800 ft (9,996 m). Empty weight, 3,217 lb (1,458 kg). Gross weight, 4,594 lb (2,082 kg). Span, 32 ft 3 in (9.80 m). Length, 27 ft 5 in (8.20 m). Wing area, 323 sq ft (29.9 m²).

Gladiator II: Introduced 825 hp Mercury VIIIA driving three-blade Fairey metal propeller, improved instruments and equipment. Production to Specification F.36/37, commencing 1939; total 318 ordered for the RAF, completed 1939. Operational in 1939 (together with some Gladiator Is) with two squadrons in BEF in France, in 1940 with one squadron in Norway, and in 1940/41 with four RAF squadrons, one RAAF squadron and three SAAF squadrons in Middle East and North Africa. Equipped 12 Meteorological Flights in UK and flew in this and other secondary roles until 1945. Foreign deliveries, ex-RAF included six for Norway (with six Mk Is), about 17 for Royal Hellenic Air Force in 1940/41, and some 42 for Egyptian Air Force, 1939/41. Twelve of 55 Swedish Gladiators — designated J8 and, when fitted with Swedish-built 740 hp Mercury VII, J8A — operated in Finland by Swedish volunteer group in Winter War of 1939/40, often on skis, alongside 30 ex-RAF Gladiator IIs used by the Finnish Air Force itself from 1940 to 1944.

Max speed, 257 mph (414 km/h) at 14,600 ft (4,449 m). Time to 10,000 ft (3,050 m), 4.5 min. Service ceiling, 33,500 ft (11,570 m). Gross weight, 4,864 lb (2,206 kg).

Above: Gladiator I K7957 serving in the Middle East with No 94 Sqn in 1940. It served there until May 1942. Below left: One of the ex-Latvian or Lithuanian Gladiators serving the Luftwaffe as a glider-tug in 1942/3. Below right: Sea Gladiator N5567 in service with No 805 Sqn, FAA, in 1941.

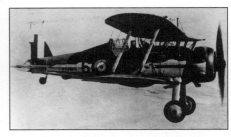

Sea Gladiator: 22 early-production Gladiator IIs modified for Naval service with arrester hook, FAA radio and equipment, delivered December 1938 and known as Sea Gladiator (Interim). Sixty production Sea Gladiators had catapult spools and additional equipment, delivered early 1939. Served operationally with five FAA squadrons from May 1939 (starting with No 801 aboard HMS *Courageous*, Feb 1939), and involved in defence of Norway and of Malta. Gross weight, 5,020 lb (2,272 kg). Dimensions as for Gladiator I.

GLOSTER F.5/34

Two prototypes of the single-seat fighter designed by H P Folland and H E Preston to Specification F.5/34 were built in 1937, the first flight being made by May of that year. Powered by the 825 hp Mercury VIII and with a design armament of eight 0.303 in (7.7 mm) Browning guns in the wings, both prototypes (K5604, K8089) were in use for experimental flying until May 1941.

Max speed, 316 mph (509 km/h) at 16,000 ft (4,876 m). Gross weight, 5,400 lb (2,449 kg). Span, 38 ft 2 in (11.5 m). Length, 32 ft (9.7 m).

Below: Second of the two Gloster F.5/34 eight-gun fighter prototypes, K8089 is seen here at Farnborough on March 28, 1938. It continued flying there until becoming an instructional airframe in March 1940.

GLOSTER F.9/37

This twin-engined fighter was designed under the direction of W G Carter to Specification F.9/37 as a single-seater carrying an armament of four 0.303 in (7.7 mm) Brownings and two 20 mm cannon in the nose. A prototype (L7999) with 1,060 hp Taurus II radials flew on April 3, 1939, being re-engined with 935 hp Taurus IIIs in 1940, and a second prototype (L8002) with 880 hp Peregrine I liquid-cooled in-line engines flew on February 22, 1940. The requirement for an aircraft in this category was dropped by the RAF and no production ensued. Data are for the Taurus version:

Max speed, 360 mph (579 km/h) at 15,000 ft (4,570 m). Time to 28,000 ft (8,534 m), 19.6 min. Service ceiling, 30,000 ft (9,144 m). Gross weight, 11,615 lb (5,269 kg). Span, 50 ft 0½ in (15.24 m). Length, 37 ft 0½ in (11.27 m).

GLOSTER E.28/39

The team led by W G Carter designed Britain's first jet-propelled aeroplane during 1940 to the requirement of Specification E.28/39, the primary object being to flight-test the Whittle-designed W.1 turbojet. Two examples were built, the first (W4041) flying on May 15, 1941, with a W.1 engine giving about 860 lb st (390 kgp), and the second (W4046) flying on March 1, 1943, with a 1,300 lb st (544 kgp) Rover-built W.2B turbojet. Other engines were fitted subsequently in both prototypes; the first survived the war but the second was lost on July 30, 1943, after entering an inverted spin.

Max speed, 466 mph (749 km/h) at 10,000 ft (3,050 m). Gross weight, 3,748 lb (1,699 kg). Span, 29 ft 9 in (8.84 m). Length, 25 ft 3¾ in (7.71 m).

GLOSTER METEOR

The Meteor was designed by a team led by George Carter during 1940 to take advantage of the still unproved Whittle turbojet, and Air Ministry Specification F.9/40 was written round the Gloster proposal for a sin-

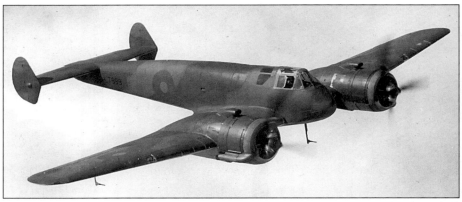

Above: *First of the two Gloster F.9/37s, L7999 (Experimental Aeroplane 108), as flown in the later months of 1940, by which time Taurus T-S(a) III engines were fitted and Type B (red and blue) roundels applied.* **Right:** *The second F.9/37, L8002 (Ex Aero 114) at the time of first flight in February 1940.*

gle-seat twin-engined fighter armed with four 20 mm British Hispano cannon. Twelve prototypes ordered February 1941, of which only eight built, with various engines. First to fly, on March 5, 1943, was DG206, powered by 1,500 lb st (681 kgp) de Havilland H.1s, and with a wing span of 44 ft 3 in (13.49 m). Next to fly, on July 24, 1943, DG202 had 1,526 lb st (693 kgp) Rover W.2B engines and span of 43 ft 0 in (13.11 m); and a prototype with 2,000 lb st (908 kgp) Metrovick F.2 axial-flow turbojets, DG204, flew on November 13, 1943. One other prototype had H.1 engines and

pressure cabin; remainder powered by Rolls-Royce built engines of Whittle type.

Meteor F. Mk I: Initial production contract for 300 F.9/40-type fighters placed June 1941, to be named Meteor and powered by 1,700 lb st (772 kgp) Rolls-Royce W.2B/23 engines named Welland. Twenty built to F Mk 1 standard with four 20 mm cannon; first flight January 12, 1944. Twelve delivered July 1944 to No 616 Squadron to become RAF's first jet fighter unit, becoming operational in August against V-1 flying bombs.

Max speed, 415 mph (675 km/h) at 10,000 ft

Left: *The first Gloster E.28/39, W4041 (Ex Aero 137) in flight and (above) at Farnborough early in 1944, with small inset fins on tailplane to improve lateral stability.* **Below:** *The first F.9/40 — prototype for the Meteor — to fly, DG206/G was fitted with Halford H.1 engines. A wide centre section gave this F.9/40 alone a span of 44 ft 3 in (13.49 m).*

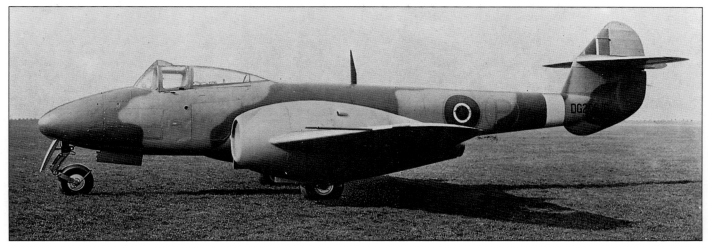

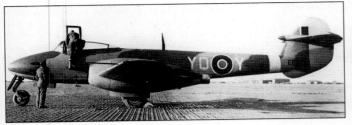

Above left: An early production Meteor F Mk 1, EE227, in the hands of No 616 Sqn, first in the RAF to fly jet fighters. Above right: Meteor III EE360/G fitted with Derwent V engines to serve as the prototype F Mk IV, flown two weeks after V-E Day. Below: Meteor IIIs of No 124 Sqn, which began flying this mark in July 1945.

(3,050 m). Time to 30,000 ft (9, 150 m), 15 min. Service ceiling, 40,000 ft (12,200 m). Empty weight, 8,140 lb (3,737 kg). Gross weight, 13,795 lb (6,258 kg). Span, 43 ft 0 in (13.11 m). Length, 41 ft 3 in (12.57 m). Wing area, 374 sq ft (34.7m²).

Meteor F Mk II: Projected with 2,700 lb st (1,226 kgp) Goblin I engines.

Meteor F Mk III: Similar to Meteor I, with 2,000 lb st (908 kgp) Derwent I (W.2B/37) engines, sliding in place of hinged canopy, increased fuel, slotted air breaks and other improvements. Total 210 built, first 15 with Welland engines; first flight September 1944. Deliveries to No 616 Squadron December 1944 and operational with 2nd TAF in Belgium with Nos 616 and 504 Sqn early 1945.

Meteor F Mk IV: Improved Mk III with 3,000 lb st (1,362 kgp) Derwent Vs in long-chord nacelles, pressurised cockpit and other improvements. First flown May 17, 1945; production deliveries of Mk IV, and development of later variants, post-war.

HAFNER A.R.III MK 2 GYROPLANE
One of a series of experimental autogiros designed by Raoul Hafner, the single-seat A.R.III (G-ADMV), powered by a 90 hp Pobjoy Niagara, first flew on February 6, 1937. It went to the RAE Farnborough in August 1939 and was used for research until mid-1941 when it was impressed by the RAF (as DG670) but not subsequently flown.
Max speed, 120 mph (193 km/h). Gross weight, 900 lb (409 kg). Rotor diameter, 32 ft 10 in (10.00 m). Overall length, 17 ft 10 in (5.44 m).

Below: A pre-war photograph of the Hafner A.R. III G-ADMV, which was at RAE Farnborough until mid-1940.

HAFNER ROTORCRAFT
As a development of the A.R.III, Raoul Hafner designed the two-seat enclosed cabin A.R.IV and three-seat A.R.V Gyroplanes, and then obtained a contract for two of the former configured to comply with Specification S.22/38 for a rotorcraft with potential Fleet or Army applications. Prototypes (V8906 and V8909) were to be built by Short Bros. Another prototype (T3005) of an entirely new, slender-profile helicopter, the P.D.6, was also ordered to Specification 10/39, and construction was again launched by Shorts. Illustrations of these types appeared in A.P.1480X as Experimental Aeroplanes 116 and 115 respectively, but work on the prototypes ceased when Hafner (as an Austrian citizen) was interned in 1939 under Defence Regulation 18B. Hafner was released in 1940 and became responsible for rotorcraft development at the Airborne Forces Experimental Establishment, subsequently designing the following types based on experience with the A.R.III and later Gyroplanes.

Rotachute: Single-seat gyroplane ('rotary glider') designed by Hafner to provide a means of landing armed personnel in enemy territory with greater accuracy than possible by parachute. After model tests starting October 1940, full-scale Rotachutes were ordered to Specification 11/42 from F

Hills & Sons (Manchester) and Airwork (Hounslow). Twenty ordered, perhaps not all built. Rotachute I had wooden aft structure with rubber fabric covering and non-rigid tailplane, all inflated by air pressure in flight; three towed flights (behind car) in February 1942. Rotachute II introduced rigid tailplane, doped fabric covering and wheeled u/c; nine flights (towed behind car) starting May 29, 1942. Rotachute III featured lengthened, rigid afterbody and made first towed flight and first free launch behind Tiger Moth on June 17, 1942. Total of 16 flights behind Tiger Moth and one behind Avro Tutor by October 1943, with designation changed to Rotachute IV after addition of endplate fins to tailplane. Six Rotachutes despatched to USA in 1945, but proposed Rotacub powered version did not proceed in UK.
Data for Rotachute III: *Rotor diameter, 15 ft*

Above: The first of the Hafner Rotachutes on tow (behind a car) showing the original configuration of the 'inflatable' fuselage fairing. Below: The final form of Rotachute, the Mk IV, showing the lengthened, rigid, after-body and added endplate fins.

Below: The sole prototype of the Hafner Rotabuggy in flight (on tow) at Sherburn-in-Elmet. Identified as Experimental Aeroplane 207 in A.P.1480X, this may have been the vehicle for which the serial number RD123 was intended.

Above: *The Handley Page H.P.42E G-AAUC after impressment as AS981, in service with No 271 Sqn at Doncaster in 1940.* Below: *A pair of Heyford IIIs serving with No 166 Sqn before the war; nearest the camera is K6889 'R' which went on to fly with No 4 Air Observers School until mid-1940.*

(4.57 m). Rotor disc area, 177 sq ft (16.4 m²). Empty weight, 76 lb (34.5 kg). Gross weight, 290 lb (131.5 kg). Max design speed, 108 mph (174 km/h). Max achieved speed, 93 mph (150 km/h). Max endurance, 40 min.

Rotabuggy: After interest in Rotachute had waned, attention switched to use of gyroplane principle to ferry vehicles or large cargo loads. Under Specification 10/42, R Malcolm Ltd (later ML Aviation), White Waltham, was contracted to produce, to AFEE designs, a free-wheeling two-bladed rotor and stabilising tail unit to be attached to a Willys 5-cwt Jeep. Single prototype made some 60 flights, first car-towed on November 16, 1943, and later behind a Whitley (always remaining attached to the tug for landing). British military prototype markings carried, but no serial number; the serials RD123 and RD127 allocated in mid-1943 for two Malcolm 'Blitz Buggys' may have been intended for later prototypes, but work ended with a flight on September 11, 1944, as development of tank-carrying gliders proved the Rotabuggy and the projected Rotatank (based on the Valentine tank) unnecessary.
Designed max speed, 150 mph (241 km/h). Max achieved speed (on tow), 72 mph (116 km/h). Empty weight, 2,675 lb (1,213 kg). Gross weight, 3,110 lb (1,411 kg). Rotor diameter, 46 ft 8 in (14.17 m). Rotor disc area, 1,711 sq ft (159 m²). Length, 21 ft (6.4 m).

HANDLEY PAGE H.P.42
Seven of these four-engined biplane transports were in service with Imperial Airways in September 1939, comprising three 38-passenger H.P.42Ws in the UK and four 24-seat H.P.42Es in the Middle East. The H.P.42Ws, with 580 hp Jupiter XFBM engines, served with National Air Communications for a few months but were soon lost in accidents; three H.P.42Es, with 550 hp Jupiter XIFs, returned to UK and were impressed for RAF service (as AS981-AS983) but none survived into 1941.
Max speed, 120 mph (193 km/h). Gross weight, 28,000 lb (12,700 kg). Span, 130 ft 0 in (39.62 m). Length, 92 ft 2 in (28.1 m).

HANDLEY PAGE H.P.50 HEYFORD
This heavy bomber biplane was designed by G R Volkert to meet Specification B.19/27

and the prototype (H.P.38) first flew on June 12, 1930. The RAF acquired 15 Heyford Is, 23 Heyford IAs, 16 Heyford IIs and 70 Heyford IIIs. About 30 remained in 1939, all Mk IIIs with 695 hp Kestrel VI engines. They were used for a year or so at Nos 3 and 4 Air Observer Schools and No 4 Bombing and Gunnery School.
Max speed, 154 mph (248 km/h). Gross weight, 17,000 lb (7,710 kg). Span, 75 ft 0 in (22.9 m). Length, 58 ft 0 in (17.7 m).

HANDLEY PAGE H.P.52 HAMPDEN
The H.P.52 twin-engined monoplane bomber was designed in 1933 under the direction of G R Volkert in response to the requirements of Specification B.9/32, having a crew of three and a slender fuselage designed to accommodate nose, dorsal and ventral turrets and a bomb-bay carrying 4,000 lb (1,816 kg) of bombs. Single prototype (K4240) ordered 1933 powered by 815 hp Pegasus XVIIIs, flown on June 21, 1936, without armament. Second prototype (L7271) flown July 1, 1937, had 835 hp Pegasus XXs and was started as the sole H.P.53 for Swedish Air Force (which later received a production H.P.52, L4036, instead).

Hampden I: First production contract for 180 placed with Handley Page August 1936 to Specification B.30/36, with Pegasus XVIIIs or XXIIs and armament of one 0.303 in (7,7 mm) Vickers 'K' gun in nose, dorsal and ventral positions plus one fixed

forward firing Browning in fuselage side, and stowage for four 500 lb (227 kg) or two 1,500 lb (681 kg) mines or two 2,000 lb (908 kg) bombs; later aircraft had twin ventral and dorsal guns on Rose mountings. First production aircraft flown June 21, 1938; deliveries began to No 49 Squadron and six squadrons operational by September 1939. Production total 500 by Handley Page plus 770 by English Electric at Preston (first flown February 22, 1940) and 160 by Canadian Associated Aircraft in Quebec and Ontario (first flown August 9, 1940). Operational 1940-42 for leaflet dropping, mine-laying and day and night bombing; thereafter for training, including about 100 transferred to Canada in 1943.
Max speed, 254 mph (409 km/h) at 13,800 ft (4,206 m). Cruising speed, 167 mph (269 km/h). Initial rate of climb, 980 ft/min (4,98 m/sec). Service ceiling, 19,000 ft (5,880 m). Range, 1,885 mls (3,160 km) with 2,000 lb (908 kg) bombs or 1,200 mls (1,930 km) with 4,000 lb (1,813 kg) bombs. Empty weight, 11,780 lb (5,345 kg). Gross weight, 18,756 lb (8,505 kg). Span, 69 ft 2 in (21.07 m). Length, 53 ft 7 in (16.35 m). Wing area, 668 sq ft (62.1 m²).

Hampden T.B.Mk I: 144 Hampden bombers converted 1942/43 as torpedo-bombers to equip five squadrons of Coastal Command, each carrying one Mk XII torpedo in open bomb-bay and one 500 lb (227 kg) bomb under each wing. Gross weight, 23,500 lb (10,669 kg) and range 1,960 mls (3,154 km) with torpedo. Twenty-three transferred to Soviet Air Force 1942 after operations from Soviet bases by Nos 144 and 455 Squadrons and then used by 3rd squadron of 24MTAP (Anti-shipping Wing) of Soviet Navy until late-1943.

Hampden Met I: Variant modified for meteorological reconnaissance, used by Nos 517, 519 and 521 Squadrons, 1943.

Hampden II: Two Hampden Is converted to have 1,100 hp Cyclone GR-1820-G102A radials (as H.P.62) in 1940.

Above: *A Hampden 1 bearing the pre-war codes of No 66 Sqn at RAF Waddington.*

Below: *Hampden TB Mk 1 in service with RNZAF-manned No 489 Sqn, in 1942. The code letters XA appear to have been overpainted.* Above right: *One of the 23 Hampden TB Mk 1s that passed into service with the Soviet Navy's air arm in 1942.*

HANDLEY PAGE H.P.52 HEREFORD

Version of Hampden powered by two 955 hp Dagger VIII in-line air-cooled engines. Second Hampden prototype L7271 (the original H.P.53) converted by Short Bros in Belfast and first flown with Daggers on October 6, 1938. Production of 150 to Specification B.44/36 by Shorts; first flight May 17, 1939, and production completed September 1940. Used only for crew-training by Nos 14 and 16 OTUs and at least 23 later converted to Hampdens. Specification similar to Hampden bomber (see previous entry).

HANDLEY PAGE H.P.54 HARROW (AND SPARROW)

The H.P.54 was designed under the direction of G R Volkert as a stop-gap night bomber to help RAF expansion in 1935 and was a derivative of the H.P.51 bomber-transport prototype to Specification C.26/31. The latter was itself a modification of the H.P.43 which had been built to C.16/28 and first flew on June 21, 1932; this same prototype, J9833, with some H.P.54 features, was in use at RAE Farnborough until January 1940. The H.P.54 was powered by Pegasus engines, carried 3,000 lb (1362 kg) of bombs, had accommodation for 20 troops and armament of two Lewis or Vickers 0.303 in (7.7 mm) machine guns each in nose and tail turrets. Production of 100 ordered 'off the drawing board' to Specification 29/35 in August 1935.

Harrow I: Initial production batch with 980 hp Pegasus X engines. First flown October 10, 1936; initial deliveries to No 214 Sqn, January 1937, and four more squadrons equipped (Mks I & II) by 1938. Twenty built, of which six modified to Mk II.

Harrow II: As Harrow I but powered by 835 hp Pegasus XX engines. Eighty built and six Mk Is converted. Not operational as bombers after early 1940, but five used by No 420 Flight to drop LAM (long aerial mines) on parachutes in path of enemy bombers. Others used for air observer and air gunnery training, for glider towing and miscellaneous duties. Many converted for transport role, operating with No 1680 Flight (later 271 Sqn) from March 1940 until April 1945 for casualty evacuation and general transport duties; some fitted with lengthened nose and tail fairings, known unofficially as Sparrows. Three converted in 1938 as aerial refuelling tankers for trans-

Above: No more than a Hampden with different engines, the Hereford saw no operational service, being used only as a trainer. Shown here, L6070 was with No 14 OTU from April 1940 to May 1941

Above: Harrow I K6941 with No 271 Sqn at Doncaster in 1940, with the then-standard yellow undersides for transport aircraft. Right: Originally K6933 and then G-AFRG as a flight-refuelling tanker, Harrow I 794 served with the RCAF for most of 1941. Below: Harrow II of No 271 Sqn in 1940, showing the Sparrow fairings in place of nose and tail turrets.

lantic experiments, of which two impressed into RCAF in 1939.

Max speed, 200 mph (322 km/h). Service ceiling, 23,000 ft (7,110 m). Range, 1,250 mls (2,150 km). Empty weight, 13,600 lb (6,760 kg). Gross weight, 23,000 lb (10,450 kg). Span, 88 ft 5 in (27.0 m). Length, 82 ft 0 in (25.1 m). Wing area, 1,090 sq ft (101.2 m²).

HANDLEY PAGE H.P.57 HALIFAX

The Handley Page H.P.57 heavy bomber was evolved by design team led by G R Volkert as final stage in process started in 1935 when a prototype of the twin-engined H.P.55 had been ordered to Specification B.1/35 but superseded by two prototypes of the H.P.56 to P.13/36, each powered by

Halifax I Srs 1 L9530 in service with No 76 Sqn — second in Bomber Command to fly the HP heavy bomber — at Middleton St George in August 1941, with no dorsal turret and with tail wheel locked down, although designed to be retractable.

Above: Early production Halifax II Srs 1, L9619, in service with No 10 Sqn, the first to become operational on the type, at RAF Leeming late in 1941. Below: Halifax II Srs 1 (Special) BB325 in the Middle East, showing 'Z' nose fairing and Boulton Paul Type C dorsal turret.

two Vultures. Substitution of four 1,145 hp Merlin Xs for the two Vultures, with increased dimensions and weights, resulted in H.P.57, with design armament of twin-gun nose and four-gun tail power-operated turrets (originally to be Frazer Nash, but finally standardised on Boulton Paul types), all with 0.303 in (7.7 mm) calibre guns and an 8,000 lb (3,632 kg) bomb load. Unarmed first prototype flown at Bicester on October 25, 1939, and second prototype with BP nose and tail turrets on August 17, 1940. Initial gross weight 47,000 lb (21,338 kg), later 50,000 lb (22,700 kg).

Halifax I: Initial production variant (H.P.57); 100 ordered to Specification 32/37 in January 1938 of which 84 delivered as Mk I, comprising 50 Mk I Series 1 with 55,000 lb (24,970 kg) gross weight and 1,392 Imp gal (6,328 l) fuel in wing tanks, 25 Mk I Srs 2 with 60,000 lb (27,240 kg) gross weight and pairs of Vickers 'K' guns firing through side hatches amidships, and nine Mk I Srs 3 with 1,636 Imp gal (7,437 l) fuel in wing tanks. All had provision to carry one, two or three 230 Imp gal (1,046 l) fuel tanks in bomb bay, in lieu of bombs, and extra bomb cells in the inner wing section. First production Mk I flown October 11, 1940; deliveries to No 35 Squadron

began November 1940 and first operational sortie flown March 10/11, 1941.
Max speed, 265 mph (426 km/h) at 17,500 ft (5,334 m). Initial rate of climb, 750 ft/min (3,81 m/sec). Service ceiling, 22,800 ft (6,950 m). Range with bomb-bay fuel and 5,800 lb (2,633 kg) bomb load, 1,860 mls (2,993 km). Empty weight, 33,860 lb (15,372 kg). Gross weight, 55,000 lb (24,970 kg). Span, 98 ft 10 in (30.21 m). Length, 70 ft 1 in (21.36 m). Wing area, 1,200 sq ft (111.4 m²).

Halifax B Mk II: Series production version (H.P.59) similar to Mk I with 1,390 hp Merlin XX engines, larger oil coolers, wing fuel capacity of 1,882 Imp gal (8,556 l) and twin-gun BP dorsal turret in place of beam guns. Prototype (Mk I conversion) flown at Radlett July 3, 1941. Production shared between Handley Page (615), London Aircraft Production Group (450) at Leavesden, Rootes Securities (12) at Speke and English Electric (900) at Samlesbury. Initial production of Mk II Series I followed by Mk II Series I (Special) with interim nose fairing replacing nose turret, first flown August 15, 1942, and operated initially for SOE sorties by No 138 Sqn and later by bomber squadrons in 4 Group using kit-modified Series I aircraft. For SOE use, fitted with parachute exit cone in rear fuselage

and retracting tailwheel; many such operated by No 148 Sqn from Brindisi to support Warsaw uprising July 1944. Later production version was Mk II Series 1A with more streamlined, largely transparent nose fairing replacing turret, and mounting one hand-held 0.303 in (7.7 mm) Vickers 'K' gun, plus low-drag nacelles incorporating Morris radiators and — usually — BP four-gun dorsal turrets. Mk II production included 299 Series IAs, from end-1942 onwards. Later production Mk IIs had 1,390 hp Merlin 22s, four-bladed propellers, gross weight of 65,000 lb (29,510 kg) and D-type rectangular fins and/or H2S bombing aid with ventral radome. H2S first flown on Halifax II on March 27, 1942. Some aircraft had modified bomb-doors to carry 8,000 lb (3,632 kg) block-busters.

Halifax B Mk III: Similar to B Mk II but with 1,615 hp Hercules VI radial engines and gross weight increased to 64,000 lb (29,056 kg). Prototype converted from first B Mk II Srs 1 (Special), flown on October 12, 1942, and first production Mk III on August 29, 1943. Production Mk IIIs (H.P.61) had retractable tailwheel, D-type enlarged fins, Hercules VI or XVI engines, Srs 1A type nose with single gun plus four-gun dorsal and tail turrets and in some cases ventral fairing containing an 0.50 in (12.7 mm) gun in Preston-Green mount. Fuel capacity increased to 1,986 Imp gal (9,028 l) and all but first few had longer wing with span increased to 104 ft 2 in (31.75 m). Max bomb load, 10,000 lb (4,540 kg) in fuselage and 3,000 lb (1,362 kg) in wings. Production totalled 326 by HP at Radlett, 900 by English Electric at Samlesbury, 260 by LAPG at Leavesden, 280 by Rootes Securities at Speke and 326 by Fairey Aviation at Stockport; first deliveries November 1943 to No 433 Sqn, RCAF and No 466 Sqn, RAAF, and used by 41 operational squadrons in 1944/45, principally in 4 and 6 Groups.

Halifax A Mk III: Thirty Rootes-built B Mk IIIs converted to serve as interim Airborne Forces glider tug and paratroop transport pending production of A Mk VII. Used to tow Horsa and Hamilcar gliders in airborne assaults on European targets after D-Day.

Halifax IV: Projected development of Mk II with 1,280 hp Merlin 60s (H.P.60A), with long-tailed inner nacelles and totally-enclosed wheel bays, enlarged fins and rudders, enlarged bomb-doors for 8,000 lb (3,632 kg) block-busters and extended span. One Mk II tested with Merlin XXs in Merlin 60 powerplants as Mk II Srs 2 in March 1943, later used as test-bed for Merlin 61s and 65s, with long-tailed inner nacelles but original fins and rudders and short span wing.

Halifax B Mk V: Same as B Mk II but

Above: Halifax II Srs 1A serving with No 78 Sqn, showing the enlarged fins of this version. Left: A Halifax GR Mk II of No 502 Sqn, Coastal Command, with H2S radar in the ventral radome, and white undersides, camouflage being restricted to the upper surfaces.

Above left: Halifax III MX954, with long-span wings and Preston-Green ventral gun mounting, of Canadian No 425 Sqn. Above right: Halifax B Mk VI NP 767 of 347 'Tunisie' Sqn, a Free French unit at RAF Elvington. Below: Halifax C Mk VII PN261 of No 298 Sqn, showing freight pannier in bomb-bay.

with Dowty main undercarriage and retraction system replacing Messier system. Prototype (Mk II converted) flown October 1941 and production (H.P.63) totalled 658 by Rootes Securities and 246 by Fairey Aviation at Stockport. Series I, Series 1 (Special) and Series 1A variants as for B Mk II. B Mk Vs used primarily by squadrons of No 6 (RCAF) Group; others converted to GR Mk V and Met Mk V for Coastal Command. Mk Vs also modified as first Halifaxes to serve with Airborne Forces as tugs for Horsa and Hamilcar, and to carry paratroops. First three modified Mk Vs to 38 Group in October 1942 for first British glider-borne operation ('Freshman'), two Horsas towed by Halifax Vs with troops to attack Norak Hydro Plant making heavy water in Norway. First 38 Group squadron equipped with Halifax Vs, No 295, in February 1943.

Halifax GR Mk II and GR Mk V: Conversion of B Mk II and B Mk V for Coastal Command, by Cunliffe-Owen, mostly of Rootes-built aircraft. Fitted with F.N.64 two-gun ventral turret and 690 Imp gal (3,137 l) extra fuel in three bomb-bay tanks; single 0.50 in (12.7 mm) Browning on Preston-Green mount later replaced the ventral F.N.64. Primarily Mk II Srs 1A standard, used by four squadrons on anti-submarine and shipping patrols, from late-1942 onwards.

Halifax B Mk VI: Similar to B Mk III powered by 1,675 hp Hercules 100s with revised fuel system for tropical operations and 2,190 Imp gal (9,956 l) basic capacity plus three-tank 690 Imp gal (3,137 l) bomb-bay option. Extended wing-tips, Series 1A nose, rectangular fins and rudders as standard. Prototype flown December 19, 1943; production first flight October 10, 1944; production totals 132 by HP and 325 by English Electric. Equipped several bomber squadrons and for radar counter-measures.

Max speed, 312 mph (502 km/h) at 22,000 ft (6,706 m) and 290 mph (497 km/h) at 10,500 ft (3,200 m). Cruising speed, 218-260 mph (351-418 km/h) at 20,000 ft (6,100 m). Time to 20,000 ft (6,100 m) at max weight, 50 min. Service ceiling at max weight, 24,000 ft (7,315 m). Range, 1,260 mls (2,027 km) with max bombs, 2,400 mls (3,867 km) with max fuel. Tare weight, 39,000 lb (17,706 kg). Gross weight, 68,000 lb (30,872 kg). Span, 104 ft 2 in (31.75 m). Length, 70 ft 5 in (21.46 m). Wing area, 1,275 sq ft (118.4 m²).

Halifax Met Mk II, Met Mk III, Met Mk V, Met Mk VI: Conversion of bomber variants for use by squadrons of Coastal Command on meteorological reconnaissance duties.

Halifax B Mk VII: As B Mk VI but with 1,615 hp Hercules XVIs, as airframe production outpaced engine availability. Fifteen

built by HP, 12 by English Electric, 90 by Fairey. Used primarily by squadrons of No 6 (RCAF) Group.

Halifax A Mk VII: Variant of B Mk VII produced for 38 Group Airborne Forces as glider tug and paratrooper, with ventral dropping hatch provided. Production totalled 120 by Rootes, 69 by Fairey, 49 by HP and eight by English Electric. Operational in UK, Middle East and Far East to August 1945 and beyond.

Halifax C Mk VIII: Unarmed passenger, freight or casualty transport version of Halifax B Mk VI, able to carry 10 stretchers, 11 passengers or paratroops (with ventral exit cone) plus 8,000 lb (3,632 kg) capacity detachable freight pannier in bomb-bay. Crew of five and dual controls; Hercules 100 engines. 100 ordered as

H.P.70, plus 304 panniers; first flown June 1945 and served post-war with five squadrons.

Halifax C Mk II, C Mk VI, C Mk VII: Bomber variants converted to carry freight, eight passengers or nine stretchers, plus six passengers in crew rest bunks. All guns, dorsal turret, H₂S scanner and radome and some radio removed. One C Mk III and C Mk VIIs could carry freight pannier as C Mk III.

Halifax A Mk IX, A Mk X: Post-war versions (Mk X not built) with Hercules XVI and Hercules 100 respectively, derived from A Mk VII.

HANDLEY PAGE H.P.75

As part of a general investigation into the characteristics of tailless aircraft, under the direction of G V Lachmann, Handley Page designed a small twin-engined research aircraft during 1937/38. Built by Dart Aircraft Ltd, it was first flown on June 25, 1943, marked H-0222, and known informally in the company as the Manx. Powered by two 130 hp Gipsy Major IIs, it was flown sporadically until April 1946 and designated H.P.75 in mid-1945.

Max speed, 146 mph (235 km/h). Gross weight, 4,000 lb (1,813 kg). Span, 39 ft 10 in (12.19 m). Length, 18 ft 3 in (5.59 m).

Above: Halifax C Mk VIII PP225 photographed whilst at the A & AEE in July 1945. Below: With a Halifax lending scale, the H.P.75 tailless research aircraft H-0222 on display at Radlett in October 1945. It was identified as Ex Aero 186 in AP1480X.

Above: A fine study of a Halifax II Srs 1 in the service of No 35 (Madras Presidency) Squadron, RAF, which began to receive early marks of the Handley Page bomber in late 1940. In 1942, No 35 was one of five squadrons forming the nucleus of Pathfinder Force, retaining Halifaxes until 1944. Left: The first production Halifax 1, L9485, serving at the A & AEE as an armament trials aircraft, with Boulton Paul Type C nose and dorsal turrets, Type E four-gun rear turret and FN 64 two-gun ventral.

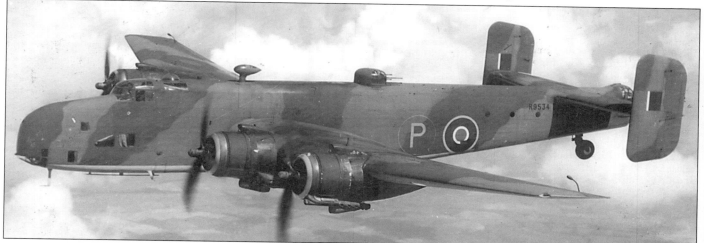

Above: The Halifax III prototype, R9534, converted from a Mk II airframe, seen here after further modification to have a Type A Mk VIII dorsal turret and D-type fins. Below: An early Halifax V in September 1942, showing the Dowty levered-suspension undercarriage that distinguished this mark.

HAWKER HORSLEY

Two-seat bomber and, later, torpedo-bomber, originally to Specification 26/23, first flown spring 1925. Ten Mk I and 102 Mk II for RAF with 665 hp Rolls-Royce Condor IIIA engines, delivered 1926 to 1931. Six Mk IIs to Greek Naval Air Service at Tatoi in December 1929, still in service 1940 but probably saw no action.
Max speed, 118 mph (190 km/h). Gross weight, 9,270 lb (4,205 kg). Span, 56 ft 5³/₄ in (17.22 m). Length, 38 ft 10 in (11.83 m).

HAWKER FURY

The single-seat Fury biplane fighter designed by Sydney Camm in 1927 had passed out of front-line service with the RAF by mid-1939, and those still in use as trainers were grounded by 1940. The SAAF received at least 22, ex-RAF, in 1940. With 640 hp R-R Kestrel V engines and two fixed forward-firing Vickers 0.303 in (7.7 mm) guns, SAAF Furies operated against Italian forces in East Africa and flew as trainers in South Africa until 1942. In Yugoslavia, Ikarus and Zmaj built 40 Furies to supplement 16 bought from Hawker for the *Jugoslovensko Kraljevsko Ratno Vazduhoplovstvo*. With 745 hp Kestrel XVI engines and four forward-firing 0.303 in (7.7 mm) guns — two in the fuselage and two under wing — the JKRV Furies operated against *Luftwaffe* forces briefly in March/April 1941, several captured examples subsequently being tested by *Regia Aeronautica* at Guidonia in Italy. Data for Fury 1:

Above: Retired from RAF front-line service, these Fury IIs (K8267, K8261 and K8262) were serving with No 8 FTS as advanced trainers when war broke out, and were retired to instructional airframe status in January 1940. Below: Four ex-RAF Fury Is in SAAF service, with serials 215-218 and lettered K, L, M and N respectively (plus Hartbees 837, letter C, extreme left), engaged in a propaganda tour in 1942.

Above: A Greek Navy Horsley in pre-war service.

Max. speed, 207 mph (333 km/h) at 14,000 ft (4,267 m). Time to 10,000 ft (3,050 m), 4 min 25 sec. Service ceiling, 28,000 ft (8,534 m). Range, 270 mls (435 km). Gross weight, 3,490 lb (1,583 kg). Span, 30 ft 0 in (9.15 m). Length, 26 ft 8.75 in (8.13 m). Wing area, 252 sq ft (23.41 m²).

HAWKER TOMTIT

Six examples of this training biplane, designed in 1928 by Sydney Camm, flew with the RAF on communications duties for much of the war. Originally built for the RAF, they had been sold for civil use in 1935, and continued to operate in civil markings without being impressed. The engine was a 150 hp Mongoose IIIC. Two similar Tomtits supplied to RCAF in 1930 (serials 139,140) served until mid-1943 with No 7 (GP) Sqn, but four supplied pre-war to RNZAF were relegated to instructional airframe status in 1939.
Max speed, 124 mph (200 km/h). Gross weight, 1,750 lb (795 kg). Span, 28 ft 6¹/₂ in (8.69 m). Length, 23 ft 8 in (7.21 m).

HAWKER HART I

Two-seat light day-bomber to Specification 12/26, was the first of the extended family of military biplanes designed by Sydney Camm. First flown June 1928 and adopted by RAF for production to Specification 9/29, with 525 hp R-R Kestrel IB (or, later 510 hp Kestrel V, VDR, X or XDR, when DR indicated de-rated). Service use began January 1930, and 937 built on Air Ministry contracts —including variants noted below with production shared between Hawker, Gloster, AWA and Vickers. Over 500 Harts of all variants still on RAF strength in September 1939, continuing to serve until declared obsolete 1943, mainly in training role and for communications. Starting early 1938, some 230 Harts (with Kestrel XDR and tropical radiators) transferred to SAAF, used for next few years primarily as trainers but also alongside Hartbees in East Africa/Abyssinia border operations against Italian forces. Two ex-RAF to South Rhodesian AF in 1938, two to RCAF in 1940 (used only as instructional airframes) and 15 to Royal Egyptian AF.

Above: G-AFIB (ex-RAF K1781), seen here in 1941, was one of six Tomtits that flew during the war with their British civil registrations, and was used for a time by Alex Henshaw at Castle Bromwich. Below: The Hart Trainer K6421 was among a miscellany of aircraft used by No 173 Sqn for communications at Heliopolis in 1942/43.

Above: Hawker Demons serving in the RAAF when war began were soon relegated to communications and training duties. These two, A1-11 'Dirty Dora' and the unidentified 'Sloppy Joe' behind, survived the war flying with the Australian No 1 FTS. Left: One of the Iraqi AF Pegasus-engined Harts at Hinaidi. Below: Built by Avro, Audax I K7424 was in RAF service with No 1 FTS (coded 67) before transfer to No 4 GTS and eventual write-off in October 1942.

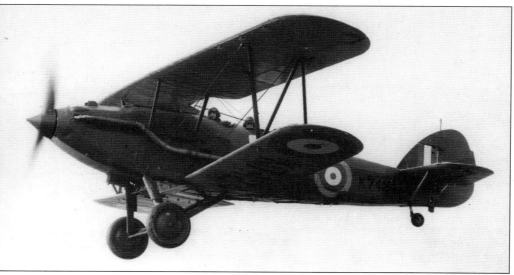

Hart (India): Equipped for RAF service in India, first flown September 7, 1931, and 57 built to Specs 9/31 and 12/33. Equipped Nos 11, 39 and 60 Sqns on NW Frontier, then used for training at No 1 SFTS (India), some transferred to Nos 1 and 2 Flights, Indian Air Force, and used for defensive patrols, 1939/40.

Hart (Special): Batch of 30 built by Gloster to Spec 9/34, based on Audax airframe with desert equipment, derated Kestrel XDR, tropical radiator and heavy duty u/c. Also 20 Audax converted or completed to this standard. Primarily for use at training schools.

Hart (Comm): Eight Hart Is modified for communications duty with No 24 Sqn, all armament removed.

Hart Trainer: Dedicated trainer without armament; windscreen for rear cockpit, and upper wing sweepback reduced from 5 deg to 2.5 deg for CG reasons. Prototype to Spec 8/32, flown April 20, 1932; production deliveries began August 1933 and of 471 built, (later batches to Spec 8/35), more than 300 in wartime service in the UK. Kestrel X or XDR, with Kestrel XVI or XVIDR later.

Max speed, 168 mph (270 km/h) at 3,000 ft (915 m). Time to 10,000 ft (3,050 m), 6.5 min. Service ceiling, 22,800 ft (6,950 m). Range, 430 mls (692 km). Empty weight, 3,020 lb (1,370 kg). Gross weight, 4,150 lb (1,882 kg). Span, 37 ft 4 in (11.38 m).

Length, 29 ft 4 in (8.94 m). Wing area, 349 sq ft (32.37 m²).

HAWKER DEMON

The Demon was developed as a two-seat fighter variant of the Hart bomber to Specification 15/30, and deliveries (initially as Hart Fighter) began in March 1931, followed by full-scale Demon production to Specification 6/32 and later 8/34. RAF acquired 128 Demons from Hawker and 106 from Boulton Paul, variously powered by 485 hp Kestrel IIS or 584 hp Kestrel VDR and many later with Frazer Nash armour-protected powered gun mounting in rear cockpit with one 0.303 in (7.7 mm) Lewis machine gun supplementing two Vickers guns in forward fuselage. A number of Demons adapted for target-towing served in the early war years. Hawker built 64 Demons for the RAAF including 10 target tugs (to Specification 1/34 and 46/36 respectively) and some of these saw brief wartime service in Australia for communication and training duties.

Max speed, 182 mph (293 km/h). Gross weight, about 4,500 lb (2,043 kg). Span, 37 ft 2 in (11.33 m). Length, 26 ft 7 in (9.02 m).

HAWKER AUDAX

Variant of Hart equipped for army co-operation role with a message pick-up hook under fuselage, initially to Specification 7/31 and first flown on December 29, 1931.

Of total production of 653 for the RAF (later batches to Specifications 19/34 and 34/34) — shared between Hawker, Avro, Bristol and Gloster — about 400 still serviceable in September 1939. Operational in East Africa with No 237 (Rhodesia) Sqn alongside SAAF units on the Kenya-Abyssinia border, and with No 4 FTS at RAF Habbaniyah during Iraqi uprising in May 1941. Wartime use in the UK continued for training, glider-towing (Hotspurs) and 'hack' duties until 1944. Production included Audax (India) for service there; Audax (Singapore) for supply to the Straits Settlements Volunteer Air Force, and 20 completed or converted as Hart (Special); examples of all variants were among the wartime survivors. Post-1939 transfers comprised 78 to the SAAF, four to South Rhodesian AF, five to RCAF (as instructional airframes) and a quantity to the Indian Air Force from 1941, used for training and coastal defence duties. Basic Audax engine was 530 hp R-R Kestrel IB; derated 520 hp Kestrel X used later. Thirty-four Audax built for Iraqi AF in 1936 had 620 hp Bristol Pegasus IIM radial engines and, known locally as the Nisr, were available for, but saw little action in, the Iraqi revolt of 1941.

Max speed, 170 mph (273.5 km/h) at 2,400 ft (732 m). Time to 10,000 ft (3,050 m), 8.65 min. Service ceiling, 21,500 ft (6,553 m). Empty weight, 2,938 lb (1,333 kg). Gross weight, 4,386 lb (1,990 kg). Span, 37 ft 3 in (11.35 m). Length, 29 ft 7 in (8.70 m). Wing area, 348 sq ft (32.33 m²).

HAWKER NIMROD

Single-seat fleet fighter, with interchangeable wheel/float undercarriage, developed under Camm's direction in 1930 to comply with Specification 16/30 and first flown on October 14, 1931. Production totalled 56 Mk I and 30 Mk II for FAA. None remained in front-line service by September 1939, but a few surviving Mk IIs flew with No 757 and, briefly, No 759 training units until 1941. The Nimrod II was powered by the 608 hp R-R Kestrel V. Twelve Nimrods (10 built in Denmark at the Orlogsvaerftet naval dockyards) delivered to the Naval Air Service (*Marine Flyvevaesenets*) in 1934-36 were front-line fighter equipment when Germany attacked Denmark in April 1940,

Above: One of the Danish-built Nimrod fighters in service with 2.Luftflotille of the Naval Air Service at the time of the German invasion in 1940. Below: Osprey I S1695 in training colours at Eastleigh, late in 1939 (courtesy FAA Museum).

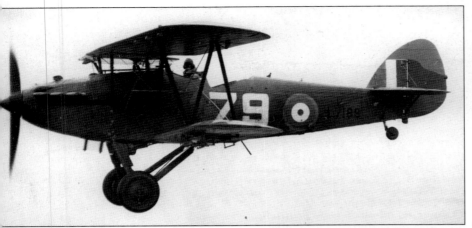

Above: Hind L7189, in service with No 1 FTS, was nearing the end of its flying life with the RAF when photographed in November 1941; it became an instructional airframe in January 1942. Below right: In camouflage-yellow training finish, Hind NZ1519 was K6787 before transfer from the RAF to the RNZAF in June 1940, and is seen here in service with No 3 FTS at Ohakea in June 1942.

but saw no action.
Max speed, 193 mph (311 km/h) at 14,000 ft (4,267 m). Gross weight, 4,059 lb (1,841 kg). Span, 33 ft 6³/4 in (10.21 m). Length, 26 ft 6¹/2 in (8.08 m).

HAWKER OSPREY
Essentially a navalised Hart, the production Osprey first flew in 1932, conforming to Specification 19/30 and featuring folding wings and interchangeable wheel/float u/c. Production for the FAA totalled 132, of which a few survived to see wartime service. Succeeded in the original fighter/reconnaissance role, they flew as target-tugs and advanced trainers with Nos 755, 758, 759 and 780 Sqns, some until early 1943. The Osprey was powered by the 630 hp R-R Kestrel IIMS (Kestrel V in Osprey IV, to Spec 26/35).
Max speed, 168 mph (270 km/h) at 5,000 ft (1,525 m). Gross weight, 4,950 lb (2,245 kg). Span, 37 ft (11.28 m). Length, 29 ft 4 in (8.94 m).

HAWKER HIND
Improved Hart purchased by RAF 1935-1938 as interim bomber, defined by Specification G.7/34 and first flown on September 12, 1934. Production of 427, of which some 360 on strength September 1939, plus eight transferred to Indian Air Force and 15 to Afghan Air Force, which also bought eight directly from Hawker. Starting early 1940, RAF transferred total of 131 to SAAF and 78 to RNZAF (of which 15 lost en route), plus four as instructional airframes to RCAF. Final 20 built as Hind Trainers, plus 124 converted to similar standard pre-war by GAL at Hanworth and other conversions by Hawker and RAF. Wartime use by RAF for training, glider-towing (Hotspur), target-towing and 'hack' duties until 1943. In New Zealand, used by FTS at Ohakea 1940-41, and about 18 for army co-operation in 1942 by Nos 20 and 21 Sqns. In South Africa, Hinds supplemented Harts in training and utility roles. Original Hind bombers used 640 hp R-R Kestrel V, derated to 599 hp Kestrel VDR in trainers (data below).
Max speed, 185.5 mph (298.5 km/h) at 15,500 ft (4,724 m). Time to 10,000 ft (3,050 m), 8.4 min. Service ceiling, 24,450 ft (7,452 m). Empty weight, 3,195 lb (1,450 kg). Loaded weight, 4,657 lb (2,112 kg). Span, 37 ft 3 in (11.35 m). Length, 29 ft 3 in (8.9 m). Wing area, 348 sq ft (32.33 m²).

HAWKER HARDY
Adapted from the Hart to conform to Specification G.23/33, the Hardy was equipped to operate in the Middle East, special features including a tropical radiator, message pick-up hook, water containers and tropical service kit. After prototype first flight on September 7, 1934, RAF bought 47 (built by Gloster) with 530 hp R-R Kestrel IB or (later aircraft) 581 hp Kestrel X. Some 30 were in the hands of No 6 Sqn in Palestine when war started; in April 1940 four transferred to South Rhodesian AF and others to No 237 (Rhodesia) Sqn for operation (alongside Harts), in army co-op and bombing roles on Kenya/Abyssinia border, and in Sudan until April 1941.
Max speed, 161 mph (259 km/h) at sea level. Gross weight, 5,005 lb (2,270 kg). Span, 37 ft 3 in (11.35 m). Length, 29 ft 7 in (9.02 m).

HAWKER HARTBEES
Based on Audax, with modifications to meet South African requirements (to Specification 22/34) for a close-support aircraft. Four built by Hawker (first flight June 28, 1935) and 65 more by the Roberts Heights Depot of SAAF. Flown by Nos 11, 40 and 41 Sqns, SAAF (alongside Harts) from Kenyan bases in action against Italian forces in Abyssinia. Survivors used for training in South Africa and Southern Rhodesia for remainder of war. The Hartbees was powered by 608 hp R-R Kestrel VFP (full power).
Max speed, 176 mph (283 km/h) at 6,000 ft (1,829 m). Gross weight, 4,787 lb (2,171 kg). Span, 37 ft 3 in (11.35 m). Length, 29 ft 7 in (9.02 m).

HAWKER HECTOR
Developed under Sydney Camm's direction during 1935 as an army co-operation aircraft to Specification 14/35, based on Hind bomber but with 805 hp Dagger IIIMS engine and suitable role equipment. Prototype flew on February 14, 1936, and production of 178 by Westland completed between February and December 1937. Entered service with No 4 (AC) Squadron February 1937 but withdrawn from all seven regular AC squadrons by 1939 and then serving only with five AAF squadrons, seeing brief operational service against German targets in N France in 1940. Many Hectors used 1940-42 as tugs for Hotspur gliders in 38 Group training units.
Max speed, 187 mph (301 km/h) at 6,560 ft (2,000 m). Time to 10,000 ft (3,050 m), 5 min 40 sec. Service ceiling, 24,000 ft (7,315 m). Gross weight, 4,910 lb (2,230 kg). Span, 36 ft 11¹/2 in (11.25 m). Length, 29 ft 9³/4 in (9.07 m).

Above: Hardy K4050 —seen here in company with K4069 serving pre-war with No 30 Sqn — later went to No 6 Sqn and was then transferred to the Southern Rhodesia AF in April 1940, surviving in service until March 1941. Below: Hartbees 104 serving with No 26 EFTS of the SAAF at Guinea Fowl, Rhodesia, used for met flights in August 1940.

Below: The Hector K9711 in service in September 1941, probably with 102 Glider Operational Training Unit. It has a Hotspur on tow, but unfortunately not recorded by the photographer! Service use, with No 4 GTS, continued until April 1943.

Above: Hurricane X AG162 came from the Canadian Car & Foundry Ltd production lines in the late summer of 1940 and was in service in the UK with No 55 OTU before the end of the year.

Above: Hurricane I V7462 in service in 1940 (as JU:T) with No 111 Sqn, which had been the first to equip on the Hawker fighter in 1937. Below: Hurricane I Z4251 of the Middle East Training squadron displays the tropical filter over the carburettor air intake.

Left: An hitherto unpublished illustration of the 'civil' Hurricane I G-AFKX, photographed at Langley in the second half of 1943, by which time it had acquired full service camouflage and markings, with the registration displayed in lieu of serial number.

HAWKER HURRICANE

First monoplane fighter to serve with RAF, the Hurricane was designed under Sydney Camm's direction as logical progression from Fury biplane, and known, in earliest project form, as Fury Monoplane with 660 hp R-R Goshawk VI steam-cooled engine. Subsequently evolved around R-R P.V.12 (Merlin) in 1934 as Interceptor Monoplane. Construction of prototype (K5083) launched in 1935, conforming to Specification F.36/34, with 890 hp Merlin C and eight 0.303 in (7.7 mm) Browning machine guns in (fabric-covered) wings. First flight at Brooklands on November 6, 1935, and prototype retired from test-flying early-1939.

Hurricane I: Production initiated March 1936 and initial contract for 600 confirmed July 1936, to Specification 15/36. First production aircraft flown October 12, 1937, with 1,030 hp Merlin II. Subsequent orders brought total Hurricane I production to 3,774 in Britain by Hawker (1,924) and Gloster (1,850), plus 160 for RAF by Canadian Car and Foundry in Canada. In

course of production, metal-covered wings replaced original fabric-covered type, and 1,030 hp Merlin III replaced Merlin II. First few aircraft had retractable tailwheel and lacked ventral fin. Service introduction late-1937 with No 111 Squadron at Northolt; up to 11 squadrons served in France 1939-40, another in Norway in 1940 and 29 squadrons of Hurricane Is available to Fighter Command for Battle of Britain in July 1940, some later transferring to night fighting role. With large filter over carburettor air intake, tropicalised Hurricane Is served in Malta, the Middle East and the Far East (Singapore and Burma) before arrival of Mk IIs in larger numbers. One Mk I armed with two 20 mm Oerlikon cannon operational in 1940; three others fitted with four-cannon wing armament in late 1940. Several export orders placed pre-1939 met by diversions from RAF contracts and subsequent run-on production; other supplies to Allied and Commonwealth forces made to meet operational needs as they arose. Thus, from 1938 onwards, 24 Hurricane Is went to Yugoslavia (where 20 more built by

Zmaj factory); 12 to Romania; 35 to Turkey; two to Persia; 12 to Finland; 15 to Belgium (plus production by Avions Fairey — see later note); 20 to the RCAF and more than 30 to SAAF. One Hurricane I (of ten intended) reached Poland in 1939 and one, with tropical filter, reached Australia in September 1941. One ex-RAF Mk I diverted to Hawker demonstrator/test-bed as G-AFKX remained in use through 1943.

Max speed, 316 mph (508 km/h) at 17,750 ft (5,410 m). Cruising speed, 272 mph (438 km/h) at 15,000 ft (4,575 m). Time to 15,000 ft (4,575 m), 6.3 min. Service ceiling, 33,200 ft (10,120 m). Range, 445 mls (716 km). Empty weight, 5,085 lb (2,308 kg). Gross weight, 6,661 lb (3,024 kg). Span, 40 ft (12.19 m). Length, 31 ft 5 in (9.58 m). Wing area, 258 sq ft (23.97 m²).

Hurricane II: Designation change to signify introduction of two-speed, single-stage supercharged 1,390 hp Merlin XX, first flown (in a Mk I) on June 11, 1940. Production switched progressively as Merlin XXs became available, with deliveries to RAF beginning early September 1940. **Hurricane IIA** retained same eight-gun wing as Mk I, with initial batch of Series 1s having same fuselage and Series 2s having strengthened fuselage to accept modified wing with later armament options. About 12 Mk IIAs had lengthened nose (7 in/18 cm), but modification not adopted for production. Introducing a 'universal' wing, **Hurricane IIB,** starting late-1940, had 12 Browning 0.303 in (7.7 mm) machine guns, and **Hurricane IIC** (first flown February 6, 1941) had four 20 mm Hispano cannon. All Mk IIs could have tropical filters for service in Middle and Far East, and could carry two 44 Imp gal (200-1) drop tanks, 88 Imp gal (400-1) ferry tanks, two 250 lb (113.5 kg) or (later aircraft) 500 lb (227 kg) bombs. A Hurricane II armed with two 40 mm Vickers Type S cannon (and two Browning machine guns) first flew on September 18, 1941 and **Hurricane IID** entered production with this armament (or a few with Rolls-Royce BF cannon). Some Hurricane IIBs and IICs carried six (later eight) 3 in (7.62 cm) rocket projectiles underwing, after tests starting February 1942. Designation **Hurricane IIE** applied to aircraft wired to accept machine guns or cannon, and bombs, without the need to change wing sets. Service use of Hurricane IIA began early September 1940; of IIB fighter in February 1941; of IIB fighter-bomber ('Hurribomber') in May 1941; of IIC in April 1941, IID in March 1942 and of IIE in September 1941. A few Hurricane IIBs and IICs fitted in 1941-42 with AI Mk IV or Mk V radar for night fighting, either in fuselage radio rack or underwing pod in place of drop tank. All Mk II variants served

Below: One of the Hurricane Is that equipped No 53 Sqn in the 5th Wing of the Romanian Air Force's No 1 Fighter Group until early 1943. Left: One of the 35 Hurricane Mk Is supplied to the Turkish Air Force (TUAF) from RAF stocks.

with UK-based squadrons and also, extensively, overseas; by November 1941, 25 Hurricane squadrons based in Middle East and others in Malta, Iceland and Soviet Union. In Middle East, some 200 Hurricanes (including 20 Mk Is re-engined with Merlin XX) modified for tac-R (with one camera and full armament) or PR (with two cameras and no armament). Hurricane II squadrons extensively engaged in India/Burma, 1942-44. Other Hurricane roles included meteorological recce in UK and ME with unarmed **Hurricane Met Mk IIC;** anti-aircraft co-operation and training, using 'war-weary' fighters. Hurricane II production in UK (shared between Hawker, Gloster and Austin Motors) totalled 8,676, comprising 451 Mk IIA, 2,948 Mk IIB, 4,711 Mk IIC, 296 Mk IID and 270 Mk IIE, plus 100 Mk Is converted (by Rolls-Royce) to Mk IIA. Several Commonwealth squadrons flew Hurricane IIs alongside the RAF, especially RAAF and SAAF units in the Middle East and RCAF in the UK, using aircraft retained on RAF strength. In India, seven squadrons of the IAF flew Hurricanes (Mks IIB, IIC and IV) from June 1942, using some 300 aircraft transferred from RAF stocks. Following on from Mk I supplies, Turkey received 38 Hurricane IIBs and 91 IICs (of which, 44 equipped for recce), and two squadrons of the Royal Egyptian Air Force flew ex-RAF Hurricane IIs (and some Is) from 1941 to 1945. Starting in 1941, several squadrons of the Free French Air Force flew Hurricanes in North and West Africa and the Middle East. Hurricane production ended with delivery of Mk IIC PZ865 (later G-AMAU) in August 1944. Data for Mk IIC follow.

Max speed, 327 mph (526 km/h) at 18,000 ft (5,486 m). Time to 15,000 ft (4,575 m), 6 min. Service ceiling, 35,600 ft (10,850 m). Range with drop tanks, 426 mls (685 km). Empty weight, 6,577 lb (2,986 kg). Gross weight, 7,544 lb (3,425 kg). Span, 40 ft (12.19 m). Length, 32 ft 3 in (9.83 m). Wing area, 258 sq ft (23.97 m²).

Hurricane III: Proposed Mk II airframe

Above: Hurricane IIA Z2836 serving with No 312 (Czechoslovak) Sqn in the RAF at Kenley in June 1941. Below: A Hurricane I converted (by Rolls-Royce) to Mk IIA standard with Merlin XX, operating in the Middle East (possibly with No 208 AC Sqn) in the photo-recce role, with camera in the ventral fairing. It has a tropical filter and overall dark PR blue finish.

with 1,390 hp Packard-Merlin 28. Not built.

Hurricane IV: Developed Hurricane IIE with uprated Merlin and 'universal' wing carrying two 0.303 in (7.7 mm) Browning guns and wiring for either two 40 mm Vickers S cannon or eight 60 lb (27.1 kg) rocket projectiles. Prototype with 1,620 hp Merlin 32, deepened ventral radiator, Rotol four-bladed propeller and tropical filter first

flown March 14, 1943. Second prototype with definitive 1,390 hp Merlin 27 and three-bladed Rotol propeller flown March 23, 1943. Service use began May 1943 (No 164 Sqn) and equipped six squadrons in the UK, one in ME and two in Burma for combat use; others for second-line duties. Production total, 524 by Hawker.

Hurricane V: Redesignation of first Mk IV (KX405) in July 1943, with Merlin 32 boosted for optimum low-altitude performance. Two more prototypes, no production.

Belgian Hurricane: Contract for 80 aircraft placed with Avions Fairey SA on behalf of the AeM (Belgian Air Force) in 1938. Similar to Hurricane I but with wing armament of four 0.50 in (12.7 mm) FN-built Browning guns. Three built and two flown by May 1940, when German invasion terminated production. Nineteen British-built Hurricane Is (including four which force-landed in Belgium in 1939) on AeM

Above: Rarely illustrated, the Hurricane IIE had a 'universal' wing wired to permit a variety of armament and stores to be carried without modification of circuits and control systems. BE485, shown with two 250 lb (113 kg) bombs, was used by No 402 Sqn. Below: Hurricane IIBs in all-black finish for night-fighting, serving with No 253 (Hyderabad) Sqn. Each aircraft has a suitably Indian-orientated name; Z3971 is 'Samasthans II'.

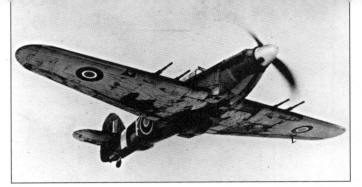

Above left: Hurricane IIC Z3778 in service (as JX:Y) with No 1 Sqn. Above right: Hurricane IIC BN354, with tropical filter and 'desert' camouflage, flown by No 213 Sqn at Alamein in late 1942. Below right: Hurricane IV KX413, with 40 mm cannon armament, serving with No 164 Sqn.

charge in May 1940, saw no action.

Yugoslav Hurricane: Production of 100 Hurricanes for Royal Yugoslav Air Force initiated 1939 by Zmaj (60) and Rogozarski (40), but only 20 built by Zmaj by April 1941, when production terminated. One Hurricane fitted in Yugoslavia with Daimler-Benz DB 601A for comparative trials.

Soviet Hurricanes: Nearly 3,000 Hurricanes supplied to Soviet Union 1941-1944 from British and Canadian production, including 210 Mk IIA (some Mk I conversions), 1,557 Mk IIB, 1,009 Mk IIC, 60 Mk IID and about 100 Mk IV. In Russia, some Hurricanes adapted to have 0.50 in (12.7 mm) machine guns of US origin, and a few modified to two-seaters for training.

Canadian Hurricanes (Mks X, XI, XII): Production of Hurricane initiated by Canadian Car and Foundry at Fort William late-1938 against British contract, and first flight of Hurricane I (P5120) on January 10, 1940. Production total of 1,451 (perhaps 1,454) included Mk Is and IIs with Merlin II/III and Merlin XX respectively, equalling British standard aircraft, and the following specifically Canadian marks.

Hurricane X: As Hurricane I with 1,390 hp Packard-Merlin 28 and Hamilton Standard propeller.

Hurricane XI: As Hurricane X, but with Canadian equipment in place of British.

Hurricane XII: As Hurricane XI, but with 1,390 hp Packard-Merlin 29 and Hurricane IIB-type 12-gun wing. Some eight-gun Hurricane Xs later fitted with Merlin 29s in Canada designated Hurricane XIIA.

From CCF production, RCAF received 400 Hurricane XIIs, of which 150 transferred to RAF, and 80 Hurricane Xs transferred *from* RAF. All other Canadian production was for supply to Britain, where many converted to Sea Hurricane (or completed as such before delivery), leading to Sea Hurricane XI, XII and XIIA designations. RCAF operational use of Hurricane began in Canada with No 1(F) Sqn in 1939 (using British-built Mk Is) and continued in UK. Ten RCAF squadrons flew Hurricanes in defensive role in Canada.

HAWKER SEA HURRICANE

Sea Hurricane IA: Starting January 1941, total of 249 Hurricane Is modified (by Hawker, Gloster and, mostly, General Aircraft) to have catapult spools, allowing launch from adapted merchant ships operating as Fighter Catapult Ships (FCSs) or Catapult Aircraft Merchantmen (CAMs). The 'expendable' Sea Hurricane IAs (or 'Hurricats') were manned by No 804 Sqn, FAA, on the FCSs or by volunteer RAF pilots. First (of eight) successful operational launches August 2, 1941.

Sea Hurricane IB: Testing began March 1941 of a Sea Hurricane IA further modified with an A-frame arrester hook to allow operations from aircraft carrier decks. Designation Sea Hurricane IB applied to over 300 conversions (mostly by GAL) of ex-RAF Hurricane Is, some of which already modified to Sea Hurricane IA, or to Hurricane IIA with Merlin XX (later sometimes referred to as Hooked Hurricane II), all with eight-gun wing armament.

Sea Hurricane IC: About 100 Mk IBs further modified to have four-cannon armament, but retaining Merlin III of Hurricane I. Operational from early 1942, including some with tropical filters.

Sea Hurricane IIB: Similar to Sea Hurricane IB, but based on Merlin XX-engined Hurricane IIB, with 12-gun wing.

Sea Hurricane IIC: Converted Hurricane IICs, with cannon armament and Merlin XX engines. Entered service in sec-

ond half of 1942. Quantities uncertain, but some 600 Sea Hurricanes of all marks eventually taken on strength by FAA, including 60 delivered as new by Hawker and remainder as conversions.

Sea Hurricane XI, XIIA: Up to 50 CCF-built Hurricane Is with Merlin IIIs, transferred from RAF to RCAF, progressively updated to have Canadian equipment and Packard-Merlin 28, then Packard-Merlin 29 engines, included some already in Sea Hurricane configuration, accounting for these designations.

Data for Sea Hurricane IIC: *Max speed, 342 mph (550 km/h) at 22,000 ft (6,075 m). Cruising speed, 212 mph (314 km/h) at 20,000 ft (6,095 m). Time to 22,000 ft (6,705 m), 9.1 min. Range, with drop tanks, 908 mls (1,461 km). Empty weight, 5,800 lb (2,631 kg). Gross weight, 7,800 lb (3,358 kg). Span, 40 ft (12.19 m). Length, 32 ft 3 in (9.83 m). Wing area, 258 sq ft (23.97 m²).*

Below: One of the first Hurricane Is off the Fairey production line at Gosselies, for service with the Belgian Air Force in 1940. Below right: Sea Hurricane IA V6756 in the markings of the Merchant Ship Fighter Unit. Above right: Sea Hurricane IB P2886 in service with No 768 Sqn, part of the Deck Landing Training School at Machrihanish in 1943.

HAWKER HENLEY

The Henley was designed under the direction of Sydney Camm as a light day bomber to Specification P.4/34, making use of many features of the Hurricane including mainplanes and tail unit. With crew of two in tandem, the Henley carried 550 lb (250 kg) of bombs internally and eight 25 lb (11.4 kg) bombs on wing racks, a wing-mounted Vickers 0.303 in (7.7 mm) gun and a Lewis gun in the rear cockpit. Powered by a 980 hp Merlin F, prototype Henley I flew on March 10, 1937, and second prototype with 1,030 hp Merlin II on May 26, 1938. Latter converted to target-tug by Gloster, which company produced to Specification 42/36, 200 Henley target-tugs with Merlin II, III or V engines, after single-engined day bomber concept had been abandoned. From late 1939 to late 1942, Henleys served primarily with Air Gunnery Schools and Anti-Aircraft Co-operation Units.

Max speed (with drogue target), 200-270 mph (322-434 km/h). Gross weight, 8,480 lb (3,850 kg). Span, 47 ft 10½ in (14.59 m). Length, 36 ft 5 in (11.09 m).

HAWKER HOTSPUR

Designed to Specification F.9/35 during 1936 as a turret fighter with armament of four 0.303 in (7.7 mm) Brownings in a B-P dorsal turret plus one Vickers gun in the front fuselage. Powered by a 1,030 hp Merlin II, the Hotspur was derived from the Henley and the prototype K8309 flew on June 14, 1938, but planned production by Avro to Specification 17/36 was abandoned and the prototype, with turret removed, served at the RAE Farnborough on miscellaneous test programmes until 1942.

Max speed, 316 mph (508 km/h) at 15,800 ft (4,816 m). Gross weight, 7,650 lb (3,473 kg). Span, 40 ft 6 in (12.34 m). Length, 32 ft 10½ in (10.02 m).

Above: The second prototype Henley, K7554, in October 1941 after its conversion (by Gloster) to target-tug configuration. Below: The single Hotspur K8309 in 1941, with dorsal turret removed, when used at the RAE for flap trials.

HAWKER TORNADO

Single-seat fighter developed under Sydney Camm's direction in response to Specification F.18/37. Variants developed in parallel with R-R Vulture and Napier Sabre engine, latter named Typhoon and described separately. Tornado IA and IB designations were to apply to Vulture-engined production versions with wing-mounted armament of ('A') 12 0.303 in (7.7 mm) Browning machine guns or ('B') four 20 mm Hispano cannon respectively. Four F.18/37 prototypes ordered early 1938 (of which two to be

Typhoons). First Tornado (P5219) flown October 6, 1939, with 'A' wing (guns not fitted) and 1,760 hp Vulture II served by ventral radiator, the latter soon replaced by chin radiator, as first flown December 6, 1939. Second prototype (P5224) first flown December 5, 1940, with 'B' wing (no guns fitted). In March 1941, 1,980 hp Vulture Vs fitted in both prototypes, and on October 23, 1941, a further prototype (HG641) flown, with 2,210 hp Bristol Centaurus C.E.4S radial engine. Production of 896 Tornados by Avro planned, but abandoned after completion of one aircraft (R7936), flown at Woodford on August 29, 1941), when production of unsatisfactory Vulture terminated. All four Tornados continued flying into 1943 on various testing, including contraprops. Data for Vulture V-engined version.

Max speed, 398 mph (640.5 km/h) at 23,000 ft (7,010 m). Time to 2,000 ft (610 m), 7.2 min. Service ceiling, 34,900 ft (10,638 m). Empty weight, 8,377 lb (3,800 kg). Gross weight, 10,668 lb (4,839 kg). Span, 41 ft 11 in (12.77 m). Length, 32 ft 10 in (10.00 m). Wing area, 283 sq ft (26.29 m²).

Above: Third prototype Tornado HG641 in its final form, with Centaurus engine. Below: Sole production Tornado IA, R7936, serving as a test-bed for de Havilland contraprops.

Below left: First Tornado prototype, P5219, with original tail unit, and ventral radiator for its Vulture engine. Below right: Second Tornado, P5224, showing the revised tail unit and nose radiator position.

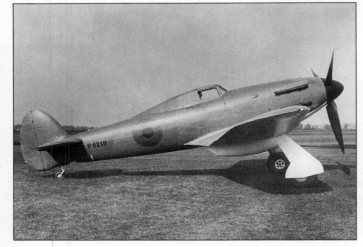

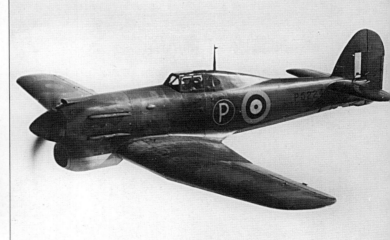

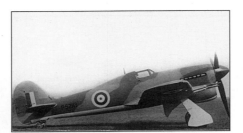

*Above left: First Typhoon prototype, P5212, with original tail unit and 'A' wing.
Above right: Second Typhoon prototype, P5216, with revised tail and 'B' wing mounting cannon armament.*

HAWKER TYPHOON

Single-seat 'heavy' fighter evolved to succeed Hurricane and designed around all-new Napier Sabre 24-cylinder sleeve-valve engine, to comply with Specification F.18/37. Four prototypes ordered early 1938, of which two with R-R Vulture (see Hawker Tornado). First prototype (P5212) flown February 24, 1940, with 2,100 hp Sabre I, 'A' wing but no armament fitted, rear-cockpit fairing and side-entrance door. Second prototype (P5216) flown May 3, 1940, with 'B' wing and cannon fitted. Pilot production batch of 15 Typhoons with Sabre I engines built by Hawker, 1941; all other production by Gloster, totalling 3,300 with 2,180 hp Sabre IIA, 2,200 hp Sabre IIB or 2,260 hp Sabre IIC engines and completed by November 1945. First production aircraft flown at Brockworth on May 27, 1941. Five Hawker and 104 Gloster aircraft completed as Typhoon IA with armament of 12 Browning 0.303 in (7.7 mm) machine guns; all others as Typhoon IB with four 20 mm Hispano cannon. First 163 aircraft retained 'solid' fairing aft of cockpit, followed by transparent fairing of similar profile and then (from aircraft No 1700) a one-piece aft-sliding 'bubble' canopy. Final batches had four-bladed propellers and enlarged tailplanes. Service introduction commenced September 1941 in No 56 Sqn, RAF, and first operation on May 30, 1942. Early operations dogged by engine prob-

lems, structural failures and some performance shortfall, eventually leading to diversion of Typhoon to fighter-bombing role, with up to two 1,000 lb (454 kg) bombs or eight (eventually 12 or 16) 60 lb (27 kg) rocket projectiles. First fighter-bomber operations late-1942 by Nos 181 and 182 Sqns and by June 1945 some 27 squadrons (including three RCAF and one RNZAF) had flown Typhoons operationally and with great success in close-support role against ground targets, entirely in European ETO. One Typhoon (R7881, first flown March 23, 1943) equipped with AI Mk IV radar to evaluate night fighting potential. Prototype P5216 flown for several months (starting on November 9, 1941) with long-span wings and long ailerons to assess potential improvement in high-altitude performance (identified as Experimental Aeroplane 174 in the recognition manual). Conversely, Typhoon IA R7577 flown (starting July 27, 1942) with clipped wings to check possible low-altitude performance improvement (Experimental Aeroplane 185).
Max speed, 405 mph (652 km/h) at 18,000 ft (5,486 m). Most economical cruising speed, 254 mph (409 km/h) at 15,000 ft (4,572 m). Time to 15,000 ft (4,572 m), 6.2 min. Service ceiling 34,000 ft (10,363 m). Empty weight, 8,800 lb (3,992 kg). Gross weight, 11,400 lb (5,171 kg). Span, 41 ft 7 in (12.67 m). Length, 31 ft 11½ in (9.73 m). Wing area, 279 sq ft (25.92 m²).

Typhoon FR Mk IB: Approximately 60 (of 200 planned) conversions for fighter-reconnaissance role, carrying one 14 in (35.6 cm) and two 5 in (12.7 cm) cameras in port wing, replacing inboard port cannon. Forward-facing cine camera replaced inboard starboard cannon in some aircraft. Used operationally, August 1944-February 1945, by Nos 268 and 4 Sqns.
Typhoon II: Renamed Tempest, described below.

HAWKER TEMPEST

Evolved under Camm's direction during 1940 as a 'second generation' Typhoon and initially known as the Typhoon II (Hawker P.1012). Combined Typhoon fuselage with new thin wing incorporating leading-edge radiators. Two prototypes ordered to Specification F.10/41 in November 1941; name changed to Tempest I in January 1942, with 2,500 hp Sabre IV engine. One prototype (HM599) completed as Tempest I with wing leading-edge radiators, first flown February 24, 1943, and planned production of 400 abandoned for want of Sabre IVs. Alternative engine installations resulted in subsequent marks, as below:
Tempest V: Essentially the Tempest I with Typhoon-type 2,180 hp Sabre IIA engine installation and nose radiator. Prototype (HM595) first Tempest to fly, in this guise, on September 2, 1942. Production initiated by Hawker and first production Tempest V flown June 21, 1943. First 100 aircraft Srs 1s with four Hispano Mk II 20 mm cannon and short barrel projections; all-round view cockpit canopies as later Typhoons and enlarged fins and tailplanes. The 700 Srs 2s had Mk V cannon with barrels flush with leading edge, and Sabre IIB or IIC; like Typhoon, Tempest V could carry two 1,000 lb (454 kg) underwing bombs or eight 60 lb (27 kg) rockets. First deliveries to Nos 3 and 486 (RNZAF) Sqns, in April 1944, operational use began in May and Tempest Vs served notably in the defence against V-1 attacks from June 1944 onwards. Seven squadrons operational by June 1945 and service use continued after war's end. Data for Mk V Srs 2.
Max speed, 435 mph (700 km/h) at 17,000 ft (5,182 m). Economical cruising speed, 246 mph (396 km/h). Time to 20,000 ft (6,100 m), 6.1 min. Service ceiling, 36,500 ft (11,125 m). Range, 740 mls (1,191 km) with standard fuel. Empty weight, 9,250 lb (4,200 kg). Normal gross weight, 11,510 lb (5,226 kg). Max overload weight, 13,640 lb (6,193 kg). Span, 41 ft 0 in (12.49 m). Length, 33 ft 8 in (10.26 m). Wing area, 302 sq ft (28.1 m²).

Below: Typhoon IB JR128 of No 183 Sqn, showing final all-round-view canopy and whip aerial.

Above: The fifth production Typhoon IA, R7580, on test at the AFDU early in 1942, showing original faired fuselage behind the cockpit. Below: Typhoon IB R8831 (with cannon removed) withdrawn from No 181 Sqn to test 500 lb (227 kg) bomb carriage

Above: Typhoon FR Mk IB EK427 of No 268 Sqn, showing armament reduced to two cannon and forward-facing camera in inboard starboard position. Left: Prototype Tempest I HM599 with its original canopy. Below: Tempest V Srs 2 SN328 at the CFE in late-1945 showing final configuration with Mk II rocket installation.

Tempest VI: Prototype (HM595) flown with 2,340 hp Sabre V on May 9, 1944, followed by two Tempest V conversions for service trials and 142 new-build Tempest VIs with this engine. Service use post-war.

Tempest II: Six Tempest airframes ordered early 1942 for prototype development, of which three to have Centaurus engine (initially under Typhoon II/Centaurus appellation), but only two proceeded as Tempest II prototypes with this engine. First flight (LA602) June 28, 1943, with Centaurus IV and (LA607) September 18, 1943, used for development flying with Centaurus IV, V, XII, XV and XVIII. First production Tempest II (by Bristol) flown October 4, 1944, with 2,520 hp Centaurus V or VI and Hispano Mk V cannon. Production totalled 452 (50 by Bristol, 402 by Hawker), continuing post-war. Operational use began after war's end.

Tempest III: Designation applicable to two prototypes with R-R Griffon IIB engine, but not built.

Tempest IV: Designation for prototypes as alternatives to Tempest III with Griffon 61 in self-contained powerplant installation.

Not built, but see Hawker Fury for further reference to LA610.

HAWKER FURY I

Conceived during 1942 as a 'lightweight' development of the Tempest, the Hawker P.1026 complied with Specification F.2/43. Two prototypes ordered during 1943, plus three airframes ordered as Tempest prototypes reassigned to this programme (but only one completed). Later named Fury, the P.1026 featured Tempest outer wing panels without a centre section, and a new small fuselage designed around a Centaurus or Griffon engine. Prototype (NX798) with Centaurus XII first flown September 1, 1944, and another (NX802) with Centaurus XV on July 25, 1945. Prototype originally planned as Tempest III (LA610) flown as Fury on November 27, 1944, with Griffon 85 and six-bladed contraprop; also flown, early 1945, with Centaurus XV and later in 1945 with 3,055 hp Sabre VII, with which a speed of 483 mph (777 km/h) at 18,500 ft (5,639 m) achieved post-war. Further development halted by war's end. Data for Centaurus XV:

Max speed, 455 mph (732 km/h) at 24,000 ft (7,315 m). Time to 20,000 ft (6,100 m), 5.5 min. Service ceiling, 43,500 ft (13,260 m). Empty weight, 8,615 lb (3,911 kg). Gross weight, 11,675 lb (5,300 kg). Span, 38 ft 4³/4 in (11.69 m). Length, 34 ft 7 in (10.54 m). Wing area, 284.5 sq ft (26.43 m²).

HAWKER SEA FURY

Navalised variant of Fury 1 (previous entry) in response to Specification N.7/43, to be developed by Boulton Paul under Hawker supervision. Three prototypes ordered 1944, of which first (SR661) flown by Hawker on February 21, 1945, with Centaurus XII engine. Subsequent prototypes, one each by Hawker and Boulton Paul, completed post-war, and Sea Fury production ordered in April 1944, to Specification N.22/43.

Max speed, 460 mph (740 km/h) at 18,000 ft (5,486 m). Gross weight, 12,500 lb (5,670 kg). Span, 38 ft 4³/4 in (11.70 m). Length, 34 ft 3 in (10.44 m).

Above: Bristol-built Tempest II MW404 photographed at Banwell immediately before first flight on May 23, 1945 — too late for wartime service. Left: The second prototype Fury, NX802, which flew in July 1945. Below: Sea Fury SR661, the only example of the navalised Fury flown by the time hostilities ended.

HELMY AEROGYPT

Four-seat cabin monoplane (G-AFFG) powered by three 22 hp Douglas Sprites, intended as scale model for passenger/freight transport to be produced in Egypt; first flown at Heston February 1939. Progressively modified to Aerogypt II and Aerogypt III, and testing continued to September 26, 1940. Further development 1943/44 at White Waltham as Aerogypt IV with two Continental A-65s and tricycle u/c; survived until November 1946 but saw no military service.

Max speed, 160 mph (257 km/h). Gross weight, 2,400 lb (1,088 kg). Span, 26 ft 4 in (8.02 m). Length, 19 ft (5.8 m).

HESTON PHOENIX

Of six examples of the five-seat Phoenix built in 1935/37, three airworthy in the UK in 1939 were impressed in March 1940, as X9393 (G-AEMT), X2891 (G-AESV) and X9338 (G-AEYX). First Phoenix flew on August 18, 1935, with a 205 hp DH Gipsy Six; those impressed had Gipsy Six Srs IIs and DH vp propellers. Two of the Phoenix used by ATA Ferry Pilot Pools were lost during the war; G-AESV survived until 1952.

Max speed, 150 mph (241 km/h). Gross weight, 3,300 lb (1,497 kg). Span, 40 ft 4 in (12.29 m). Length, 30 ft 2 in (9.19 m).

HESTON T.1/37

One prototype (L7706) built in 1938 to requirements of Specification T.1/37, for a primary RAF trainer powered by a 205 hp DH Gipsy Queen I. On test at A & AEE in September 1939, then transferred to Boscombe Down, but performance found unsatisfactory and became instructional airframe late 1940 after T.1/37 requirement dropped. Second prototype (L7709) may not have been completed and a third (P8804) was certainly not built.

Right: The all-yellow Heston T.1/37 protype L7706 as tested at the A & AEE in 1939. Below: The ill-fated Heston Racer G-AFOK, which was lost on its first flight in 1940.

Above: The Helmy Aerogypt in the form in which it was tested until September 1940, with the three Sprite engines, supplementary fins fitted and original lifting surface above the cabin roof removed. Below left: Heston Phoenix G-AESV – seen here pre-war – it flew as X2891 until 1945 and then returned to civil use. (Photo, AJ Jackson Collection)

Max speed, 159 mph (256 km/h). Time to 10,000 ft (3,050 m), 24 min. Service ceiling, 12,800 ft (3,901 m). Empty weight, 2,653 lb (1,203 kg). Gross weight, 3,250 lb (1,474 m). Span, 42 ft (12.8 m). Length, 31 ft 8 in (9.65 m). Wing area, 227 sq ft (21.1 m²).

HESTON-NAPIER RACER

Designed, at Napier's instigation, in 1938 for an attempt on the World Speed Record for aircraft, the Racer was of wooden construction and powered by a 2,000 hp Sabre engine. Remarkably, work on prototype (G-AFOK) proceeded through first nine months of war, leading to first flight on June 12, 1940. However, with engine overheating, the flight was curtailed to a few minutes, and aircraft stalled just before touchdown, suffering irreparable damage. Construction of second Racer (G-AFOL) meanwhile abandoned.

Estimated max speed, 480 mph (772 km/h). Gross weight, 7,200 lb (3,266 kg). Span, 32 ft

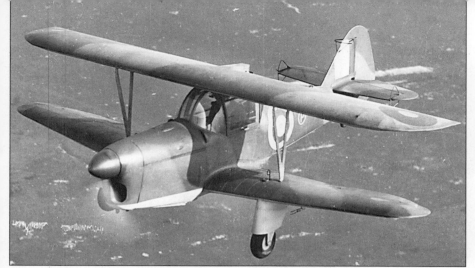

Above: The intriguing Bi-Mono (Experimental Aeroplane 133) in the form which a successful 'slip' of the upper wing was demonstrated in July 1941. Above right, upper: As first flown, the Bi-Mono had a longer-span upper wing. Above right, lower: The Bi-Mono in monoplane configuration. Below: Hurricane I serial 321 arranged as a biplane (Experimental Aeroplane 205).

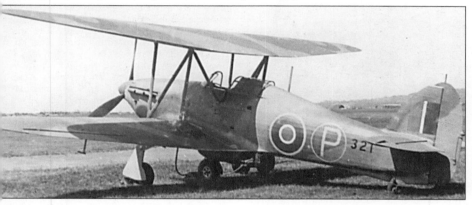

0¹/₂ in (9.77 m). Length, 24 ft 7¹/₄ in (7.49 m). Wing area, 167.6 sq ft (15.6 m²).

HILLSON BI-MONO

Small single-seat cabin aircraft, intended as scale model for a light/cheap fighter, built in 1940 by F Hills and Sons Ltd as a PV and powered by 205 hp DH Gipsy Six. Extra area of upper wing was to allow take-offs from grass fields or roads at 'overload' weights, wing then to be 'slipped' (jettisoned) to allow good fighting performance and maneouvrability. Single Bi-Mono prototype (with no serial number but in military prototype finish) flown extensively in both monoplane and biplane configuration at Squires Gate — upper wing initially with greater span, later reduced to same span as lower wing. Single, successful, 'slip' made on July 16, 1941, at height of 4,500 ft (1,372 m) over sea off Blackpool.
Span, 20 ft (6.1 m). Length, 14 ft 6 in (4.4 m). Wing area (each wing), 66 sq ft (6.13 m²).

HILLS F.H.40

In continuation of work on Bi-Mono, F Hills and Sons obtained Air Ministry permission to fit a 'slip-wing' to a Hurricane I. Aircraft used was early Mk I, one of 20 transferred to Canada in 1939 and returned to UK in 1942 (originally L1884, but retaining RCAF serial 321 for 'slip-wing' trials). First taxi-trials and flights at RAF Sealand, May 25-28 1943; ferried to A & AEE September 15, 1943. Upper wing, of same span as lower, never slipped in flight.

MARENDAZ TRAINER

Small low-wing monoplane with tandem open cockpits, designed by D M K Marendaz and built at Barton-in-the-Clay, Beds, during 1939. Powered by a 90 hp Cirrus Minor I and intended as a primary trainer, sole example (G-AFZX) first flew December 1939. With no prospect for use during the war, the trainer was given to ATC unit at Halton in 1940.
Max speed, 124 mph (200 km/h). Gross weight, 1,500 lb (680 kg). Span, 34 ft 0 in (10.36 m). Length, 22 ft 4 in (6.81 m).

MARTIN-BAKER M.B.2

Single private-venture prototype broadly responding to Specification F.5/34 and first flown at Denham on August 3, 1938. Powered by a 725 hp Napier Dagger IIIM, the M.B.2 carried eight 0.303-in (7.7-mm) Brownings in the wings and had a fixed,

Below: In its final configuration with small fin and enlarged rudder, the Martin-Baker M.B.2 acquired the serial number P9594 and is seen here in the summer of 1939. Above right: The Marendaz trainer made its first flight at the end of 1939 but had no military application.

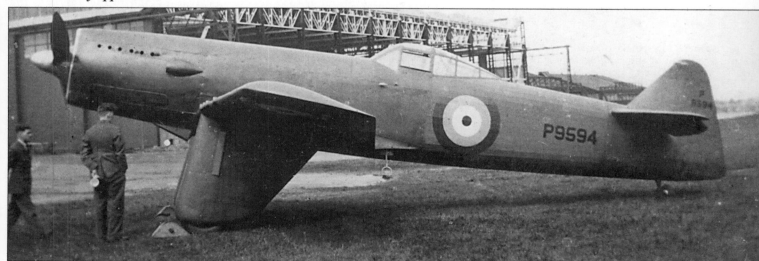

Above: Only a few flights were made by the Martin-Baker M.B.3 (Ex Aero 120) before it was lost in a dead-stick landing on September 12, 1942. Below: Ordered as the second prototype to follow the M.B.3, R2496 emerged as the much-developed M.B.5 in 1944, one of the fastest piston-engined aircraft of World War II.

trousered undercarriage. Initially tested with markings M-B-l (G-AEZD not carried), the M.B.2 was acquired by Air Ministry in June 1939 as P9594 and returned to A & AEE for second assessment after mods to tail control surfaces. It also spent some time at the AFDU, Northolt, before returning to Martin-Baker late in 1939, where it still survived in December 1941, although probably flown little or not at all after outbreak of war.

Max speed, 320 mph (515 km/h). Gross weight, 5,537 lb (2,512 kg). Span, 34 ft 0 in (10.36 m). Length, 34 ft 6 in (10.51 m).

MARTIN-BAKER M.B.3

First of three prototypes ordered mid-1939 to conform to Specification F.18/39 for a heavily-armed high-performance fighter. Powered by a 2,300 hp Napier Sabre II, the M.B.3 (R2492) first flew at Wing on August 31, 1942, but was lost 12 days later when making a dead-stick landing. Second prototype appeared two years later as M.B.5 (next entry).

Max speed (estimated), 415 mph (668 km/h). Gross weight, 11,497 lb (5,215 kg). Span, 35 ft 0 in (10.67 m). Length, 35 ft 4 in (10.77 m).

MARTIN-BAKER M.B.5

Second of the F.18/39 fighter prototypes ordered in 1939 (see M.B.3 entry), the M.B.5 (R2496) was a much-developed version, featuring a 1,900 hp R-R Griffon 83 with contra-props, and four cannon armament. First flown at Harwell on May 13,1944, but requirement overtaken by advent of jet-powered fighters, and second M.B.5 (R2500) not built. Flight demonstrations with R2496 continued until end-1947.

Max speed, 460 mph (740 km/h) at 20,000 ft (6,100 m). Rate of climb, 3,800 ft/min (19.3 m/sec). Service ceiling, 40,000 ft (12,192 m). Range, 1,100 mls (1,770 km). Empty weight, 9,233 lb (4,192 kg). Max gross weight, 12,090 lb (5,489 kg). Span, 35 ft 0 in (10.67 m). Length, 37 ft 0 in (11.30 m). Wing area, 263 sq ft (24.4 m²).

MILES AIRCRAFT

The series of light aircraft and trainers widely known as Miles types were, in fact, products of Phillips & Powis Aircraft Ltd until 1943. The latter company had formed in 1929 to own and operate Reading Aerodrome at Woodley, and became responsible for the production of aircraft designed by F G Miles in 1932. Starting with the prototype M.2 in March 1933, the aircraft built and flown at Woodley were almost universally referred to as Miles types and are included as such in this review - although the Air Ministry contracts for their production or acquisition were with Phillips & Powis until October 1943, when the name was changed to Miles Aircraft after the Miles family aquired a majority holding in the company.

It is of interest to note also that a greater diversity of Miles aircraft types was flown during the war than those of any other single British manufacturer.

MILES M.2 HAWK SERIES

First of a series of Miles-designed light air-craft to achieve quantity production, the M.2 was a low-wing monoplane with tandem open cockpits, first flown on March 29, 1933. Production (by Phillips & Powis Ltd at Woodley) totalled 55 in 16 months before more powerful Hawk Major appeared, most of the earlier aircraft being powered by the 90 hp Blackburn Cirrus IIIA. Two M.2s impressed for RAF in September 1940 and a third in January 1941 saw little use before becoming instructional airframes.

Hawk Major: With the 130 hp DH Gipsy Major I and metal engine mounts, variants of the Hawk Major followed the original Hawk into production at Woodley in mid-1934. Some 18 M.2Fs and 47 M.2Hs built, latter introducing split trailing-edge flaps. Small numbers of other, more specialised, versions, starting with M.2R Hawk Trainer I, led to development of M.14 Magister (described later). From late 1939, nine M.2F/M.2H Hawk Majors impressed in the UK, plus single M.2P with increased wing span, and single, generally similar, M.2R. Several survived entire war period serving in communications and station 'hack' roles. One other M.2F impressed in June 1942 for Communications Flight, Levant, to support Arab Legion ops in Middle East; and one other M.2H impressed in India in 1942. Two M.2Hs in South Africa impressed for SAAF; two Hawk Majors in Australia similarly joined RAAF; and four assorted M.2 variants impressed for RNZAF.

Data for M.2H: Max speed, 150 mph (241 km/h). Service ceiling, 20,000 ft (6,100 m). Empty weight, 1,150 lb (521 kg). Gross weight, 1,800 lb (816 kg). Span, 33 ft 0 in (10.06 m). Length, 24 ft 0 in (7.32 m). Wing area, 169 sq ft (15.7 m²).

Hawk Trainer II: For primary training use at No 8 E & RFTS, Woodley, Miles adapted the M.2H Hawk Major to have enlarged cockpit openings, to permit use of parachutes. Twelve built as M.2W Hawk Trainer IIs in 1935, one similar M.2X and eight virtually identical M.2Ys, of which two to Reading Aero Club and remainder to the E & RFTS. The two former impressed in 1941, by which time remainder of Hawk Trainer IIs all retired, but one original M.2W impressed in 1943 after overhaul at Woodley. Ten M.2Zs built for Romanian Air Force in 1936 and probably still in service when Romania entered the War. Further development of Hawk Trainer II led to M.14 Magister.

Miles M.2F Hawk Major HK863 served the Arab Legion in the hands of the Communications Flight, Levant, in 1942. It had been exported to Egypt as SU-AAP in late 1934. (Photo, via The Earl Bathurst).

MILES M.3 FALCON

With an enclosed cabin seating four in side-by-side pairs, the M.3 was in most other respects similar to the M.2 Hawk Major, and initially used the same 130 hp Gipsy Major I. First flown on September 23,1934, basic M.3A Falcon Major was joined in 1935 by the Falcon Six with 200 hp DH Gipsy Six engine. Some 35 Falcons of all types built by 1937. Five assorted Falcons impressed 1940-41 for the RAF and one for the FAA Communications Unit at Lee-on-Solent, No 781 Sqn. Several others flew for most of the war retaining their British civil registrations. Two Falcon Majors and a Falcon Six impressed for the RAAF served in Communications Units. In April 1936, RAE took delivery at Farnborough of Falcon Six K5924, with three sets of wings to investigate laminar flow; this remained in use at Farnborough until 1944. A second Falcon Six, the M.3E L9705, reached Farnborough in April 1938, testing highly-tapered wings of three different aerofoil sections and three sets of low-tapered wings with three different aerofoil biconvex tip sections. Returned to Miles in 1943, L9705 became the 'Gillette Falcon', first flown August 11, 1944, to test features of very thin wing projected for Miles M.52 supersonic research aircraft. A third Falcon Six, ex-civil, reached the RAE in November 1939 as R4071 for research into spoilers, and survived the war there.

Data for Falcon Six: Max speed, 180 mph (290 km/h). Range, 560 mls (901 km). Empty weight, 1,550 lb (703 kg). Gross weight, 2,650

Above: Miles M.3B Falcon Six G-ADTD retained its civil registration whilst serving throughout the war as a communications 'hack' for Vickers-Armstrongs Ltd. Right: Falcon L9705 with a thin bi-convex wing as designed for the M.52. Below: The only M.4 Merlin in military guise, A37-2 was VH-UXN before impressment for RAAF service.

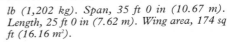

Left: Falcon K5924 acquired in April 1936 for research with Piercy laminar flow wing sections, was at the RAE Farnborough until 1944.

lb (1,202 kg). Span, 35 ft 0 in (10.67 m). Length, 25 ft 0 in (7.62 m). Wing area, 174 sq ft (16.16 m²).

MILES M.4 MERLIN

In effect a five-seat derivative of the Falcon, the Merlin first flew on March 24, 1935, with a 200 hp DH Gipsy Six engine. Four more built, of which one went to Australia in 1936 and was impressed by the RAAF (as A37-2) in 1940 for the Communications Unit.

Max speed, 155 mph (249 km/h). Gross weight, 3,000 lb (1,361 kg). Span, 37 ft 0 in (11.28 m). Length, 25 ft 10 in (7.87 m²).

MILES M.5 SPARROWHAWK

Using standard M.2 components, the Sparrowhawk was a single-seat open-cockpit racing aircraft, first flown on August 19, 1935, and powered by a 138 hp Gipsy Major I Srs II. Of five examples built, two were purchased in February 1940 for high-speed flap testing at the RAE Farnborough, to which they were delivered with Class B markings of U-3 and U-5. The former became G-AGDL in December 1941 and survived the war as a company 'hack'.

Max speed, 180 mph (290 km/h). Gross weight, 1,750 lb (794 kg). Span, 28 ft 0 in (8.53 m). Length, 23 ft 6 in (7.16 m).

MILES M.7 NIGHTHAWK

Conceived as a multi-purpose military trainer/communications aircraft, the Nighthawk was first flown in civil guise on October 26,1935. Three more examples built in 1936, of which two for Romanian Air Force still in service in 1939. The other aircraft went to Air Ministry under Specification

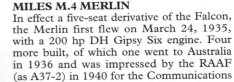

Above: Sparrowhawk G-ADNL, first of five built, was used for much of the war as the personal mount of Geoffrey Alington, and is here at Elmdon in May 1944. Below: The hybrid M.7A Nighthawk, with Mohawk wings; it was later flown as U-0225.

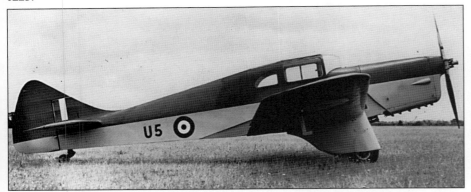

MILES M.12 MOHAWK

Two-seat tandem cabin monoplane built to the order of Charles Lindbergh and flown as G-AEKW on August 22, 1936. Impressed for RAF use as HM503 in November 1941, but little used other than by Maintenance Command Comm Sqn, September 1943-January 1944, because of difficulties with 200 hp Menasco Buccaneer B6S engine. Second set of M.12 wings used in M.7A hybrid (which see).

Max speed, 185 mph (298 km/h). Gross weight, 2,620 lb (1,188 kg). Span, 35 ft 0 in (10.67 m). Length, 25 ft 6 in (7.77 m).

MILES M.14 MAGISTER AND HAWK TRAINER III

Elementary trainer for the RAF, produced to Specification 40/36 on basis of M.2Y Hawk Trainer II experience at No 8 E & FTS at Woodley. First low-wing monoplane trainer for the RAF. Civil prototype (U-2/G-AETJ) first flown March 20, 1937, as Hawk Trainer III, with 130 hp DH Gipsy Major I. Production Magister deliveries to RAF began June 1937; total contracts for 1,210 to Specification 37/37. Initial M.14 followed by definitive M.14A Magister I with taller rudder, deeper rear fuselage and, eventually, anti-spin strakes on rear fuselage. Equipped 16 Elementary Flying Training Schools, and widely used for communications and 'hack' duties, including some by FAA units. M.14B designation applied to aircraft with 135 hp Blackburn Cirrus Major II; five RAF Magisters to this standard. In June 1940, some 16 Magisters adapted each to carry eight 25-lb (113-kg) bombs under centre-section, for emergency use against expected German invasion forces. Two Magisters fitted with Maclaren castering (crosswind) undercarriages for demonstration to Army Co-operation squadrons; another used by Miles in 1941 to test-fly a 'towed wing', attached aft of tailplane by twin booms from the mainplane and intended to carry (in application on other aircraft types) extra fuel or bomb-load. RAF diverted 23 Magisters to Royal Egyptian Air Force in 1940 and 15 to Irish Air Corps in 1939. In 1943, 30 ex-RAF Magisters transferred to Turkish Air Force.

Max speed, 140 mph (225 km/h). Cruising speed, 122 mph (196 km/h). Initial climb, 750 ft/min (3.8 m/sec). Service ceiling, 16,500 ft (5,030 m). Range 367 mls (591 km). Empty weight, 1,286 lb (583 kg). Gross weight, 1,900 lb (862 kg). Span, 33 ft 10 in (10.31 m). Length, 24 ft 7½ in (7.51 m). Wing area 176 sq ft (16.35 m²).

Hawk Trainer III: Aircraft built to

Above: In its final guise, after it had been acquired for Air Ministry testing as N3300, the M.9 Kestrel was effectively the prototype for the Master I. Left: The sole M.12 Mohawk saw limited service after impressment as HM503. Below: Whitney Straight G-AERV was impressed as EM999 and is seen at Abingdon in 1945.

24/36 but grounded a few months before war began. In 1940, Miles used a spare Nighthawk fuselage plus set of M.12 Mohawk wings to produce M.7A hybrid with 205 hp Gipsy Six Srs II engine and four seats. Initially marked U-5, the M.7A flew as U-0225 as a company transport, surviving the war to become G-AGWT in 1945.

Max speed, 180 mph (290 km/h). Gross weight, 2,650 lb (1,202 kg). Span, 35 ft 0 in (10.67 m). Length, 25 ft 0 in (7.62 m).

MILES M.9 KESTREL

Single private-venture prototype advanced trainer of wooden construction, inspired by specification T.6/36, powered by 745 hp R-R Kestrel XVI and first flown as U-5 (registration G-AEOC not used) on June 3, 1937. Successively modified, then acquired by Air Ministry in October 1938 for official trials, marked N3300. Provided basis for produc-

tionised M.9A Master, and used until 1943 for investigation of wing slots and slats.

Max speed, 296 mph (476 km/h). Gross weight, 5,340 lb (2,422 kg). Span, 39 ft 0 in (11.88 m). Length, 30 ft 6 in (9.29 m).

MILES M.11 WHITNEY STRAIGHT

Side-by-side cabin monoplane for club and private flying, first flown at Woodley on May 3, 1936. Production totalled 50 up to 1938, of which 21 impressed in 1940/41 for the RAF and three others used as company 'hacks' throughout the war, with civil registrations. One other impressed in India, one in Egypt and one (with civil registration) for the Malayan Volunteer Air Force. Three impressed in New Zealand for RNZAF duty all survived the war. Standard M.11 powered by 130 hp DH Gipsy Major I.

Max speed, 145 mph (233 km/h). Gross weight, 1,896 lb (860 kg). Span, 35 ft 8 in (10.87 m). Length, 25 ft 0 in (7.62 m).

Below right: A pair of Magister Is in definitive form, serving in the summer of 1940 at No 15 EFTS and photographed near Kingston, Cumberland. Below left, upper: A Magister I at Debden in 1937, showing the original fin and rudder shape, and wheel fairings. Below left, lower: Originally G-AEZS and later U-0229, this M.14A was used to test the thick wing for the M.18.

Above: Mentor I L4393, the second of the production batch of 45 aircraft, pictured whilst serving at the A & AEE Boscombe Down. Below: In overall yellow finish, the second of two M.15 prototypes, P6326, was on test at the A & AEE when the war began.

M.14 (later, M.14A) standard for users other than RAF, including civil and export, identified by Miles as Hawk Trainer III although some used Magister name later in military service. Some 54 built, of which eight later impressed for RAF from UK civil use. Two of latter, plus one other used by Blackburn as engine test bed, had Cirrus Major II engines as M.14B Hawk Trainer IIs. Exports included one each to Estonia and Soviet Union, six to New Zealand of which two impressed for RNZAF, eight to South Africa of which six impressed for SAAF and one to Australia in 1938 for RAAF evaluation, serving until mid-1940. Twenty Hawk Trainer IIIs went to Royal Egyptian Air Force 1937/38, prior to Magisters from RAF.

MILES M.15

Basic trainer to Specification T.1/37, with tandem open cockpits and 200 hp DH Gipsy Six Srs I engine. First of two prototypes (L7714) flown September 1938. Second aircraft (L7717) abandoned but components then used to complete prototype (U-0234, then P6326) with 210 hp Gipsy Queen I. Under test at A & AEE

Martlesham Heath and transferred to Boscombe Down in September 1939, but no further development.
Gross weight, 2,530 lb (1,147 kg). Span, 33 ft 5 in (10.19 m). Length, 29 ft 6 in (8.99 m).

MILES M.16 MENTOR

Developed M.7 to meet Air Ministry Specification 38/37 as a three-seat radio/navigation trainer and communications aircraft, first flown on January 5, 1938.

Total of 45 built by early 1939, of which 42 available for service when war began. Used by No 24 Sqn, Station Flights and other UK-based units, only one surviving to 1945. Powered by 205 hp DH Gipsy Queen I.
Max speed, 156 mph (251 km/h). Gross weight, 2,710 lb (1,229 kg). Span, 34 ft 9 1/2 in (10.60 m). Length, 26 ft 1 3/4 in (7.97 m).

MILES M.17 MONARCH

Three-seat development of M.11 Whitney Straight, first flown February 21, 1938, and final pre-war Miles product for civil use. Eleven built, of which one, exported to Belgium in 1938, was returned to UK in 1940 and used for communications by Miles as U-0226 until becoming TP819 in March 1945 when used by Allied Flight of Metropolitan Communications Sqn. Four others impressed for RAF and one used in civil marks by Rolls-Royce, all of which survived the war. Standard M.17 engine was the 130 hp DH Gipsy Major I Srs I.
Max speed, 140 mph (224 km/h). Gross weight, 2,150 lb (975 kg). Span, 35 ft 7 in (10.85 m). Length, 25 ft 11 3/4 in (7.92 m).

MILES M.18

Prospective successor for Magister designed as private venture and first flown December 4, 1938, with 130 hp DH Gipsy Major I Srs I, combining basic M.14 fuselage with new thick-section wing, initially tested on ex-civil M.14A (U-6). Three further M.18s flown late 1939-1942, with 150 hp Blackburn Cirrus Major III engine and variety of trial features such as tricycle u/c (on Mk I), cabin enclosure over tandem cockpits (on Mk III) and full-span slots and large-chord flaps with inset ailerons (on Mk IV) as designed for use on Supermarine S.12/40 Seagull.
Max speed, 135 mph (217 km/h). Gross weight, 1,903 lb (863 kg). Span, 31 ft 0 in (9.45 m). Length, 24 ft 10 in (7.57 m).

Below: The third Monarch built went to Belgium in 1938 as OO-UMK but returned to Britain in the hands of the Finance Minister of the Belgian Government in exile, becoming first U-0226, then G-AGFW and eventually TP819, before being returned to Belgium in 1946 again as OO-UMK.

Below: The second M.18, which first flew in November 1939 and acquired the serial number HM545 late in 1941. Below right: The fourth M.18, JN703 (Ex Aero 147) was built for the RAE to study full-span slots and flaps designed for use on the Supermarine Seagull. Lower right: The first M.18 U-0222 after modification with nosewheel undercarriage (Ex Aero 173).

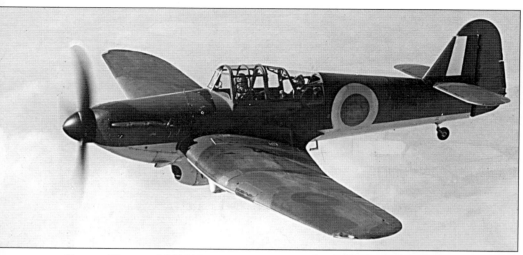

Above: Master I N7547, transferred from RAF to FAA in February 1940, here shows the original long wing span, and the later raised canopy line.

Below: Master I N7809, with the early, low, canopy line, was one of some 24 armed as emergency fighters in 1940. Right: Master III W8513 reveals the late-standard 'clipped' wing. It served first with 1 FTS, later with 9 (P)AFU.

MILES MASTER

Advanced trainer based on M.9 Kestrel, ordered for RAF to Specification 16/38 in June 1938 with 720 hp R-R Kestrel XXX. First production M.9B Master I flown March 31, 1939, and seven delivered by time war began; total production 900, of which three became prototypes for Master II and III and 60 transferred to FAA. Remainder used primarily at Nos 5, 8, 9, 14 and 15 FTS, and in smaller numbers by (P)AFUs and OTUs. Starting in 1939, sliding canopy replaced earlier upward-hinged type, and in 1942 all remaining aircraft converted to M.9C Master IA with wing tips clipped to reduce span to 35 ft 9 in (10.89 m). In 1940, up to two dozen Master Is fitted with six 0.303-in (7.7-mm) Browning guns in wings as emergency fighters (retrospectively designated Miles M.24).
Max speed, 226 mph (363 km/h). Cruising speed, 160 mph (257 km/h) at 10,000 ft (3,050 m). Endurance, 3 hrs. Empty weight, 4,370 lb (1,982 kg). Gross weight, 5,573 lb (2,528 kg). Span, 39 ft 0 in (11.89 m). Length, 30 ft 5 in (9.29 m). Wing area, 235 sq ft (21.83 m²).
M.19 Master II: As Master I but powered by 810 hp Bristol Mercury XX engine, to overcome shortage of Kestrels. First of two prototypes (Mk I conversions) flown in November 1939, and first production Mk II on April 8, 1941. Total production 1,748 (1,250 at Woodley, 498 at South Marston and Doncaster), completed in 1942. Most Master IIs built with long-span wings, later reduced to 35 ft 9 in (10.89 m) as for Master IA. Service use primarily at (Pilot) Advanced Flying Units and, from 1942, as tugs for Hotspur gliders at Glider Training Schools. Several hundred Master IIs converted, or delivered new, for the glider-towing role, with bottom of rudder cut away to allow fitting of towing hook. Diversions from RAF stocks included 426 to SAAF, 5? to FAA, nine to USAAF in UK, 23 to [R] Egyptian AF and, early in 1945, 23 to Turkey. Eleven also went to Irish Air Corps and two to Portugal.
Max speeed, 242 mph (389 km/h) at 6,000 f (1,828 m). Rate of climb, 2,120 ft/min (10.8 m/sec). Service ceiling, 25,100 ft (7,650 m). Range, 393 mls (632 km). Endurance, 1.8 hrs. Empty weight, 4,293 lb (1,947 kg). Gross weight, 5,573 lb (2,528 kg). Span, 39 ft 0 in (11.89 m). Length, 29 ft 6 in (8.99 m). Wing area 235 sq ft (21.83 m²).
M.27 Master III: Similar to Master II, with 825 hp P & W R-1535-SB4G Twin Wasp Junior engine. Prototype (Mk I conversion) first flown December 17, 1940 (or earlier). Production total 602 (at South Marston) and used primarily at (P)AFUs. At least 12 to USAAF in UK and ten to Portugal. Like Master IIs, Master IIIs had wings clipped during their service life.

MILES M.20

Prototype low-cost fighter designed for rapid production, using many standard Master components, conceived, built and flown (as M.20/2) in 65 days during 1940. Powered by 1,390 hp R-R Merlin XX and armed with eight 0.303-in (7.7-mm) Browning wing guns; first flown September 15, 1940 as U-9 and tested at A & AEE as AX834 in compli-

Left: Master II DM434 in service with 3 GTS shows the rudder modifications to allow fitment of a glider-towing hook. Below: The original M.20 private-venture (Ex Aero 118) as first flown and (bottom) the M.20/4 (Ex Aero 138) second prototype, designed to meet a Naval requirement.

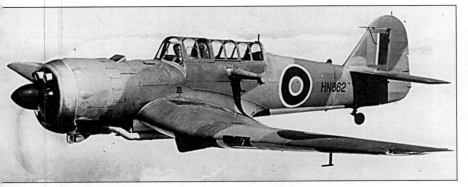

Above: Martinet I HN862, showing the fuselage side-mounted winch to retrieve towed sleeve or drogue targets. A spin-recovery parachute is fitted for trials at the A & AEE. Below: The second M.28, used by Miles for communications after receiving serial HM583.

ance with Specification F.19/40. Later scrapped at Woodley. Second prototype (as M.20/4) to conform with Specification N.1/41 for naval fighter, first flown April 8, 1941 as U-0228 and later allotted serial DR616 for testing at A & AEE.

Data for M.20/4: Max speed, 333 mph (536 km/h) at 20,400 ft (6,218 m). Initial climb, 2,300 ft/min (11.7 m/sec). Time to 20,000 ft (6,100 m), 9.6 min. Service ceiling, 32,800 ft (9,997 m). Max range, 200 mls (322 km). Empty weight, 5,870 lb (2,663 kg). Gross weight, 8,000 lb (3,629 kg). Span, 34 ft 7 in (10.54 m). Length, 30 ft 8 in (9.35 m). Wing area, 234 sq ft (21.74 m²).

MILES M.25 MARTINET

Specialised target-tug (first in the RAF) derived from Master II for production to Specification 12/41, with controls removed from rear cockpit, canopy modified to facilitate operation of side-mounted winch for flag or sleeve drogue targets stowed in rear fuselage, and lengthened front fuselage. First of two prototypes (LR241) flown on April 24, 1942, followed by total of 1,722 Martinet T.T.Mk Is delivered from July 1942 to 1945, to serve primarily at Air Gunnery Schools, AA Co-operation Sqns and OTUs. A few also used on ASR duties (No 269 Sqn) and 506 diverted from RAF contracts for FAA use. Ten ex-RAF to Portugal starting September 1943 (final three post-war).

Max speed, 240 mph (386 km/h) at 5,800 ft (1,768 m). Time to 10,000 ft (3,050 m), 10 min. Range, 694 mls (1,117 km). Empty weight, 4,640 lb (2,105 kg). Gross weight, 6,750 lb (3,062 kg). Span, 39 ft 0 in (11.89 m). Length, 30 ft 11 in (9.40 m). Wing area, 242 sq ft (22.48 m²).

M.50 Queen Martinet: Radio-controlled target drone version of Martinet inspired by Specification Q.10/43. First of two prototypes (PW979) flown late 1944 and 69 built before production contracts terminated in 1946 (but four scrapped before delivery). Three to FAA and 18 more

Martinet TT Mk Is converted to Queen Martinet post-war.

MILES M.28

Private-venture design in 1939 for communications and training aircraft to succeed Whitney Straight. Four examples built during wartime period, as follows, and two more post-war.

M.28 Mk I: Prototype U-0232 with 130 hp DH Gipsy Major I, two seats side-by-side with dual controls and thickened wing centre-section to enclose wheels fully when retracted. Built at Liverpool Road works in Reading, so also known as L.R.l. First flight July 11, 1941. Retained in use by Miles until 1942.

M.28 Mk II: Prototype U-0237 (later HM583), with 140 hp DH Gipsy Major IIA, third seat in cabin and extra side windows. Flown September 1942 and used by company for communications duty.

M.28 Mk III: Configured as three-seat trainer (instructor in rear) with 150 hp Blackburn Cirrus Major III, more rear cabin window area, and thinner wing centre-section leaving wheels projecting when retracted. Flown June 1943 as U-0242, evaluated in training role as PW937 and returned to Miles.

M.28 Mk IV: Similar to Mk III, but with four seats and used by Miles for communications, with 145 hp DH Gipsy Major IIA engine. First flown July 1944, and marked as U-0243.

Data for Mk II: Max speed, 159 mph (259 km/h). Time to 10,000 ft (3,050 m), 14 min. Range, 408 mls (656 km). Empty weight, 1,658 lb (752 kg). Gross weight, 2,500 lb (1,134 kg). Span, 30 ft 8 in (9.35 m). Length, 24 ft 0 in (7.31 m). Wing area, 162 sq ft (15.05 m²).

MILES M.30 X-MINOR

Flying-scale model to investigate blended (aerofoil-section) fuselage/wing design planned for a series of large commercial transport aircraft projects, from X-1 in 1936 to X-15 in 1944 (the latter proposed to Specification 2/44 in competition with Bristol Brabazon). Powered by two 130 hp DH Gipsy Major I Srs I engines, two-seat M.30 (U-0233) was too small to represent all full-scale X features, but provided useful data following first flight in February 1942, until later becoming instructional airframe at company's Aeronautical Technical School. In the course of testing, span was increased to 38 ft 6 in (11.73 m).

Empty weight, 2,710 lb (1,229 kg). Gross weight, 4,240 lb (1,923 kg). Span (original), 33 ft 0 in (10.06 m). Length, 26 ft 3 in (8.00 m).

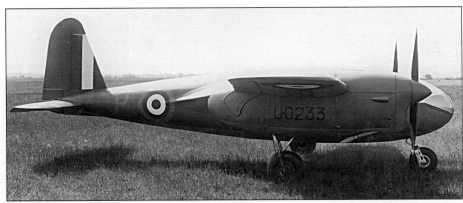

Above: Flown during 1942, the M.30 or 'X-Minor' (Ex Aero 172) was built to test Miles' blended fuselage/wing configuration. Below: Monitor TT Mk II NP407, the second production example of the first dedicated British aircraft designed as a target-tug

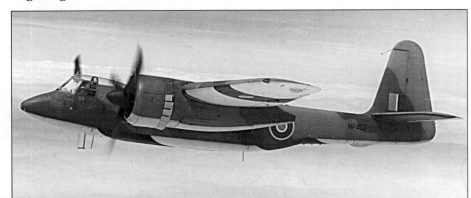

Above: The M.35 (Ex Aero 177), first to test Miles' libellula (tandem-wing) layout, flew only a few times in 1942. Below: Messenger I RH374 was the seventh of 11 built at Woodley.

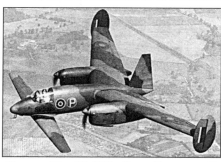

Above: The M.39B, first flown as U-0244 and here seen on test as SR392 (Ex Aero 217), was in effect a scale model of a bomber designed to Specification B.11/41. Below: M.48 U-0247 was essentially a Messenger with retractable flaps.

MILES M.33 MONITOR

Optimised twin-engined target-tug to Specification Q.9/42, combining wooden wings with metal fuselage (Miles' first use of stressed-skin construction). Powered by two 1,700 hp Wright R-2600-31 Cyclone engines, the Monitor had a crew of two and an internal hydraulic winch for drogue targets trailed through ventral hatch.

Monitor TT Mk I: RAF version. Prototype (NF900) first flown April 5, 1944. Planned production cancelled.

Monitor TT Mk II: RN version, introducing dive brakes and dorsal cupola. Prototype (NF904) first flown December 2, 1944. Planned production of 500 cut to 20, none of which entered service.

Max speed, 330 mph (531 km/h) at 15,000 ft (4,572 m). Time to 15,000 ft (4,572 m), 6.4 min. Service ceiling, 29,000 ft (8,839 m). Max range, 2,750 mls (4,426 km). Empty weight, 15,850 lb (7,190 kg). Gross weight, 21,075 lb (9,560 kg). Span, 56 ft 3 in (17.15

m). Length, 47 ft 8 in (14.53 m). Wing area, 500 sq ft (46.45 m²).

MILES M.35

Small-scale research aircraft, built as company PV to investigate potential advantages of tandem wing 'libellula' configuration. Prototype U-0235 built at Liverpool Road works (as L.R.2) and first flown (with difficulty) by George Miles on May 1, 1942. Powered by single 130 hp DH Gipsy Major I Srs I.

Empty weight, 1,456 lb (660 kg). Gross weight, 1,850 lb (839 kg). Span (front), 20 ft 0 in (6.10 m). Span (rear), 20 ft 5 in (6.32 m). Length, 20 ft 4 in (6.19 m).

MILES M.38 MESSENGER

Adaptation of M.28 design in 1942 to meet perceived Army need for an AOP for frontline use, able to operate from small unprepared fields. Prototype modified from M.28 Mk I, flown as M.28/38 (U-0223) on September 12, 1944, featuring new thinner wing with external trailing-edge flaps and 145 hp Gipsy Major II engine. First flown with M.28 twin tail unit; large single fin and rudder tested later as alternative to definitive triple tail unit.

M.38/II: Further redesign of M.28/38 to conform with Specification A.17/43 for four-seat Army AOP/communications aircraft. Definitive triple tail unit. Prototype U-0245 flown early 1944.

Messenger I: Production form of M.38/II. Two prototypes (RG327 and RG333) flown early 1944, of which one temporarily assigned as personal aircraft for Field Marshal Montgomery. Production order for 250, with 138 hp Gipsy Major I Srs II engine; first deliveries late-1944, used primarily in communications role, including one for FM Montgomery. Production, mostly post-war, terminated with 21 aircraft built, of which 10 from new Miles factories in Northern Ireland (Banbridge and Newtownards).

Max speed, 116 mph (187 km/h). Rate of climb, 660 ft/min (3.35 m/sec). Time to 10,000 ft (3,050 m), 30 mins. Service ceiling, 14,000 ft (4,267 m). Range 260 mls (418 km). Empty weight, 1,518 lb (689 kg). Gross

weight, 1,900 lb (862 kg). Span, 36 ft 2 in (11.02 m). Length, 24 ft (7.32 m). Wing area, 191 sq ft (17.74 m²).

M.38A Mariner: Prototype M.28/38 modified to evaluate potential of Messenger to operate from 60-ft (18,3-m) square decks on merchant ships. Fitted with two rockets for assisted take-off, and lightweight arrester hook. Aircraft flown into deck-edge safety net (with gap for propeller) to cater for 'missed-wire' case, during trials at Woodley in 1943.

M.48 (M.38 Mk III): Single prototype (U-0247), flown September 1944, based on M.38 with four seats, retractable trailing-edge flaps and 150 hp Blackburn Cirrus Major III engine.

MILES M.39B

Single-seat research aircraft of 'libellula' configuration (see M.35), built as five-eighths model of M.39 designed to Specification B.11/41 for a lightly-armed, high-altitude high-speed bomber. Powered by two 140 hp DH Gipsy Major IC engines. M.39B was built at Liverpool Road (as L.R.3) and first flown on July 22, 1943, as U-0244. Transferred to RAE Farnborough in January 1944 as SR392, for official evaluation: returned to Woodley for modifications in February 1945 and remained with Miles for the remainder of the war, becoming marked as U-4.

Max speed, 164 mph (264 km/h). Rate of climb, 1,100 ft/min (5.5 m/sec). Empty weight, 2,405 lb (1,091 kg). Gross weight, 2,800 lb (1,270 kg). Span (front), 25 ft 0 in (7.62 m). Span (rear), 37 ft 6 in (11.43 m). Length, 22 ft 2 in (6.76 m).

MILES M.57 AEROVAN

A 1944 design for a small, cheap, short-haul freighter with military potential, operating from small landing strips. Of all-wooden construction and powered by two 150 hp Blackburn Cirrus Major IIA engines, prototype (U-0248) built at Liverpool Road (as L.R.4) and first flown at Woodley on January 26, 1945. Entered production for civil use post-war.

Max speed, 130 mph (209 km/h). Gross weight, 5,900 lb (2,676 kg). Span, 50 ft 0 in (15.24 m). Length, 36 ft 0 in (10.97 m).

MILES M.64

Two-seat side-by-side tourer/trainer with tricycle undercarriage, intended for post-war club use, designed and built at Liverpool Road as L.R.5. Prototype U-0253 (later U-6) first flown at Woodley on June 3, 1945. No production.

Gross weight, 1,550 lb (703 kg). Span, 36 ft 0 in (10.97 m).

Above: Aimed at post-war civil sales, the prototype Aerovan I (Ex Aero 242) flew in January 1945. Below: The final Miles design flown before V-J Day was the M.64, marked as U-0253.

MOSSCRAFT M.A.2

Second sports lightplane produced by Moss Bros Aircraft Ltd, this low-wing monoplane with tandem open cockpits first flew in spring 1939, with registration G-AFMS. Powered by 90 hp Blackburn Cirrus Minor I, it was tested as potential flying observation post (FOP) by School of Army Co-operation at Old Sarum, January/February 1940. After reverting to civil role, exported to Canada later in 1940.
Cruising speed, 110 mph (177 km/h). Gross weight, 1,400 lb (635 kg). Span, 34 ft 0 in (10.36 m). Length, 23 ft 3 in (7.09 m).

PARNALL HECK IIC

Three-seat tourer developed from prototype Hendy 3308 Heck, first flown in July 1934. Six built 1936-37, with 200 hp DH Gipsy Six, of which three used for war-time communications by Parnall and, later, British Parachute Co, in civil markings as G-AEGH, G-AEGI and G-AEMR. One (G-AEGH) impressed March 1943 (as NF749) for No 17 Group Comm Flt. One other Heck IIC acquired by Air Ministry in 1936 as K8853, with Gipsy Six Srs II engine, used for gunsight development, for which

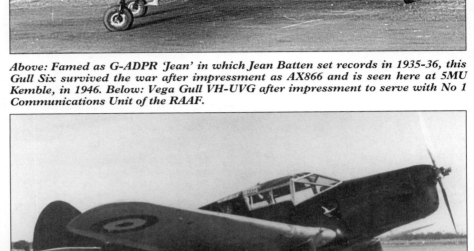

Above: Famed as G-ADPR 'Jean' in which Jean Batten set records in 1935-36, this Gull Six survived the war after impressment as AX866 and is seen here at 5MU Kemble, in 1946. Below: Vega Gull VH-UVG after impressment to serve with No 1 Communications Unit of the RAAF.

Above: In the form shown here, the Mosscraft M.A.2 was evaluated for the FOP role early in 1940.

Above: The sole Parnall 382, built as a private venture to meet Specification T.1/37. Below: Hendy Heck IIC K8853 serving in the communications role, after pre-war use for the development of Parnall gunsights.

fitted with 0.303-in (7.7-mm) Browning guns in wings; later disarmed for general communications.
Max speed, 185 mph (298 km/h). Ceiling, 16,700 ft (5,090 m). Range, 605 mls (972 km). Empty weight, 1,750 lb (794 kg). Gross weight, 2,700 lb (1,225 kg). Span, 31 ft 6 in (9.60 m). Length, 26 ft 1$^{1}/_{2}$ in (7.96 m). Wing area, 105.2 sq ft (9.77 m²).

PARNALL 382 HECK III

Ab initio trainer with tandem open cockpits, built as PV to conform to Specification T.1/37. Used components of Heck IIC including outer wing panels, tail unit, u/c and 200 hp DH Gipsy Six engine. Flown late in 1938, in B-class marking as J1 (G-AFKF not used), and serial R9138 applied later. Served with No 24 Sqn June-August 1941.
Cruising speed, 135 mph (217 km/h). Gross weight, 2,450 lb (1,111 kg). Span, 33 ft 6 in (10.21 m). Length, 28 ft 8 in (8.73 m).

PERCIVAL GULL

Three-seat sporting/touring aircraft, flown in prototype form in 1932 and 29 built in initial Gull Four form, followed by 19 of Gull Six version powered by 200 hp DH Gipsy Six engine. Two of latter impressed in 1940 for RAF, but one destroyed before so used. One Gull Four (G-ADOE, with 130 hp Gipsy Major Srs I) and one Gull Six (G-ADFA) retained civil marks for wartime service with Blackburn and Vickers-Armstrongs. One other British-registered Gull Six impressed in 1940 to serve in Middle East and two (perhaps three) Indian-registered aircraft impressed in India, 1942. One Gull Six (the last produced) impressed in South Africa in 1940. One Gull Four impressed in New Zealand, November 1939, written-off in service with Communications Flight, July 1940.
Cruising speed, 160 mph (257 km/h). Gross weight, 2,450 lb (1,111 kg). Span, 36 ft 2 in (11.03 m). Length, 24 ft 9 in (7.54 m).

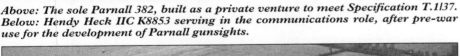

Above: The last of six built, Mew Gull G-AFAA is believed to have been flying at Hatfield until damaged in a forced landing early in 1940.

Above: Percival Q.6 P5639 was one of a batch of seven built for the RAF to Specification 25/38 and delivered in June 1939. It served variously at Andover, 61 OTU, Northolt, Speke and finally with the Metropolitan Communications Squadron before it was sold for civil use in 1946. Above right: The first of two Q.6s supplied to the Royal Egyptian Air Force in 1939, to fly with No 3 (Comm) Sqn.

PERCIVAL VEGA GULL

Four-seat development of Gull, first flown November 1935 and powered usually by 200 hp DH Gipsy Six Srs I or 205 hp Gipsy Six Srs II. Pre-war production included 14 to Specification 20/38 for RAF communications use, of which 11 initially to No 24 Sqn, two to FAA and one to British Air Attache in Lisbon; earlier, one other civil-standard Vega Gull acquired by Air Ministry for use by Air Attache in Buenos Aires. Another (civil-registered) Vega Gull used by Air Attache in Berlin abandoned there at outbreak of war; subsequent use in Germany unconfirmed. Two Vega Gulls retained civil registration for war-time use in Britain, and 21 others impressed 1939-40 for RAF and FAA. Two more impressed for RAF use in India. Two Vega Gulls impressed for RAAF served in Australia with No 1 Communications Unit throughout the war and a single example impressed for the RNZAF similarly survived.

Max speed, 174 mph (282 km/h). Cruising speed, 150 mph (241 km/h). Ceiling, 17,000 ft (5,182 m). Range, 660 mls (1,062 km). Empty weight, 1,740 lb (789 kg). Gross weight, 3,250 lb (1,474 kg). Span, 39 ft 6 in (12.04 m). Length, 25 ft 6 in (7.77 m). Wing area, 184 sq ft (17.09 m²).

PERCIVAL MEW GULL

Single-seat sporting and racing monoplane, first flown in March 1934. Six built by 1937, of which three in UK at outbreak of war. A scheme to fit pairs of Vickers 0.303-in (7.7-mm) machine guns to each of these for use as 'panic' fighters in 1940 did not proceed. Mew Gull G-AFAA reportedly loaned to de Havilland at Hatfield (possibly for propeller development), severely damaged in forced landing in 1940, and subsequently written off. The engine was a 205 hp DH Gipsy Six Srs II.

Max speed, 235 mph (378 km/h). Gross weight, 2,125 lb (964 kg). Span, 22 ft 9 in (6.93 m). Length, 20 ft 3 in (6.17 m).

PERCIVAL Q.6

Six/seven-seat twin-engined light transport/business aircraft, first flown September 14, 1937, with 205 hp DH Gipsy Six Srs II engines. Total of 27 built, of which two for Royal Egyptian Air Force and seven for RAF to Specification 25/38. Used in Egypt by No 3 Communications Sqn and the Royal Flight, at least one surviving the war. RAF aircraft delivered mid-1939 and used principally by station communications flights; one transferred to FAA in June 1943. Name Petrel, often associated with the RAF Q.6s, was never official. From September 1939, nine civil Q.6s impressed for RAF and FAA in the UK, and one other used with civil registration. Two more British civil Q.6s impressed in Middle East, 1940-41, and a third, acquired pre-war for the King of Iraq, taken over from Iraqi Air Force in 1941 for RAF use until early 1943. One of the UK impressments and one in Middle East had retractable u/cs; all others had fixed, trousered u/cs. Two Q.6s sold pre-war to a Lithuanian airline taken over by Aeroflot in June 1940, and one of these reported to have ended up in German hands.

Max speed, 195 mph (314 km/h). Cruising speed, 175 mph (282 km/h). Ceiling, 21,000 ft (6,400 m). Range, 750 mls (1,207 km). Empty weight, 3,500 lb (1,588 kg). Gross weight, 5,500 lb (2,495 kg). Span, 46 ft 8 in (14.22 m). Length, 32 ft 3 in (9.83 m). Wing area, 278 sq ft (25.83 m²).

Above: Delivered in mid-1940, P6123 was among the first ten Proctor Is to enter RAF service, spending the entire war at Heliopolis in Egypt. Right: One of the 100 Proctor IIs for the FAA, BV539 shows the folding wing feature. Below: Hills-built Proctor III R7572.

Above: Proctor IV NP210, serving with No 1 Radio School, displays high-visibility yellow panels on fuselage and wings. Below: A private-venture attempt to interest the RAF in a light twin-engined trainer, the R.S.1 G-AEOD served Reid and Sigrist as a 'hack' for most of the war.

PERCIVAL PROCTOR

Closely following the issue of Specification 20/38 for Vega Gulls in the communications role, Specification 26/38 called for the Vega Gull to be adapted to meet OR65 for an aircraft equipped for radio or navigation training, and fitted with dual controls for initial deck-landing instruction. Powered by the 205 hp Gipsy Queen II (Gipsy Six Srs II in military guise), the new aircraft, named Proctor, was to have only one rear seat, instead of the Vega Gull's two. Production ordered without waiting for prototype testing, and following variants built:

Proctor I: Three-seat communications aircraft for RAF, first flown October 8, 1939. Fitted with D/F loop for navigation equipment, dual controls, and third seat in rear of cabin. Entered service early 1940, and 166 built, including 25 by F Hills & Sons. In 1940, one aircraft fitted with racks for 16 x 20 lb (9.08 kg) bombs as potential 'anti-invasion' light bomber. Six used by USAAF units in UK.

Proctor IA: Version of Mk I for FAA use as radio trainer, with R/T operator on swivel seat in rear of cabin, with radio equipment. Eighty-one delivered in 1940.

Proctor II: As Mk IA, primarily for FAA, with R/T operator and equipment alongside pilot to improve CG. Percival built 100, of which 34 to RAF, and Hills built 100 for FAA (often called Proctor IIA), of which four to RAF. Two (at least) used by USAAF in UK, and 18 (or more) converted to Mk III.

Proctor III: Differed from Mks I and II in having no D/F loop, no nav equipment and no dual controls. Percival modified a Mk II as a prototype and Hills produced 437 Mk IIIs, of which 20 used by USAAF in UK, a few by FAA and one to RNZAF in November 1944. Series 1 was three-seat communications version, some with radio and operator in rear cabin. Series 2 was two-seat R/T trainer, with operator facing aft, alongside pilot.

Max speed, 170 mph (274 km/h). Cruising speed, 155 mph (250 km/h) at 6,000 ft (1,830 m). Range, 540 mls (865 km/h). Empty weight, 2,180 lb (989 kg). Gross weight, 3,250 lb (1,475 kg). Span, 39 ft 6 in (12.04 m). Length, 25 ft 10 in (7.87 m). Wing area, 197 sq ft (18.3 m²).

Proctor IV: Completely revised design, to Specification T.9/41, for which name Preceptor initially proposed. Dual role, three-seat R/T trainer with operator alongside pilot, or four-seat communications, with dual controls. Increased overall dimensions. Two prototypes and six pre-production by Percival; 250 by F Hills. First flight March 16, 1942, and deliveries continued through end of war.

Max speed, 160 mph (257 km/h). Cruising speed, 140 mph (225 km/h) at 3,000 ft (914 m). Service ceiling, 14,000 ft (4,267 m). Range, 500 mls (805 km). Empty weight, 2,370 lb (1,075 kg). Gross weight, 3,500 lb (1,588 kg). Span, 39 ft 6 in (12.04 m). Length, 28 ft 2 in (8.58 m). Wing area, 202 sq ft (18.77 m²).*

REID AND SIGRIST R.S.1

Twin-engined three-seat advanced trainer, powered by two 205 hp DH Gipsy Six Srs II engines, first flown early 1939. Further development arrested by war, and single prototype G-AEOD used by manufacturers for communications duty until 1944. Known as Snargasher.

Max speed, 205 mph (330 km/h). Gross weight, 4,900 lb (2,222 kg). Span, 36 ft 4 in (11.07 m). Length, 25 ft 4 in (7.72 m).

REID AND SIGRIST R.S.3 DESFORD

Twin-engined two-seat trainer, similar in configuration to R.S.1 and conceived in late-war period for post-war needs. Single prototype G-AGOS first flown July 9, 1945, shortly before V-J Day.

Max speed, 162 mph (261 km/h). Gross weight, 3,300 lb (1,497 kg). Span, 34 ft 0 in (10.36 m). Length, 25 ft 6 in (7.77 m).

ROBINSON REDWING

Side-by-side two-seat lightplane, first flown mid-1930. Powered by 80 hp AS Genet II; 12 built through 1933, of which one (G-ABNX) survived the war in the UK, but not flown during war-time. In New Zealand, Redwing II ZK-ADD impressed in August 1941 for (ground) use by Invercargill ATC, eventually acquiring serial INST 112.

Max speed, 95 mph (153 km/h). Gross weight, 1,500 lb (680 kg). Span, 30 ft 6 in (9.3 m). Length, 22 ft 8 in (6.91 m).

SARO A.17 CUTTY SARK

Four-seat touring and training amphibian, first flown July 4, 1929. Of 12 built, two, with 145 hp AS Genet Major IA engines, used by No 3 E & RFTS operated at Hamble by AST. Registered G-ACDP and G-AETI, they survived until early 1942.

Max speed, 115 mph (185 km/h). Gross weight, 3,900 lb (1,770 kg). Span, 45 ft 0 in (13.72 m). Length, 34 ft 4 in (10.46 m).

Below: Continuing the concept of a light trainer for multi-engine pilot training, Reid and Sigrist built and flew the R.S.3 just before the end of the war. (Photo courtesy of 'The Aeroplane'). Above right: Saro Cutty Sark G-ACDP was one of two used by AST-operated No 3 E & RFTS until early 1942.

SARO A.19 CLOUD

Transport amphibian for up to eight passengers, first launched at Cowes on July 16, 1930. One of four civil examples, G-ABHG (at one time fitted with auxiliary aerofoil above the two 425 hp P & W Wasp C engines, and non-standard twin fins and rudders) acquired by Imperial Airways in November 1939; used by the airline's School for Basic Marine Instruction at Hythe until June 1940, and finally at Poole for crew training from September to December 1940. Beyond economic repair, it was dismantled by May 1941. The last of 17 A.29 Clouds operated by the RAF were withdrawn from service in July 1939.
Cruising speed, 98 mph (158 km/h). Gross weight, 10,000 lb (4,536 kg). Span, 64 ft 0 in (19.5 m). Length, 47 ft 9 in (14.55 m).

SARO A.27 LONDON

Twin-engined GP and patrol flying-boat developed to meet Specification R.24/31; prototype first flown in March 1934. Production totalled 30, initially Mk I with 690 hp Bristol Pegasus IIIM.3 but principally Mk II to Specification R.3/35 with 980 hp Pegasus X engines. All but two still in service in September 1939, with Nos 201 and 240 Sqns for North Sea patrols and No 202 at Gibraltar. Operational until early 1941, then in training role at No 4 (Coastal) OTU until summer 1942. Armament comprised three 0.303-in (7.7-mm) machine guns in bows and dorsal cockpit, plus 2,000 lb (907 kg) of bombs.
Max speed, 155 mph (249 km/h) at 6,250 ft (1,905 m). Cruising speed, 100 mph (161 km/h). Range, up to 2,600 mls (4,184 km). Empty weight, 12,800 lb (5,806 kg). Gross weight, 22,000 lb (9,980 kg). Span, 80 ft 0 in (24.38 m). Length, 56 ft 9 in (17.30 m). Wing area, 1,425 sq ft (132.4 m²).

Above: London K5910 in service with No 240 Sqn, flying from Sullom Voe in the Shetlands for patrols over the North Sea. Right: A London II of No 201 Sqn seen through the nose of a Heinkel He 111 over the North Sea on February 10, 1940. Below: A pre-war shot of Cloud G-ABHG; the auxiliary upper aerofoil was later removed.

Below: The Saro A.37 in early 1940. It had been hastily camouflaged after first flight in October 1939, and would soon acquire fin stripes and a yellow outline to the fuselage roundels.

The R.5/39 programme did not go ahead, but the A.37 was completed in time to make its first flight at Cowes in October 1939, with registration G-AFZS. Powered by four 85 hp Pobjoy Niagara III engines, it was later modified to have a single fin and rudder, and other features representative of the Shetland flying-boat jointly developed by Shorts and Saro. In this guise, it acquired

Above: The first Lerwick L7248 as tested in early 1940 with twin fins and rudders.

Below: Lerwick L7257, one of only 27 produced, in the markings of No 4 OTU shortly after this unit (previously the FBTS) had moved from Stranraer to Invergordon (Alness) in Scotland.

SARO A.37

After designing the S.38 four-engined patrol flying-boat to Specification R.5/39, Saro built, as a private venture, a half-scale model as the A.37, often called the Shrimp.

the serial TK580, and was tested from early 1944 until after the war had ended.
Max speed, 130 mph (209 km/h). Gross weight, 6,250 lb (2,835 kg). Span, 50 ft 0 in (15.24 m). Length, 42 ft 3¼ in (12.88 m).

SARO S.36 LERWICK

Twin-engined GR flying-boat to meet Specification R.1/36, powered by two 1,375 hp Bristol Hercules IM (first four aircraft), II or IV. Crew of six/seven, and armament of seven 0.303-in (7.7-mm) machine-guns in nose, dorsal and tail Frazer Nash powered turrets; 2,000 lb (907 kg) of bombs or depth charges. First of 21 production aircraft flown early November 1938, with first three assigned to prototype development and used to test a number of tail configurations and other modifications to overcome early shortcomings. Deliveries to No 209 Sqn began December 1939 but Lerwicks unsatisfactory and little used. Transferred to No 4 (Coastal) OCU by April 1941, but eight used briefly in summer of 1942 by No 422 (Canadian) Sqn pending arrival of Sunderlands. All aircraft retired by early 1943.

Above: Short Scion Z7190 in service in 1941 with the Comm Flt, Lydda, where it had been in service, before impressment, with Palestine Airways as VQ-PAB.

Max speed, 215 mph (346 km/h). Cruising speed, 165 mph (266 km/h). Service ceiling, 15,000 ft (4,572 m). Range, 1,500 mls (2,414 km). Gross weight, 33,200 lb (15,060 kg). Span, 80 ft 10 in (24.64 m). Length, 63 ft 7½ in (19.40 m). Wing area, 845 sq ft (78.5 m²).

SHORT S.16 SCION

Six-seat light transport, first flown August 18, 1933. Production totalled five Scion I with two 85 hp Pobjoy Niagara I or II and 17 Scion II (including four built by Pobjoy) with 90 hp Niagara IIIs. Eleven British-registered Scions (three Mk I, eight Mk II) impressed by RAF during 1940, to serve primarily with Anti-Aircraft Co-operation Units and Ferry Pilots Pool. Three others retained British civil registrations for wartime use, including one in Aden. Two Scion IIs exported pre-war to Palestine Airways impressed for RAF use in August 1940 at Lydda, written off respectively in April 1941 and December 1942. Data for Scion II.
Max speed, 126 mph (203 km/h). Gross weight, 3,200 lb (1,452 kg). Span, 42 ft 0 in (12.8 m). Length, 31 ft 6 in (9.6 m).

SHORT S.17/L

Two 38-seat transport biplanes built for Imperial Airways as landplane derivatives of S.17 Kent flying-boat; first flown (*Scylla*) on March 26 and (*Syrinx*) on May 17, 1934. Powered by four 900 hp Bristol Pegasus XC engines. Both aircraft used by National Air Communications, 1939-40, flying stores and personnel to France. Impressed for RAF March 1940, but *Syrinx* grounded from December 1939 and *Scylla* damaged beyond repair in April 1940 before transfer to RAF.
Max speed, 137 mph (220 km/h). Gross weight, 33,500 lb (15,200 kg). Span, 113 ft 0 in (34.4 m). Length, 83 ft 10 in (25.5 m).

SHORT S.19 SINGAPORE III

Six-seat general reconnaissance flying-boat produced for RAF on basis of single S.12

Above: Short S.17/L Scylla in pre-war service with Imperial Airways and, below, at RAF Drem in April 1940 after it had been blown over in a gale and damaged beyond repair.

Singapore II developed in 1930-32. Four pre-production Singapore IIIs to Specification R.3/33 and a further 33 to Spec R.14/34 with 675 hp R-R Kestrel VIII pusher and two Kestrel IX tractor engines. First Mk III flown June 15, 1934; entered service 1935 with No 203 Sqn. Latter unit flying Singapores on anti-shipping patrols at Aden when war began, continuing to February 1940. No 205 Sqn used Singapores from Seletar until March 1941, then transferred four to RNZAF for use by latter's No 5 Sqn at Fiji until April 1943.
Max speed, 136 mph (219 km/h) at 5,000 ft (1,524 m). Service ceiling, 15,000 ft (4,570 m). Range, 1,000 mls (1,610 km). Empty weight, 20,364 lb (9,237 kg). Gross weight, 32,390 lb (14,692 kg). Span, 90 ft 0 in (27.4 m). Length, 64 ft 2 in (19.5 m). Wing area, 1,834 sq ft (170.5 m²).

SHORT S.22 SCION SENIOR

Eleven-seat light transport conceived as enlarged derivative of S.16 Scion, first flown October 22, 1935, and powered by four 90 hp Pobjoy Niagara III engines. Six built, and used primarily in floatplane configuration. One (seaplane) exported to Sierra Leone, lost in August 1939. Three (seaplanes) exported to Rangoon, of which one later to Palestine and (converted to landplane) impressed by RAF in August 1940 for service at Lydda until September 1942. One (landplane) exported to Iraq, impressed by RAF February 1942 and lost in Egypt in September 1943. Sixth aircraft bought by Air Ministry as L9786 for research into hull design, fitted with central float (half-scale model of Sunderland hull) and strutted wing-tip floats. First flown October 18, 1939, and survived until 1944. Data for landplane.

Above: Singapore III K6912 was one of four transferred from No 205 Sqn, RAF, in Seletar to serve with the RNZAF. The latter formed No 5 Sqn to operate the Singapores from Suva Bay, Fiji, marked as OT:A, B, C and D, with RAF serials painted out.

Left: The last of six Scion Seniors, L9786 was used to investigate hydrodynamics of flying-boat hulls, its central float being a half-scale representation of the Sunderland's hull.

Max speed, 140 mph (226 km/h). Gross weight, 5,750 lb (2,607 kg). Span, 55 ft 0 in (16.75 m). Length, 42 ft 0 in (12.8 m).

SHORT S.20/S.21

Composite aircraft pair conceived in accordance with patents by Major Mayo and supported by Air Ministry and Imperial Airways, to provide a heavily-loaded mailplane with transatlantic range. Under Specification 13/33, Shorts designed a variant of the Empire flying-boat (see S.23 entry) as the carrier (S.21) of a small two-seat seaplane (S.20). Powered by four 900 hp Bristol Pegasus XC engines, S.21 G-ADHK *Maia* first flown on July 27, 1937; powered by four 340 hp Napier Rapier Vs, S.20 G-ADHJ *Mercury* first flown September 5, 1937; and first combined S.20/S.21 flight on January 20, 1938. After outbreak of war, S.20 *Mercury* used for training, including a spell with Fokker T-8-W-equipped No 320 (Netherlands) Sqn at Pembroke Dock, until returned to Rochester and scrapped late 1941. S.21 *Maia* used by BOAC for training at Poole until destroyed in enemy air raid on May 11, 1941.

Data for S.20: *Max speed, 212 mph (339 km/h). Range, 3,900 mls (6,240 km). Gross weight, 20,800 lb (9,443 kg). Span, 73 ft 0 in (22.2 m). Length, 51 ft 0 in (15.5 m).*

Data for S.21: *Max speed, 200 mph (322 km/h). Range, 850 mls (1,360 km). Gross weight, 38,000 lb (17,252 kg). Span, 114 ft (34.7 m). Length, 84 ft 11 in (25.9 m).*

SHORT C-CLASS EMPIRE BOATS

Long-range passenger and mail transport flying-boat designed for use on Empire routes operated by Imperial Airways and developed in parallel with S.25 Sunderland for RAF. Produced in three principal variants, as follows:

S.23: Powered by four 900 hp Bristol Pegasus XC radial engines and designed to carry 3½-ton payload (including 24 passengers). First flown July 3, 1936, and total of 25 built for Imperial Airways plus six for Qantas by December 1937. Eight of these lost pre-war; remainder used principally by Imperial Airways' successor BOAC (retaining British civil registrations) throughout the war on segments of Empire routes, from Durban to India and Australia. Two impressed by RAAF in September 1939 (original IA 'boats; two to IA from Qantas in exchange). Two more ex-Qantas impressed in July 1940, and all four used by No 11 Sqn, RAAF, for coastal patrols and transport duty, with underwing bomb racks and a miscellany of guns. Later served with No 33 Sqn as transports; three lost in 1942; fourth returned to Qantas July 1943 and lost January 1944. Two S.23s (ex-BOAC) impressed for RAF 1940 and delivered Spring 1941 to No 119 Sqn, fitted with dorsal and tail turrets and ASV radar; one lost August 1941 and other returned to BOAC December 1941 after brief service with No 413 (RCAF) Sqn. Of the remainder, seven lost and ten survived the war.

Max speed, 200 mph (322 km/h). Service ceiling, 20,000 ft (6,100 m). Range, 760 mls (1,245 km). Empty weight, 23,500 lb (10,670 kg). Gross weight, 40,500 lb (18,380 kg). Span, 114 ft 0 in (34.7 m). Length, 88 ft 0 in (26.8 m). Wing area, 1,500 sq ft (139.5 m²).

S.30: Long-range version intended for transatlantic service; fitted with 815 hp Bristol Perseus XIIC engines, with gross weight of 46,000 lb (20,866 kg) and first flown September 28, 1939. Nine built, including four equipped for in-flight refuelling (from HP Harrow tankers) and airborne weights up to 53,000 lb (24,040 kg). One lost before war. Two impressed for RAF early 1940, for ASV radar development trials with Special Duty Flight at Invergordon; then used to ferry supplies and troops to Norway in April 1940, where both lost. Others used by BOAC and (two) by Tasman Empire Airways, four surviving the war.

S.33: Final two Empire boats, ordered for Imperial Airways as attrition replacements, with strengthened hulls. First flown April/May 1940, later fitted with 835 hp Pegasus XXII engines and gross weight increased to 53,000 lb (24,040 kg). One operated by BOAC survived the war; second impressed by RAAF in March 1942 and armed to serve with No 33 Sqn, then with No 41 (Sea Transport) Sqn before return to Qantas in July 1943; lost January 1944.

Above: The S.30 Empire Boat Awarua was used mainly between Auckland and Sydney after delivery in 1940 to Tasman Empire Airways as ZK-AMC. Below: First of the two S.33 Empire Boats, BOAC's G-AFPZ Clifton became A18-14 in RAAF service, here with No 33 Sqn in July 1942 operating from Townsville, Queensland.

SHORT S.25 SUNDERLAND

Four-engined general-purpose flying-boat designed during 1933/34 in response to Specification R.2/33, which spelt out the needs of Operational Requirement 8 as a replacement for the biplane 'boats then in service. Designed under direction of Arthur Gouge, S.25 retained overall configuration and geometry of Scion Senior, and was in many respects the military counterpart of S.23 Empire Boat, which was the first to fly. A single prototype S.25 ordered in 1934 for competitive evaluation against Saro A.33. Powered by four 950 hp Bristol Pegasus X engines, prototype K4774 first flew on October 16, 1937. After four flights, sweepback of 4.5 deg introduced on the mainplanes, and 1,010 hp Pegasus XXIIs fitted; testing in this form resumed on March 7, 1938.

Sunderland I: Initial production version of S.25, the first 11 being ordered to Specification 22/36 and OR.42 at the same time as 11 Saro A.31s ordered to Specification 21/36 (the latter being cancelled after A.31 prototype damaged beyond repair on October 25, 1938). Further contracts brought total of Sunderland Is built to 74 by Shorts at Rochester and 15 by Blackburn at Dumbarton. First of development batch flew on April 21, 1938 and 42 Sunderland Is flying by September 1939; first by Blackburn flew late-1941. Sunderland I was powered by four 1,010 hp Pegasus XXII engines and carried a crew of 9-10. Armament comprised a single (later, two) guns in FN11 nose turret, four guns in FN13 tail turret and (later aircraft) two Vickers 'K' guns in dorsal hatches, all of 0.303-in (7.7-mm) calibre. A 2,000 lb (908 kg) bomb-load was carried. Service use began June 1938 with No 230 Sqn at Seletar and No 210 Sqn at Pembroke Dock, the latter unit flying the first wartime sortie – a convoy patrol – on September 3. At that time, No 228 Sqn also flying Sunderlands at

Alexandria, Egypt, and No 204 at Mount Batten. Nine Mk Is released by RAF to equip No 10 Sqn, RAAF, still in UK when war began, becoming operational with Australian crews (but retaining RAF serials in place of A18-1 to A18-9 allocated). Two further squadrons, Nos 95 and 201, equipped from 1940.

Max speed, 210 mph (338 km/h). Rate of climb, 1,200 ft/min (6.1 m/sec). Ceiling, 20,500 ft (6,248 m). Range, 2,910 mls (4,686 km). Empty weight, 28,290 lb (12,832 kg). Gross weight, 45,700 lb (20,730 kg). Span, 112 ft 8 in (34.34 m). Length, 85 ft 8 in (26.11 m). Wing area, 1,487 sq ft (138.14 m²).

Sunderland II: Operationally-improved Mk I with 815 hp Pegasus XVIII engines and two-speed superchargers, FN7 two-gun dorsal turret in place of open 'K'-gun mounts, and FN4A tail turret with double rpg. Most Mk IIs also fitted with ASV Mk II

radar, indicated by aerial masts and transmitter loops on rear fuselage, and central and underwing Yagi homing aerials. Prototype conversion of (first Blackburn-built) Mk I, T9083, followed by 23 by Shorts at Rochester, five by Blackburn and five by Short & Harland in Belfast (where first flew on April 24, 1942). Served alongside Mk Is in four squadrons and as initial equipment of four more.

Sunderland III: Principal war-time production and service version, featuring impoved low-drag hull design and faired main step. Other features as Mk II. Prototype (Mk I conversion) T9042 flown at Rochester on June 28, 1941, and first production Mk III, also at Rochester, on December 15, 1941. Production totals, 186 from Rochester, 71 from Belfast, 170 from Blackburn Dumbarton and 71 from Short-operated factory on Lake Windermere. Early in 1943, centimetric ASV Mk III

Above: Sunderland III ML868 of No 230 Sqn operating over the Bay of Bengal, late 1944; note dorsal turret and ASV radar aerials. Below: Sunderland I L2163 in service in 1940 with No 210 Sqn, flying convoy protection patrols from Oban.

Above: Sunderland III ML727 in 'civil' guise as G-AGHZ for use by BOAC on services between Poole, Dorset, and West Africa. Left: A Blackburn-built Sunderland V, showing the underwing radomes for the ASV Mk VIC scanners.

replaced ASV Mk II; later, ASV Mk VIC, with fairings for underwing scanners, was fitted in Sunderland IIIAs. From late 1943, Mk IIIs fitted with four additional forward-firing machine guns in the nose, and a further modification provided pairs of 0.50-in (12.7-mm) guns to fire through beam hatches aft of dorsal turret, bringing the total to 18 machine guns. Sunderland IIIs served with some 15 squadrons of the RAF, including one French-manned, one Norwegian, two Canadian, one Australian and one New Zealand. Also, No 10 Sqn, RAAF, progressed from Mk Is to Mk IIIs. Between January 1943 and August 1944, BOAC received 24 Sunderland IIIs (diverted from RAF contracts), stripped of armament and military equipment, and fitted with austere bench-and-mattress seating. First conversion flew at Rochester on December 26, 1942, and these aircraft, in camouflage and with civil registrations, used initially on the UK-West Africa route to Lagos. Operating later on the route through Egypt to Karachi, they acquired RAF roundels and Transport Command style four-letter codes. Four similar austere transport conversions diverted from RAF to RNZAF late-1944 for use by the Flying Boat Transport Flight in the Pacific.

Sunderland IV: See separate entry for S.45 Seaford.

Sunderland V: As Mk III but fitted with 1,200 hp Pratt & Whitney R-1830-90 engines. Prototype conversions of Mk IIIs by Shorts at Rochester (ML765) and by No 10 Sqn (RAAF) at Mount Batten (ML839), flown in March and May 1944 respectively. Existing Mk III contracts switched to Mk Vs, with deliveries starting late-1944, all with ASV Mk VIC and full 18-gun armament. Short built 47 at Rochester where the last one flew on September 27, 1945; Short and Harland built 47 at Belfast, completed June 1946; and Blackburn built 60 at

Dumbarton, where last Mk V flew on November 8, 1945. Entered service February 1945 and used (mostly post-war) by nine RAF squadrons.

Max speed, 213 mph (343 km/h). Rate of climb, 840 ft/min (4.27 m/sec). Service ceiling, 17,900 ft (5,455 m). Cruising endurance, over 15 hours. Empty weight, 37,000 lb (16,783 kg). Gross weight, 60,000 lb (27,216 kg). Dimensions as Mk I.

SHORT S.26 G-CLASS

Large transport flying-boat for commercial service with non-stop transatlantic capability. Three ordered by Imperial Airways, with Air Ministry subsidy in view of potential for military use. First flight, July 21, 1939; second and third aircraft flown February 24 and July 8, 1940. Powered by four 1,400 hp Bristol Hercules IV engines, the S.26s, intended to form Imperial Airways' G-Class with names *Golden Hind, Golden Horn* and *Golden Fleece*, were all impressed for RAF and modified to S.26/M military configuration before delivery as X8275, X8273 and X8274 respectively. Armament comprised eight 500 lb (227 kg) bombs under wings, two dorsal and one tail Boulton Paul four-gun turrets and internal stowage for flares and smoke floats. ASV radar fitted. Served with No 119 Sqn from early 1941 and with No 10 Sqn, RAAF, flying stores to Gibraltar and Middle East, during which X8274 was lost. Remaining two returned to civilian status as G-AFCK and G-AFCI, used by BOAC with 40-seat layout between UK and Nigeria. G-AFCK lost January 1943; G-AFCI on other routes in UK and West Africa until war's end.

Max speed, 209 mph (336 km/h). Range, 3,200 mls (5,120 km). Empty weight, 37,705 lb (17,100 kg). Gross weight, 74,500 lb (33,800 kg). Span, 134 ft 4 in (40.9 m). Length, 101 ft 4 in (30.9 m). Wing area, 2,160 sq ft (201 m²).

SHORT S.31

After receiving orders for two prototypes and 100 production aircraft to the S.29 design which became the Stirling, Shorts built in 1938 a ½-scale prototype at its own expense. Powered by four 90 hp Pobjoy Niagara III engines, this S.31 was mostly of wooden construction apart from a semi-monocoque fuselage, and seated two in tandem. In overall silver finish and marked M4, the S.31 flew on September 19, 1938, at Rochester. It later acquired a lengthened u/c (as adopted meanwhile on the S.29 to give greater effective wing incidence during take-off and landing); then in January 1939 it was fitted with 115 hp Niagara IVs and in March with a larger tailplane. In 1940, now in green/brown camouflage with yellow undersides, the S.31 was fitted with ½-scale mock-ups of the Boulton Paul Type O ventral and Type H dorsal twin-cannon turrets proposed for a version of the Stirling II, and was tested in the RAE 24 ft (7.3 m) wind tunnel. Further flights were made from March 13, 1942, onwards (with a shortened u/c), and the S.31 was scrapped after a take-off accident at Stradishall in February 1944.

Max speed, 180 mph (290 km/h). Gross weight, 5,700 lb (2,586 kg). Span, 49 ft 6½ in (15.09 m). Length, 43 ft 7½ in (13.31 m).

Above: Photographed in June 1940, the S.31 half-scale Stirling in the 24-ft (7.3 m) RAE wind tunnel. Scale mock-ups of the Boulton Paul Type O ventral and Type H dorsal turrets, fitted for these tests, were removed before the S.31 flew again.

SHORT S.29 STIRLING

The S.29 was designed under the direction of Arthur Gouge as Short's response to Specification B.12/36, which defined a heavy bomber to meet Operational Requirement OR.40 drawn up by the Air Staff in 1936. Two prototypes ordered 1937, for competitive evaluation with Supermarine Type 316. Powered by four 1,150 hp Bristol Hercules Is, the first Stirling, L7600, flew at Rochester on May 14, 1939, but was damaged beyond repair when u/c collapsed on landing. Second prototype, L7605, flew on December 3, 1939, by which time Shorts had flown a ½-scale Stirling (see S.31 entry above), and first Stirling production order had been placed.

Stirling I: Initial production version, with orders eventually totalling 267 by Shorts at Rochester, 266 by Short & Harland at Belfast and 191 by Austin Motors at Longbridge. First production Stirling flown on May 7, 1940, at Rochester, and first at Belfast on October 28, 1940. Initial aircraft were Series 1 (320 built) with 1,375 hp Hercules II engines and armament of eight 0.303-in (7.62-mm) m/gs in FN5A nose, FN4A tail and FN25A retractable ventral turrets. Bomb-load was up to 14,000 lb (6,350 kg), and crew of seven carried. Found operationally unfit, first ten Srs 1s classified as Stirling Trainers.

Below: Laid down as G-AFCJ Grenadier but renamed Golden Fleece before completion, this was the third of the G-class boats to fly. As X8274, it was fully-armed with three turrets, and went from Rochester to Dumbarton for installation of radar before joining No 119 Sqn.

Above: Stirling I Srs 3 W7455 was built by Austin Motors at Longbridge and entered service with No 149 Sqn late in 1941, at Mildenhall, but flew only four operational sorties. It was eventually shot down over the UK by enemy aircraft on September 7, 1943, whilst serving as a trainer. Right: Third production Stirling I Srs 1, N3638 – one of the ten Stirling Trainers.

Stirling I Srs 2 (117 built) introduced 1,590 hp Hercules XI engines with two-speed superchargers in Short-designed powerplants, and had two beam m/gs in FN55A mounts to replace ventral turret. The Srs 3 (307) had Hercules XIs in Bristol-designed powerplants and FN7A or FN50A two-gun dorsal turret in place of beam guns; some aircraft (perhaps Srs 4) later had provision for a remotely-controlled FN64A ventral turret, and an FN20A rear turret. Stirling Is also used 1,400 hp Hercules III and 1,420 hp Hercules X engines. Deliveries began late 1940 to No 7 Sqn, which flew first operation on night of February 10/11, 1941. No 7 later became only Stirling unit in Pathfinder Force; all other Stirling bomber squadrons, comprising four by end-1941, three more in 1942 and further four in 1943, served in No 3 Group, Bomber Command; seven of these squadrons flew Stirling Is.

Stirling II: Proposed Canadian production version to be built at St Hubert, PQ, by Canadian Associated Aircraft, with 1,600 hp Wright R-2600-A5B Cyclone engines. Three Mk I airframes completed as Mk II prototypes in UK, with first flight at Rochester August 1941. Planned production of 140 in Canada cancelled, as also was proposed Mk II production at new shadow factory operated by Shorts at South Marston, near Swindon. One Mk II later converted to Mk III prototype.

Stirling III: Improved Mk I Srs 3 with 1,615 hp Hercules VI (and, later, Hercules XVI) engines in powerplants with underslung oil coolers. Two Mk Is converted to Mk III prototypes (one having previously served as third Mk II), the first flying at Rochester in June 1942. Production switched from Mk I to Mk III late 1942 and 1,037 built (266 by Shorts at Rochester/South Marston, 342 at Belfast and 429 by Austin). A few Mk Is also converted to Mk IIIs. Standard armament comprised FN5A nose, FN50A dorsal and FN20A tail turrets; provision for FN64A ventral turret, seldom fitted. Installation of H2S with distinctive ventral radome soon became standard on Mk IIIs, and in early 1944 aircraft in at least five squadrons fitted with additional 0.50-in (12.7-mm) gun in aft escape hatch for rear defence. Mk III operations began in February 1943 and this variant used by nine squadrons.
Max speed, 200 mph (322 km/h) at 15,000 ft (4,572 m). Time to 15,000 ft (4,572 m), 30

min. *Ceiling, 20,000 ft (6,096 m). Range, 590 mls (949 km) with 14,000 lb (6,350 kg) bomb-load. Empty weight, 44,000 lb (19,504 kg). Gross weight, 70,000 lb (31,751 kg). Span, 99 ft 1 in (30.2 m). Length, 87 ft 3 in (26.59 m). Wing area, 1,322 sq ft (122.81 m²).*

Stirling IV: Adaptation of Mk III as glider tug and/or paratroop transport. Nose and dorsal turrets removed. For glider-towing, fitted with coupling on stirrup mount round tail turret (which sometimes removed). As paratrooper carrying 20, had glazed cupola in place of tail turret, and no coupling; exit hatch in rear fuselage aft of bomb cells. One prototype of each version converted from Mk IIIs, flown in August 1943. Production of Mk IIIs thereafter switched to Mk IVs and delivery commenced in last quarter of 1943.

Production totals were ten by Short and 450 by Short & Harland, with at least a further 130 Mk IIIs converted. Deliveries began early 1944 and operational use, on SOE sorties, started by March; two squadrons in UK and one in North Africa flew Mk IVs (and some Mk IIIs) for this purpose. Eleven other squadrons eventually flew Stirling IVs in troop-transport and GT role; as a tug, could tow one Hamilcar, two Horsas or up to five Hotspurs.

Stirling V: Unarmed personnel, cargo and vehicle transport derivative of Mk III, to carry 20 paratroops, 40 troops, two jeeps with trailers or 12 stretchers and 14 sitting wounded. Lengthened nose fairing, hinged to give access to cargo compartment, and large loading door in starboard side. One prototype conversion of Mk III, first flown at Rochester August 1944, and 160 built at Belfast (ending November 1945) principally to be used by Tiger Force in Far East. Deliveries began September 1944, and five squadrons flying Mk Vs when war with Japan ended.
Max speed, 280 mph (451 km/h) at 6,000 ft (1,829 m). Gross weight, 72,000 lb (32,659 kg). Span, 99 ft 1 in (30.2 m). Length, 90 ft 7 in (27.61 m).

Above: A formation of Stirling IV glider tugs in the markings of No 620 Sqn, with crudely-applied invasion stripes for operations after June 1944. Below: Stirling V PJ943, which entered service with No 242 Sqn in 1945.

Above: The first of two prototypes of the Seaford, MZ269, after the fitting of the taller fin with dorsal extension. Below: First flown in December 1944, the Shetland (Experimental Aeroplane 212) was intended to succeed the Sunderland but found no role in the post-war RAF.

SHORT S.45 SEAFORD

Improved Sunderland variant responding to OR.118 (which stressed the need for more range) and as defined by Specification R.8/42 issued at the end of 1942. Featured lengthened hull with improved hydrodynamics; dihedral tailplane; 1,700 hp Bristol Hercules XIX engines with four-bladed propellers, and armament of two 20-mm cannon in Bristol B.17 dorsal turret plus 0.50-in (12.7-mm) m/gs in nose and tail twin-gun turrets and one in each beam hatch, and two 0.303-in (7.7-mm) guns fixed forward-firing in nose. Two prototypes ordered as Sunderland IVs; first (MZ269) flown at Rochester on August 30, 1944, after which enlarged tailplane, taller fin and dorsal fin fitted. Initial production order for 30 reduced to eight, all completed post-war, with name Seaford.
Max speed, 242 mph (389 km/h). Range, 3,100 mls (4,990 km). Gross weight, 75,000 lb (34,020 kg). Span, 112 ft 9¹/₂ in (34.37 m). Length, 88 ft 7 in (27.0 m).

SHORT S.35 SHETLAND

High-speed very long-range heavily-armed reconnaissance flying-boat designed to OR.91 in compliance with Specification R.14/40. Two prototypes ordered after selection of Short design in favour of competing Saro S.41, and Saro made responsible for detail design and manufacture of wing. At time of first flight on December 14, 1944, prototype DX166 was largest British aircraft to have flown. Powered by four 2,400 hp Bristol Centaurus VII engines, the Shetland had a crew of 11 and was to be armed with nose, dorsal and tail turrets each carrying a pair of 0.50-in (12.7-mm) guns; the bomb-load was to be

18,000 lb (8,165 kg). The war ended before completion of the second prototype.
Max speed, 263 mph (424 km/h). Gross weight, 125,000 lb (56,700 kg). Span, 150 ft 4 in (46.75 m). Length, 110 ft 0 in (33.5 m).

SLINGSBY T.1 FALCON I

Single-seat sailplane, designed in Germany as the Schleicher Falke. Nine built, to German designs, by Slingsby in Yorkshire

from 1931 onwards, of which one impressed for ATC late-1942 and four more by early-1945. One converted to flying-boat glider in 1942 and tested on Lake Windermere to assess possibility of establishing ATC schools with waterborne gliders.
Gross weight, 506 lb (230 kg). Span, 42 ft 0 in (12.6 m).

SLINGSBY T.3 PRIMARY

Single-seat primary glider based on RRG Kassel Zogling and almost identical RFD Dagling (see page 52) which preceded production by Slingsby. Total of 67 built by Slingsby 1934-1939, some fitted with cockpit nacelle round pilot's seat. At least 33 impressed for ATC use during 1942, and a further six or so later. (Often noted, incorrectly, as Slingsby T.2 in official records.)
Gross weight, 380 lb (172 kg). Span, 33 ft 11 in (10.35 m) with rounded tips or 33 ft 0 in (10.06 m) with square tips.

SLINGSBY T.4 FALCON III

Two-seat derivative of Falcon I. Nine built from 1935 onwards, of which four impressed in 1940 for use at Central Landing Establishment and transferred to ATC in 1942. Four more in ATC service by early 1945.
Gross weight, 899 lb (408 kg). Span, 58 ft 0 in (17.69 m).

SLINGSBY T.5 GRUNAU BABY

Single-seat intermediate sailplane designed in Germany by Schneider. Slingsby built 15 under licence, but 13 impressed for ATC between 1942 and 1945 may have included examples built by other UK companies and individuals.
Gross weight, 550 lb (250 kg). Span, 44 ft 6 in (13.57 m).

SLINGSBY T.6 KIRBY KITE I

Single-seat sailplane derived from Grunau Baby design, first flown August 1935. Twenty-five built, including one with non-metallic control system, for early RAF radar experiments. Fifteen impressed for Central Landing Establishment in 1940 for early glider pilot training. Five in ATC use early 1945.

Below: In camouflage finish, this impressed Slingsby T.4 Falcon III was in service in late 1942 at the London Command School of Gliding, the first such school formed for ATC cadets' use. It may be the Falcon III allocated the serial NF744 in December 1942 (after this photo was taken).

Gross weight, 509 lb (231 kg). Span, 46 ft 6 in (14.1 m).

SLINGSBY T.7 KIRBY CADET

Single-seat intermediate training glider, first flown January 1936. From pre-war production of 22, two went to local Slingsby ATC squadron at Kirkbymoorside and several others impressed from 1942 onwards. In late 1943, OR.142 was drawn up for a training glider to be suitable for ATC use and Specification 20/43 required that it should be capable of being flown at heights up to 100 ft (30.5 m) by unskilled cadets. The T.7 was selected to meet this requirement and the type was then named Cadet TX Mk.I. Production totalled 376, by Slingsby (226), Fox and Davies (30), Ottley Motors Ltd (30) and Papworth Industries and Enham Industries (90); six of this total were exported to Canada and more than 100 of the Slingsby batch were delivered post-war.
Gross weight, 513 lb (233 kg). Span, 38 ft 6 in (11.73 m).

SLINGSBY T.8 KIRBY TUTOR (CADET)

Training glider similar to Kirby Cadet, with (interchangeable) tapered wing of greater span. First flown July 1937 and seven built pre-war, all of which believed to be in ATC service by early 1945. Slingsby delivered 62 more post-war as Cadet TX Mk 2, built to complete earlier contract for T.7 Cadet TX Mk 1s.

Above: The prototype T.7 Cadet TX Mk I TS291, the first of a batch of 50 ordered from Slingsby in 1943 to Specification 20/43. Further contracts kept the Cadet in production into 1946, joined by (left) the similar T.8 Cadet TX Mk 2 with tapered outer wing panels.

Gross weight, 549 lb (249 kg). Span, 43 ft 3³/₄ in (13.24 m).

SLINGSBY T.9 KING KITE

High-performance single-seat sailplane first flown in April 1937. Of three built, one in service with ATC gliding schools by 1945.
Gross weight, 580 lb (263 kg). Span, 51 ft 0 in (15.5 m).

SLINGSBY T.12 GULL I

High-performance sailplane first flown April 1938. Nine built pre-war, of which one impressed in 1942 for the ATC.
Gross weight, 624 lb (283.5 kg). Span, 50 ft 3³/₄ in (15.33 m).

SLINGSBY T.14 GULL II

Two-seat high-performance sailplane derived from T.12 design. Single example built, flown April 1940 and impressed for the ATC in 1942.
Gross weight, 1,011 lb (459 kg). Span, 65 ft 4 in (19.91 m).

SLINGSBY T.18 HENGIST

Troop transport glider designed in accordance with OR.98 and to Specification X.25/40 issued in February 1941. Designed

Right: The Hengist prototype DG570 (Ex Aero 143), first of four completed during 1942. Below: Slingsby Hengist I DG676, one of the 14 production examples, served briefly at the AFEE.

to carry 15 troops (including the pilot) and to be towed at max speed of 150 mph (241 km/h) EAS, in trains of three (loaded) or five (unloaded). Four prototypes ordered late 1940, of which the first flew at Dishforth in January 1942, behind a Whitley. Fourteen production Hengist Is delivered February 1943-March 1944, of which two reached the Glider Pilots' Exercise Unit and others remained at experimental units or in store until struck off strength in 1946. A strengthened undercarriage used on production aircraft was identified as the Mk III by Slingsby; this designation did not apply to the Hengist, which remained the Mk I throughout.
Towing speed, 130 mph (209 km/h). Empty weight, 4,629 lb (2,100 kg). Gross weight, 8,350 lb (3,788 kg). Span, 80 ft 0 in (24.38 m). Length, 56 ft 5¹/₂ in (17.22 m). Wing area, 780 sq ft (72.46 m²).

SLINGSBY TYPE 20

Two-seat intermediate training glider with tandem seating, built as private venture for potential ATC use, and first flown in 1944. Not adopted for production, but used May 1945 to investigate airflow in wake of aircraft carriers, towed behind HMS *Pretoria Castle* and, later, HMS *Illustrious*.
Gross weight, 1,000 lb (454 kg). Span. 54 ft 6 in (16.61 m).

SLINGSBY TYPE 21

Two-seat training glider with side-by-side seating, designed for ATC as alternative to Type 20. Prototype flown in 1944 (later identified as T.21P), leading to post-war production of Type 21B Sedbergh TX Mk 1 for ATC use.
Span (prototype only), 50 ft 0 in (15.24 m).

SPARTAN CRUISER

Three-engined light transport, based on Saro-Percival Mailplane of 1931 and produced by Spartan in collaboration with

Above: The sole Slingsby Type 20 engaged in carrier wake trials aboard HMS Pretoria Castle in May 1945. Right: The prototype Type 21P, tested for ATC use in 1944, survived into 1946 in civilian use.

Saunders-Roe. Production comprised one Cruiser I prototype, 12 six-passenger Cruiser IIs and three eight-passenger Cruiser IIIs, completed by May 1935. In September 1939, three Cruiser IIs and one Cruiser III powered by 130 hp DH Gipsy Major I Srs I engines, serving with Scottish Airways on Highland and Island routes; of these, one Mk II (G-ACSM) flew for a few months in civil marks and the other three impressed in April 1940 to serve with Nos 6 or 7 AACU, but little used as airframes badly deteriorated.

Cruising speed, 115 mph (85 km/h). Gross weight, 6,200 lb (2,812 kg). Span, 54 ft 0 in (16.46 m). Length, 39 ft 2 in (11.94 m).

SPARTAN CLIPPER

Two-seat lightplane powered by a 75 hp Pobjoy R and using outer wing panels based on Monospar ST-4. First flown at East Cowes on December 14, 1932, as S-3, later registered G-ACEG. With 90 hp Pobjoy Niagara III, used in civil guise for communications by Spartan Aircraft until destroyed by enemy action in May 1942.

Max speed, 110 mph (177 km/h). Gross weight, 1,300 lb (590 kg). Span, 34 ft 0 in (10.36 m). Length, 28 ft 2 in (8.58 m).

SUPERMARINE SCAPA

General reconnaissance flying-boat developed to Specification R.20/31 as the Southampton IV and produced to Specification 19/33. Powered by two 535 hp Rolls-Royce Kestrel IIIMS engines, the

Above: The Cruiser II G-ACSM and (left) Cruiser III G-ADEL were impressed as X9433 and X9432 respectively, but saw little service with the RAF. Below: The Clipper G-ACEG, used by Spartan for communications.

Scapa (Supermarine Type 221) was first flown in 1932 and 14 were built for RAF in 1934-36. Served with Nos 202, 204, 228 and 240 Sqns until 1938. Three Scapas remained with training units when war began and two of these at the FBTS survived until August 1940, although possibly not flown after war began.

Max speed, 142 mph (229 km/h). Gross weight, 16,080 lb (7,290 kg). Span, 75 ft 0 in (22.85 m). Length, 53 ft 0 in (16.2 m) on chassis.

Below: Stranraer K7295 serving with No 240 Sqn in 1940; it survived in No 4 OTU until September 1942. Right: Canadian-built Stranraer 914 serving in 5(BR) Sqn, RCAF, in 1940 at Dartmouth, NS.

SUPERMARINE STRANRAER

An improved general reconnaissance flying-boat developed from the Southampton (initially as the Supermarine Type 227, Southampton V) to meet requirements of Specification R.24/31. Prototype flown July 27, 1934, and production of 17 Stranraer Is to Specification 17/35 ordered in 1935. Powered by two 920 hp Bristol Pegasus X engines, the Stranraers (as Supermarine Type 304) carried a crew of five and an armament of three 0.303-in (7.7-mm) machine guns in bow, midships and tail positions plus 1,000 lb (484 kg) of bombs underwing. Deliveries began April 1937 and service use with four squadrons, of which Nos 209 and 240 flew the type operationally from UK bases until spring 1941. Training use with No 4 OTU continued until late 1942.

Canadian Stranraer: In November 1936, RCAF placed an order with Canadian Vickers Ltd for licence production of the Stranraer, eventually buying 40 of a version almost identical with RAF Stranraer I. Deliveries were spread from late 1938 to late 1941, with 835 hp Pegasus XXIIs in later aircraft. Service use with eight RCAF squadrons, initially with No 2 Sqn which flew patrols out of Dartmouth, Nova Scotia, starting September 10, 1939. Served later in training role, continuing until 1944.

Max speed, 165 mph (266 km/h). Time to 20,000 ft (6,096 m), 37.6 min. Service ceiling, 20,000 ft (6,096 m). Range, 1,140 mls (1,834 km). Empty weight, 12,534 lb (5,690 kg). Gross weight, 19,900 lb (9,035 kg). Span, 85 ft 0 in (25.81 m). Length, 54 ft 6 in (16.61 m). Wing area, 1,457 sq ft (135.35 m²).

Above: A Scapa serving with No 202 Sqn pre-War. Two of these boats survived at the FBTS, Calshot, into 1940.

SUPERMARINE WALRUS

Single-engined naval reconnaissance amphibian developed during 1932 in continuation of the Seagull family, initially to satisfy Australian requirements. Private venture prototype (Supermarine 228) first flown June 21, 1933, as Seagull V, marked N-1 and powered by 625 hp Bristol Pegasus IIL.2P in pusher configuration. Marked N-2 in July 1933 for tests at MAEE Felixstowe and purchased by Air Ministry in January 1935 as K4797 with 625 hp Pegasus IIM2 engine.

Seagull V: Name used by RAAF for 24 aircraft similar to Type 228 prototype, ordered August 1934 and built in accordance with Specification 6/34, with 625 hp Pegasus IIM2 engine. Crew of three and single Vickers 'K' 0.303-in (7.7-mm) machine guns in bow and dorsal open cockpits. First Seagull V flown June 25, 1935, and deliveries completed mid-1937. Served throughout the war with No 101 Fleet Co-operation Flight (later No 5 Sqn), No 9 Sqn and aboard RAN cruisers. Supplemented by 37 Walrus, ex-RAF contracts, delivered 1939-1944. Six Seagull Vs also acquired by Turkey, delivered 1938.

Max speed, 125 mph (201 km/h) at 3,280 ft (1,000 m). Gross weight, 6,847 lb (3,106 kg). Span, 46 ft 0 in (14.02 m). Length, 38 ft 0 in (11.6 m) on chassis.

Walrus I: The Seagull V adopted for use by the FAA as a fleet general reconnaissance amphibian. First order for 12 placed early 1935, in accordance with Specification 2/35, and first of these (Supermarine Type 236) flown March 18, 1936, with Pegasus IIM2 engine; 690 hp Pegasus VIP then adopted as standard. Subsequent aircraft produced in accordance with Specification 37/36, bringing total production by Supermarine to 281 (of which four undelivered, probably destroyed by enemy action during assembly). Additional production by Saro of 270 (but six not delivered) brought Mk I total to 551, plus two for Argentina in 1939. In the FAA, Walrus Is equipped Catapult Flights and Catapult Squadrons aboard battleships and cruisers for spotting, aided after 1942 by addition of ASV Mk II radar on some aircraft; last operated in this role from HMS *King George V* in November 1944. Also used in training and miscellaneous support roles by some 29 second-line FAA squadrons and by two others for air-sea rescue. Also extensively used in latter role by 12 RAF squadrons in the UK, Mediterranean, India and Ceylon. Ten aircraft (including one Mk II) transferred to RNZAF 1943-44 as flying-boat trainers, and 37 (including some Mk II) transferred to RAN, 1939-44. One Mk I (and four Mk II) to RCN (plus one Mk I and two Mk II in 1946).

Max speed, 135 mph (217 km/h) at 4,750 ft (1,448 m). Time to 10,000 ft (3,050 m), 12.5 min. Rate of climb, 1,050 ft/min

Above: Walrus I W2784, built by Saunders-Roe, in the hands of No 700 Sqn, FAA, from HMS Kenya, in the second quarter of 1942.

Above: Walrus II HD908 serving in the ASR role with Gravesend-based No 277 Sqn, RAF, in 1944.

Below: The second of the RAAF's 24 Seagull Vs, which served throughout the war.

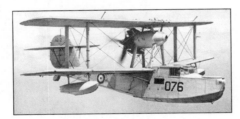

Below: Sea Otter JM879 serving in the communications role with No 740 Sqn from Machrihanish in early 1945.

(5.3 m/sec). Service ceiling, 18,500 ft (5,639 m). Empty weight, 4,900 lb (2,233 kg). Gross weight, 7,200 lb (3,266 kg). Span, 45 ft 10 in (13.97 m). Length, 37 ft 7 in (11.45 m) on chassis. Wing area, 610 sq ft (56.67 m²).

Walrus II: Similar to Mk I but with wooden hull and rubber-tyred tailwheel. Two prototypes were rebuilds of Mk Is by Supermarine, with Saro-built hulls and new serials (X1045, X1046), the first of which flew on May 2, 1940. All production by Saro, totalling 190 (of which one not delivered, probably destroyed in enemy air raid on Cowes). Served primarily in training role. Transfers to RNZAF, RAN and RCN (see under Mk I entry).

SUPERMARINE SEA OTTER

A developed version of the Walrus, evolved early-1936 to meet OR.33 for a spotting amphibian to operate from cruiser/battleship catapults or from the decks of aircraft carriers. Two prototypes (Supermarine Type 309) ordered April 1936 to conform to Specification 5/36, which called for a Bristol Pegasus engine to be used, in tractor configuration. With a crew of three, the Type 309 lacked the bow gun of the Walrus and had twin guns in the dorsal cockpit. First prototype K8854 flew on September 23, 1938, with a 745 hp Bristol Perseus XI engine and was re-engined with a 920 hp Bristol Mercury XX in 1940; a 965 hp Mercury 30 was fitted in January 1941 and latter engine specified for production aircraft ordered January 1942. Second prototype destroyed by enemy action at Woolston in September 1940, possibly before being flown.

Above: Sea Otter JN185 was the first completed to ASR Mk II standard, this designation being adopted in May 1945. Service use of this air-sea rescue variant by FAA squadrons was exclusively post-war.

Sea Otter ABR Mk I: Initial production version, 'amphibian boat reconnaissance', built by Saro and first flown January 1943 at Cowes. First contract for 250, of which nine (or more) completed as Mk II. Entered service early 1944 for ASR and communications duties in FAA.

Sea Otter ASR Mk II: Second contract for 100 placed with Saro in September 1943, of which only 41 built, plus nine (or more) from previous contract for Mk Is. Dedicated and equipped for ASR role, with armament removed. Delivered from May 1945.

Max speed, 163 mph (262 km/h) at 4,500 ft (1,371 m). Time to 5,000 ft (1,525 m), 7 min. Rate of climb, 870 ft/min (4.4 m/sec). Service ceiling, 17,000 ft (5,181 m). Range, 690 mls (1,110 km). Empty weight, 6,805 lb (3,086 kg). Gross weight, 10,000 lb (4,536 kg). Span, 46 ft 0 in (14 m). Length, 39 ft 10³/₄ in (12.2 m). Wing area, 610 sq ft (56.7 m²).

SUPERMARINE SPITFIRE
(Merlin, Fighter)

Single-seat high-performance fighter, initially evolved by R J Mitchell as private venture to improve on unsuccessful Supermarine 224 prototype built to Specification F.7/30 – which gave effect to the first designated Air Ministry Operational Requirement (OR.1). By 1934, PV Supermarine 300 design had been developed to meet OR.17 and single prototype ordered on December 1, 1934, to conform with Specification F.37/34. Powered by a 990 hp Rolls-Royce Merlin C with DH two-bladed fixed-pitch wooden propeller, unarmed prototype K5054 first flown at Eastleigh on March 5, 1936. Successively fitted with 1,035 hp Merlin F and 1,030 hp Merlin II and with full armament of eight 0.303-in (7.7-mm) machine guns, before being written off on second day of World War II, September 4, 1939.

Spitfire I: Initial production version, built to Specification 16/36; first contract placed June 3, 1936. First aircraft flown May 14, 1938, with 1,030 hp Merlin II; Merlin III introduced at 175th aircraft. Early aircraft with two-bladed Airscrew Co wooden propeller; three-bladed metal propeller soon standardised – DH two-position, then DH or (few only) Rotol constant speed unit. Entered service August 1938 with No 19 Sqn at Duxford and nine squadrons operational by September 1939, with ten more by mid-1940. Designation **Spitfire IA** adopted retrospectively in 1940 after 30 aircraft designated **Spitfire IB** when fitted with two Hispano 20-mm cannon each in place of four of the machine guns. Total Mk I production (excluding conversions to prototypes of later marks), 1,519 by Supermarine and 50 by Westland. One Mk I exported to France, mid-1939; 18 ex-RAF Mk Is to Portugal in 1942. One RAAF, one RNZAF and two RCAF squadrons flew Spitfire Is that remained on RAF strength.

Max speed, 346 mph (557 km/h) at 15,000 ft (4,575 m). Time to 15,000 ft (4,575 m), 6.85 min. Service ceiling, 30,500 ft (9,296 m).

Above: Spitfire Is, including L1043, DW:0, from No 610 County of Chester Sqn, Aux AF, on patrol from RAF Gravesend in June 1940. Right: One of the two Spitfire Is (P9566 and '67) destined for Turkey but diverted back to RAF Middle East in May 1940 and given new serial numbers HK854 and HK856.

Above: Spitfire IIB P8327, named Java, displaying the standard 'B' wing armament of cannon and machine guns. It was lost whilst serving with No 308 Sqn in July 1941. Below: Spitfire IIA (LR) P8077, with extra fuel tank under port wing (only), in service with No 19 Sqn at Fowlmere, summer 1941.

Range at normal cruising speed of 304 mph (489 km/h), 415 mls (668 km). Empty weight, 4,517 lb (2,049 kg). Gross weight, 5,844 lb (2,651 kg). Span, 36 ft 10 in (11.23 m). Length, 29 ft 11 in (9.12 m). Wing area, 242 sq ft (22.48 m²).

Spitfire II: Similar to Mk I but powered by 1,175 hp Merlin XII and with operational refinements progressively introduced on Mk Is. Three (or more) Mk Is flown with Merlin XIIs before first production Mk II (Supermarine Type 329) completed in June 1940 at Castle Bromwich Aircraft Factory. Operational use began August 1940 with No 611 Sqn and production totalled 751 **Spitfire IIA** with eight machine guns and 170 **Spitfire IIB** with two cannon and four machine guns. For extended range, **Spitfire IIA (LR)** carried a 30-Imp gal (136-l) fuel tank flush-fitting under the port wing leading-edge; limited use by five RAF squadrons in mid-1941. The **Spitfire IIC** (later, **ASR Mk II**) was adapted for air-sea rescue duties, with 1,240 hp Merlin XX in place of Merlin XII,

rescue packs in the flare chutes and marker bombs under the port wing. About 50 conversions flown by RAF squadrons from 1943. Spitfire IIs from RAF stocks made available for squadrons of RAAF, RCAF and RNZAF in Fighter Command, together with, in 1941, three US-manned Eagle squadrons and units of the *Forces Aériennes Françaises Libres*. Later marks flown by most of these units as they became available.

Spitfire III: Single Mk I airframe (N3297) flown March 1940 with Merlin R.M.3SM (ie, Merlin XX) and operational/performance improvements including structural strengthening, retractable tailwheel and short-span wing of 30 ft 6 in (9.30 m). Production plans cancelled and prototype (Supermarine Type 330) later fitted with Merlin 60/61-series two-speed two-stage engine. Second Mk III conversion (Type 348) in 1941, based on Mk V airframe and used to develop new u/c with main wheels raked forwards 2 in (1.5 cm) and, later, four-cannon wing armament.

Above: First of the two Spitfire IIIs, N3297, introduced improvements including retractable tailwheel and uprated Merlin. It first flew with short-span wing shown here, but later had standard wing and two-stage, two-speed Merlin fitted.

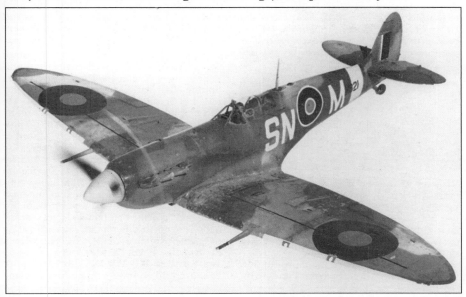

Above: The classic lines of the Spitfire, displayed by a standard Mk VB, EN821, in the markings of No 243 Sqn flying from Ouston, Northumberland, summer 1942.
Below: Spitfire VC BR537, with tropical filter, of No 452 Sqn, RAAF, after that unit returned to Australia in June 1942. It carries the new code QY:A, but awaits serial A58-43.

Spitfire V: Third major production version, combining Mk I/II airframe features with 1,185 hp Merlin 45 single-stage single-speed engine. Prototype installation in a Mk I first flown December 1940 and 154 Mk I and Mk II conversions made in 1941. First production Mk V (Supermarine Type 331) flown from CBAF in June 1941 and production totalled 4,489 at that factory, 1,363 by Supermarine and 635 by Westland. In addition, some 200 Mk I/II converted to Mk V standard. Service use began mid-May with No 92 Sqn. Production included 94 **Spitfire VA** with eight-gun armament, 3,911 **Spitfire VB** with two-cannon/four-mg armament, and 2,467 **Spitfire VC** introducing new wing (Supermarine Type 349) in late 1941 that could carry four cannon without mgs, or two-cannon/four mg arrangement as Mk VB. Total production also included 15 photo-recce **Spitfire PR Mk V** (see separate entry for photo-recce Spitfires). For service in Middle and, later, Far East, tropical versions introduced large Vokes dust filter over carburettor air intake under nose, or small filter developed and fitted at Aboukir in Egypt. To extend range, Spitfire Vs (and later marks) carried flush-fitting belly tanks of 30- or 45-Imp gal (136- or 205-l) capacity on regular operations, 90-Imp gal (409-l) for special ferry flights or 170-Imp gal (773-l) version used by 17 aircraft flown from Gibraltar to Malta in late 1942. From end-1942, 'fighter' role prefix resulted in **Spitfire F Mk VA, F Mk VB** and **F Mk VC** designations, using

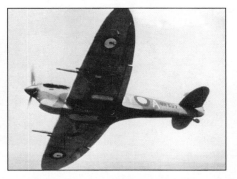

Merlin 45, 46, 50, 50A, 55 or 56 medium-altitude engines. For lower altitude operations, **Spitfire LF Mk VB** used Merlin 45M, 50M or 55M, with cropped supercharger impellers and combat boost rating of 1,585 hp. Many Spitfire Vs had wing tips removed ('clipped'), reducing span to 32 ft 2 in (9.80 m). Starting 1942, Spitfire Vs were adapted to carry one 250-lb (113-kg) bomb under each wing, or one 500-lb (227-kg) bomb under fuselage in place of long-range tank. Some aircraft were fitted with hooks to tow Hotspur gliders at training schools. One radio-controlled drone version was tested in 1944, and one captured Mk VB was fitted in Germany with 1,475 hp Daimler-Benz DB 605A. In Egypt, two Spitfire VCs fitted with extended wing-tips, boosted Merlin 46s and four-blade propellers operated up to 50,000 ft (15,240 m) to intercept Ju 86P-2s. Spitfire Vs operated in Europe and Middle East by RAF, RCAF, RNZAF and RAAF squadrons from 1941 onwards; in India/Burma from late 1943, and in Australia, where 245 Spitfire VCs and one VB were transferred from RAF to RAAF in 1942-43 (plus 11 lost en route). Starting late-1942, ten squadrons of the SAAF flew Spitfire Vs (and/or Mk IXs) in North Africa, Sicily and Italy, including No 40 Sqn operating in the 'Tac R' role for which Spitfires carried an oblique camera just behind the cockpit. From mid-1942, some 600 Spitfires (mostly Mk Vs) supplied to USAAF units flying in the UK and North Africa on 'reverse lend-lease' basis, retaining RAF serials. Two (or more) Mk VAs to USA in 1941 for evaluation. Supply of Spitfires to Soviet Union began early-1943 with transfer of 143 Mk VBs; in late-1943 the RAF released 33 Mk VBs to Portugal. One squadron of the R Egyptian AF was equipped with Spitfire VCs.

Spitfire VI (F Mk VI): High altitude version of Spitfire VB (Supermarine Type 350), featuring pressurised cockpit with sealed, jettisonable hood, 1,415 hp Merlin 47 with four-bladed propeller, and extended wing-tips giving 40 ft 2 in (12.24 m) span. Prototype conversion of Mk V during 1941 and 100 built by Supermarine in 1942; entered service April 1942 with Nos 616 and 124 Sqns.

Below: Spitfire VB EP689 serving with No 601 Sqn in North Africa in 1943, showing the 'clipped' wing and 'Aboukir' filter. Above right: Spitfire VB EP688, configured as EP689 below, serving with No 40 Sqn, SAAF, in the Tac-R role, with locally-installed camera in fuselage aft of cockpit.

Spitfire VII: High-altitude fighter evolved from Spitfire VC (Supermarine Type 351) with pressurised cockpit, sliding hood, increased fuel capacity, rectractable tailwheel, two-stage, two-speed 1,565 hp Merlin 61 or 1,710 hp Merlin 64 (in **Spitfire F Mk VII**) or 1,475 hp high-altitude Merlin 71 (**Spitfire HF Mk VII**). Extended wing-tips usually fitted and, later aircraft, broad-chord rudder with extended tip. Prototype conversions of Mk VCs flown second half of 1942; 140 produced by Supermarine, first deliveries September 1942 and operations began same month. One Mk VII to USAAF at Wright Field in April 1943.

Spitfire VIII: Similar to Mk VII but without pressurised cockpit. Armament as Mk VC, structural and systems improvements as Mk VII, enlarged rudder (except first few aircraft) and compact Aero-Vee tropical filter as standard. Prototype development included Mk III (N3297) fitted with Merlin 61 early-1942. Production (Supermarine Type 360) totalled 1,658 by Supermarine in three designated sub-variants according to altitude rating of engine: **Spitfire LF Mk VIII** with 1,705 hp Merlin 66; **Spitfire F Mk VIII** with 1,565 hp Merlin 61 or 1,710 hp Merlin 63; and **Spitfire HF Mk VIII** with 1,655 hp Merlin 70. Most Spitfire VIIIs flew with standard-span wing, but extended or clipped tips used as required operationally without change of designation. Service introduction, mid-1943, principally in North Africa, Sicily and Italy, including some SAAF squadrons. Later, Spitfire VIIIs replaced Mk VCs in squadrons operating in the CBI theatre and equipped units of the Indian Air Force. In 1944, RAAF took on charge 251 LF Mk

Above: An early Spitfire F Mk VI (Experimental Aeroplane 152), AB200, showing extended wing-tips and, below the exhaust ports, extra air intake for Marshall cabin blower. Below left: Spitfire HF Mk VII MD159 (with cannon removed) in service with No 518 Sqn in Northern Ireland, 1945.

VIIIs for its squadrons in New Guinea; 159 more Mk VIIIs were received post-war. In fighter-bomber role, some Mk VIIIs carried two 500-lb (227-kg) bombs under fuselage; later aircraft used 45-Imp gal (205-l) teardrop long-range tanks in place of earlier slipper type.

Spitfire IX: Fourth major production fighter variant (Supermarine Type 361), combining Mk VC airframe with two-stage two-speed Merlin 60 series engine but lacking other improvements designed for (later) Spitfire VIII. Early Merlin 60 and 61 flight-tested in Spitfire III (from August 19, 1941) and a Spitfire IA, followed by conversion by Rolls-Royce of two Mk VCs to Mk IX prototypes with Merlin 61s early-1942. Further 282 conversions of Mk V airframes by Rolls-Royce; production totals 5,095 by CBAF and 561 by Supermarine. Service use began June 1942 in No 64 Sqn. Early standard aircraft had 'C' wing armament, standard wing span, Merlin 61 and provision for wing and fuselage bomb racks. Later, designations used to differentiate altitude rating of engine: **Spitfire LF Mk IX** with Merlin 66, **Spitfire F Mk IX** with Merlin 61 or 63 and **Spitfire HF Mk IX** with Merlin 70. Broad-chord, pointed-tip rudder became

Above: Tropicalised Spitfire F Mk VIII JF330, with long-span wing, as personal mount of AV-M Harry Broadhurst, 1943. Below: RAAF Spitfire LF Mk VIIIs, drawn from No 1 APU (nearest camera) and No 548 Sqn, RAF, on training exercise, early 1944.

Above: A standard production Spitfire F Mk IX, EN133 (FY:B) in service with No 611 Sqn at Biggin Hill in September 1942. Below: Spitfire VC AB196 after conversion to Mk IX prototype and still with four-cannon armament fitted. It first flew in this form on March 27, 1942. In service, the Mk IX more usually had two cannon and four machine guns.

Above: An ex-RAF Spitfire IX (with cannon removed) in service with No 60 Sqn, SAAF, carrying an oblique camera in the fuselage. Right: A Spitfire XVI with clipped wings, pointed rudder, tropical filter, 45-Imp gal (205-l) belly tank and 'E'-wing armament, serving in No 416 Sqn, RCAF, early-1945. Below: Converted from a Mk V by Rolls-Royce, BS553 still had 'B'-wing armament when serving with No 93 Sqn in Sicily in 1943.

standard later, as did compact Aero-Vee tropical filter. Late-production CBAF Mk IXs had cut-down rear fuselage with 360-deg vision canopy, and **Spitfire IXE** designation (with LF, F or HF prefix) indicated new wing armament of two 20-mm cannon and two 0.50-in (12.7-mm) machine guns. More than 50 RAF and Commonwealth squadrons flew Spitfire IXs, primarily in European theatre, and 1,188 Mk IXs were supplied to the Soviet Union in 1943-44; at least one Mk IX was modified in Russia to two-seat training configuration. A small number of Spitfire IXs supplemented Mk Vs in USAAF service in Twelfth Air Force. *Max speed, 408 mph (657 km/h) at 25,000 ft (7,620 m). Time to 20,000 ft (6,100 m), 5.7 min. Initial climb, 3,950 ft/min (20.1 m/sec). Service ceiling, 43,000 ft (13,106 m). Range, internal fuel, 434 mls (698 km). Empty weight, 5,634 lb (2,556 kg). Gross weight, 9,500 lb (4,309 kg). Span, 36 ft 10 in (11.23 m) or 32 ft 9 in (9.80 m). Length, 31 ft 1 in (9.47 m). Wing area, 242 sq ft (22.48 m²).*

Spitfire XVI: CBAF production of 1,054 Spitfires similar to LF Mk IX but with US Packard-built Merlin 226 engine. Initially with 'C' wing armament, later with 'E' wing, broad-chord rudder and cut-down rear fuselage, most operated with clipped wings and all designated **Spitfire LF Mk XVI** regardless of configuration. Deliveries began October 1944 and service use from November onwards, particularly by four RAF squadrons attacking V-2 sites with bombs.

SUPERMARINE HIGH-SPEED SPITFIRE

Single Spitfire I (K9834) diverted from RAF contract in 1938 and modified (as Supermarine Type 323) for attempt on World Air Speed Record for landplanes. First flown December 14, 1938, and speed of 408 mph (656 km/h) achieved at 3,000 ft (914 m), but record objective abandoned in 1939. Fitted with Merlin XII engine and three-bladed propeller, and single F.24 oblique camera behind cockpit, used by PRU at Heston (later Benson) for one operational sortie and then as station hack throughout war. Span reduced to 33 ft 8 in (10.25 m).

SUPERMARINE SPITFIRE
(Merlin, photo-reconnaissance)

Unarmed (and later, in some cases, armed) versions of Spitfire, equipped with vertical and/or oblique cameras, operated with RAF from November 1939 until after the war had ended. Initially known as **Spitfire Mk I PR**, with Types A to H distinguishing variations of camera, fuel capacity and armament. At the end of 1941, Air Ministry adopted a system of mark number prefix letters to indicate aircraft role, and Types A to H then became – at least notionally – Spitfire PR Mk I to PR Mk VIII respectively; by this time, however, no Type A or Type B remained in service, and Type H was never produced.

Spitfire I PR, Type A: Two Mk I fighters (N3069, N3071) modified for Heston Flight (later No 2 Camouflage Unit, then Photographic Development Unit), with guns removed and one F.24 (5-in/12.7-cm) vertical camera in each wing. First operation November 18, 1939. Lost on operations, March 19 and April 21, 1940, respectively.

Spitfire I PR, Type B: Some eight-ten Mk I fighters modified with F.24 (8-in/20.3-cm) cameras in wings, as Type A, and extra 29-Imp gal (132-l) tank in rear fuselage. Operational by February 1940, No 212 Sqn in France.

Spitfire PR Mk III (initially, Type C): Up to 20 converted Mk I fighters, with two F.24 cameras in blister under starboard wing and 30-Imp gal (136-l) blister tank under port wing, plus rear fuselage tank as Type B. Operational by April 1940, PDU and No 212 Sqn.

Spitfire PR Mk IV (initially Type D): First production photo-recce version, developed by Supermarine (as Type 353) based

Above: The original High-Speed Spitfire after its reconversion to serve – mostly as a station 'hack' – at PRU Benson. Below: In overall pink finish, N3117 was one of numerous PR Spitfires that flew in several configurations, and is here a Type E (PR Mk V) with oblique cameras in underwing fairings.

Above left: Another of the 'pink' Spitfires, this PR Mk VII (note ports for wing guns) carries the codes of No 140 Sqn. Above right: Originally a Type C conversion, X4492 became a PR Mk VI before transfer to RCAF in mid-1943; note deepened nose and underwing blister tanks. Below: Spitfire PR Mk XI PA892 in service with USAAF's 14th Photographic Sqn, 7th PG, at Mount Farm, Oxon, 1944.

on Mk I fighter airframe, with Merlin III engine, 133-Imp gal (605-l) fuel in wing leading edges and extra oil in port wing. Two cameras in rear fuselage, F.24 (8-in/20.3-cm or 20-in/51-cm) or F.8 (20-in/51-cm). First of two prototype conversions (P9551, P9552) flown September 15, 1940. Starting mid-1941, Supermarine delivered 12 Type D based on Mk I airframes with Merlin 45 engines, and 217 PR Mk IVs based on Mk V airframes with Merlin 45 or 46 engines, all delivered by March 1943. For service in Middle East, some fitted with Aboukir-developed tropical filter. After RAF detachments of PR Mk IVs to Northern Russia, two/three transferred to Soviet Air Force, May 1944.

Spitfire PR Mk V (*initially* Type E): First low-altitude photo-recce variant, with oblique instead of vertical cameras. One F.24 in blister fairing under each wing; rear fuselage tank. Conversions from PR Mk III or F Mk V; in service with PDU April 1940.

Spitfire PR Mk VI (*initially* Type F): Interim long-range variant pending introduction of PR Mk IV. Based on Mk V airframe with Merlin 45; one 30-Imp gal (136-l) blister tank under each wing, rear fuselage tank and extra oil tank in deepened nose cowling. Two F.24 (8-in/20.3-cm) or F.8 (20-in/51-cm) cameras behind cockpit; some later with oblique F.24 (14-in/35.5-cm) camera. In service July 1940 and first RAF aircraft to photograph Berlin (X4712 on March 14, 1941). Fifteen Type F con-

verted from Mk V during production by Supermarine, and other conversions from Type C. One to RCAF, 1943.

Spitfire PR Mk VII (*initially* Type G): First armed photo-recce version, with eight 0.303-in (7.62-mm) wing machine-guns; 29-Imp gal (132-l) rear fuselage tank. Two F.24 (14-in/35.5-cm and 5-in/12.7-cm) vertical cameras and one F.24 (14-in/35.5-cm) oblique, mounted port or starboard. Merlin 45. About two dozen conversions by Heston Aircraft; in service mid-1940.

Spitfire PR Mk VIII (*initially* Type H): Proposed Spitfire I PR variant with Merlin 32. Not built; see PR Mk XIII.

Spitfire PR Mk X: Unarmed long-range photo-recce variant (Supermarine Type 362) based on F Mk VII (fighter) fuselage with pressurised cockpit, Merlin 64 engine, leading-edge wing fuel tanks as PR Mk IV, and oil tank in deepened nose cowling. Two F.52 (36-in/91-cm or 20-in/51-cm) or F.8 (20-in/51-cm) vertical cameras or two F.24 (14-in/35.5-cm) plus one F.24 (14-in/35.5-cm or 8-in/20.3-cm) oblique camera. Sixteen built, in service from May 1944 with Nos 541 and 542 Sqns (following PR Mk XI into service).

Spitfire PR Mk XI: Basically unarmed photo-recce variant of F Mk IX (fighter), using wing leading-edge tanks as on PR Mk IV, extra oil tank in nose as PR Mk VI and X, camera options as PR Mk X. First few PR Mk XIs by conversion of F Mk IXs in production by Supermarine (Type 374) with Merlin 61 or Merlin 63; later aircraft

(Type 365) with retractable tailwheel, broad-chord rudder and Merlin 70. First flight November 21, 1942; total 471 delivered. Served with some 14 RAF squadrons and 21 transferred to USAAF for use by 7th PG in UK, 1943-45.

Max speed, 417 mph (671 km/h) at 24,000 ft (7,376 m). Initial climb, 4,350 ft/min (22.0 m/sec). Time to 20,000 ft (6,100 m), 5 min. Service ceiling, 44,000 ft (13,411 m). Ferry range, 2,300 mls (3,701 km). Empty weight, 5,575 lb (2,523 kg). Gross weight, 7,930 lb (3,597 kg). Span, 36 ft 10 in (11.23 m). Length, 31 ft 4¹/₂ in (10.47 m). Wing area, 242 sq ft (22.48 m²).

Spitfire PR Mk XIII: Armed low-altitude photo-recce variant (Supermarine Type 367) to succeed PR Mk VII, with 1,645 hp Merlin 32 engine. Based on F Mk VA airframe, but only four 0.303-in (7.7-mm) guns in wings. Cameras as PR Mk VII. Total of 25 conversions from F Mk II, F Mk VA or (four only) PR Mk VII airframes. Eleven later transferred to FAA. Entered service April 1943, used by Nos 541, 542 and 543 Sqns.

SUPERMARINE SPITFIRE FLOATPLANE

Floatplane fighter version of Spitfire initiated during 1942, based on Mk VB airframe using floats designed by Supermarine (as Supermarine Type 355). Conversion by Folland Aircraft, with four-bladed propeller on Merlin 45 engines, tropical filter and extra ventral fin. First flown October 12, 1942, and later fitted with extra dorsal fin and Aero-Vee tropical filter. Two further Mk VB conversions by Folland during 1943; all three to Egypt late-1943 and flown from Great Bitter Lake, but no operational use. One Spitfire LF Mk IXB, with Merlin 66 and four-bladed propeller (Type 385), similarly converted by Folland, first flown June 18, 1944, later reconverted to landplane.

Data for Mk VB floatplane: *Max speed, 324 mph (521 km/h) at 19,500 ft (5,944 m). Initial climb, 2,240 ft/min (11.38 m/sec). Service ceiling (estimated), 33,400 ft (10,180 m). Empty weight, 6,014 lb (2,728 kg). Gross weight, 7,580 lb (3,438 kg). Span, 36 ft 0 in (11.23 m). Length, 35 ft 4 in (10.76 m).*

Below: One of the Spitfire VB floatplanes (ex Aero 181), EP754, operating from the Great Bitter Lake. Right: The sole Spitfire IX floatplane, MJ892.

SUPERMARINE SEAFIRE
(Merlin, fighter)

Single-seat, high-performance naval fighter initiated during 1941 as Sea Spitfire, based at first on Spitfire VB airframe fitted with 'A'-frame arrester hook and catapult spools for accelerated take-offs from carrier decks. First Spitfire VB with arrester hook (BL676) flown October 1941; two further prototypes (AB205, AD371) converted, with hooks and spools, in January/February 1942. Name Seafire then adopted for fully-navalised version of Spitfire, as described below. In addition, from 1942 onwards, FAA received some 77 Spitfire IAs, four Spitfire IIAs, 26 Spitfire VAs, 149 Spitfire VBs and 11 Spitfire PR XIIIs. Most of these un-navalised, but including about 40 (mostly Spitfire VBs) hooked for airfield training. FAA also took on charge single Spitfire HF Mk IX in May 1945, and tested three (or more) Spitfire VIIIs fitted with 'sting' arrester hooks in April 1944.

Seafire F Mk IB: Total of 166 Spitfire VBs converted (and given new serial numbers) by Air Service Training at Hamble (136) and Phillips & Powis or Supermarine at South Marston (30). As Supermarine Type 340, fitted with 'A'-frame arrester hooks; no catapult spools on first 48. Armament and equipment as Spitfire VB, with Merlin 45 (few with Merlin 46). Deliveries from mid-1942; principally used for training, but No 801 Sqn fully-equipped aboard HMS *Furious* October 1942 as second operational Seafire squadron.

Seafire II: First naval production variant, based on Spitfire VC airframe, with 'A'-frame hook, catapult spools and fuselage strengthened, armament of two cannon/four mgs in 'C' wing (alternative provision for four cannon). Provision for RATOG and, like Spitfire VC, could have tropical filter and carry bombs, and/or have 'clipped' wing tips. One original Seafire prototype (AD371) converted to Seafire IIC prototype, flown February 1942. Production (Supermarine Type 357) by Supermarine (262) and Westland (110); first production aircraft flown May 28, 1942. Initial **Seafire F Mk IIC** had Merlin 45, 46, 50 or 55, and entered service with No 807 Sqn (first Seafire unit in FAA) in mid-1942, operating in Operation *Torch* from HMS *Furious* with additional Seafire squadrons. After successful testing late-1942 of Spitfire I (L1004) fitted with 1,645 hp Merlin 32 with cropped impeller for better low-altitude performance, combined with four-bladed propeller, this engine adopted for **Seafire L Mk IIC** (Supermarine Type 375), with at least 60 of production total to this standard; first operational May 1943 with No 807 Sqn. About 10 aircraft were **Seafire FR Mk IIC** (provisionally, PR L Mk IIC or LR Mk IIC), fitted by Heston Aircraft with one F.24 (20-in/51-cm) vertical and one F.24 (14-in/35.5-cm) oblique cameras in fuselage. First conversion flown July 1943.

Seafire III: Developed from Seafire II with double-folding wings (mainplanes up, tips down) for improved stowage aboard car-

Above: The first Spitfire IV, DP845 (Experimental Aeroplane 168), in original form with Griffon IIB and slotted flaps, as flown in November 1941. Below: The second Spitfire IV, DP851, completed as the Mk XX and here serving as interim prototype F Mk 21 in October 1942.

riers. Prototype (MA970) converted from first production F Mk IIC, first flown November 1942. Basic production **Seafire F Mk III** (Supermarine Type 358) normally powered by Merlin 55 (but Merlin 45, 46 and 50 also used), and four-bladed propeller; featured improved u/c for deck operations and, after first small batch, deletion of outer cannon bays in 'C'-type wing. Provision for RATOG and bombs, as Seafire II. Major variant was **Seafire LF Mk III** (often also called L Mk III) fitted for low-altitude operations with Merlin 55M. Small number of LF Mk IIIs fitted with vertical and oblique cameras, as in FR Mk IIC, and designated **Seafire FR Mk III**; first conversion, by Heston Aircraft, completed June 1943. Total Seafire III production, 1,263, by Westland (913) and Cunliffe Owen (350), included about 30 initially with fixed wings, known as L Mk IIC Hybrid until converted. First production Seafire III completed May 1943; service use began November 1943, with No 894 Sqn.

Data for LF Mk III: *Max speed, 348 mph (560 km/h) at 6,000 ft (1,830 m). Initial climb, 4,160 ft/min (21.13 m/sec). Time to 5,000 ft (1,525 m), 1.9 min. Service ceiling, 24,000 ft (7,315 m). Range (with drop tanks), 513 mls (825 km). Empty weight, 6,204 lb (2,814 kg). Gross weight, 7,640 lb (3,565 kg). Span, 36 ft 10 in (11.23 m). Length, 30 ft 2¹/₂ in (9.21 m). Wing area, 242 sq ft (22.48 m²).*

SUPERMARINE SPITFIRE
(Griffon, fighter)

Two prototypes ordered early-1940 to allow development of version of the Spitfire powered by the Rolls-Royce Griffon, offering

Above: Westland-built Seafire LF Mk III, NF547, with 'clipped' wings – when fitted, the tips folded downwards.

Right: Seafire L Mk IIC MB245 of No 880 Sqn landing on HMS Indomitable, May 1943.

Below: Hooked Spitfire VB BL676, which was the first to be fitted with an arrester hook, in October 1941, was later converted to Seafire IB and given the new serial number MB328.

Above: Spitfire F Mk XII MB878 on test from the A&AEE in September 1943 with 500-lb (227-kg) bomb. Right: One of the Mk VIII airframes used as prototypes for the Mk XIV, JF321, here with enlarged fin and DH contra-props. Below: A standard F Mk XIV, RM958, in India, early 1945.

some 50% more power than 1940-standard Merlin for little increase in frontal area.

Spitfire IV: Initial designation for two Griffon-engined prototypes defined by Specification F.4/41, developed in parallel with Spitfire III (see earlier entry) with similar airframe features, as Supermarine Type 337. First aircraft (DP845) flown November 27, 1941, with Griffon IIB, four-bladed propeller, retractable tailwheel, and standard-span wing with slotted flaps. Redesignated Spitfire XX early-1942 and then modified to Mk XII prototype. Second prototype (DP851) flown on August 8, 1942, as Mk XX (which see). Production order for 750 Spitfire IVs placed August 1941, later cancelled.

Spitfire F Mk XII: Interim Griffon-engined fighter for low-altitude operations, put into production pending availability of Mk XIV. Mk XX (DP845) flown as Mk XII prototype on April 10, 1942, with Griffon IIB, Mk VC armament, broad-chord, pointed, rudder; also flown with reduced-span wings and fixed tailwheel. Production (Supermarine Type 366) of 100 by Supermarine, with 1,735 hp Griffon III or Griffon IV; a few early aircraft flown with full-span wing and fixed tailwheel; reduced-span wing, retractable tailwheel were later

standardised. Deliveries began late-1942; in service February 1943, used by Nos 41 and 91 Sqns until September 1944.
Max speed, 397 mph (639 km/h) at 17,800 ft (5,425 m). Gross weight, 7,415 lb (3,363 kg). Span, 32 ft 7 in (9.93 m). Length, 30 ft 9 in (9.37 m).

Spitfire XIV: Second Griffon-engined production variant, combining 2,035 hp two-stage, two-speed Griffon 65 with features of Mk VIII airframe. Development (Supermarine Types 369 and 373) based on six Spitfire VIIIs fitted with various Griffon 60-series engines, flown during 1943. Initial (Supermarine Type 379) production configuration, **Spitfire F Mk XIV**, featured full-span wing with 'C'-type armament of two 20-mm cannon and four 0.303-in (7.7-mm) machine guns; retractable tailwheel; enlarged fin-and-rudder; extra leading-edge fuel tank and structural improvements. The **Spitfire F Mk XIVE** had 'E'-wing armament of two 20-mm cannon (outer bays) and two 0.50-in (12.7 mm) machine guns (inner bays); later aircraft, without change of designation, used cut-down rear fuselage with 360-deg vision canopy, requiring further enlargement of rudder chord and height. **Spitfire FR Mk XIV** and **FR Mk XIVE** were fighter-reconnaissance versions with oblique F.24 camera and extra fuel

tank in rear fuselage; all had 360-deg vision canopy. Production of all four Mk XIV variants totalled 957, by Supermarine. Deliveries began October 1943 and service use January 1944, with No 610 Sqn. F and FR variants operational in Europe up to end of war, some in fighter-bomber role with underwing rockets and/or bombs. Introduction into Far East theatre too late for wartime use.
Max speed, 448 mph (721 km/h) at 26,000 ft (7,925 m). Time to 20,000 ft (6,100 m), 7 min. Service ceiling, 44,500 ft (13,564 m). Max range, 850 mls (1,368 km). Empty weight, 6,600 lb (2,994 kg). Gross weight, 8,500 lb (3,856 kg). Span, 36 ft 10 in (11.23 m) or 32 ft 7 in (9.93 m). Length, 32 ft 8 in (9.96 m). Wing area, 242 sq ft (22.48 m²) or 231 sq ft (21.46 m²).

Spitfire XVIII: Fully productionised Griffon-Spitfire, similar in general to F Mk XIVE with cut-down rear fuselage and enlarged rudder. Also featured lengthened fuselage (33 ft 3¼ in/10.14 m); stronger wing and u/c, and additional fuel in rear fuselage. Production totalled 200 **Spitfire F Mk XVIII** and 100 **Spitfire FR Mk XVIII**, the latter with one oblique and two vertical cameras in rear fuselage. No prototype; first production aircraft flown June 1945 and in service too late for wartime use.

Spitfire XX: Redesignation of Spitfire IV first prototype (which see). Second prototype (DP851) first flown August 8, 1942, with Griffon IIB and full-span wing, plus structural changes leading towards Spitfire 21 (next entry).

Spitfire 21: Major redesign (Supermarine Type 356) of basic Spitfire, launched in 1942 to take full advantage of two-speed, two-stage Griffon engine variants. Spitfire XX (DP851) modified to serve as preliminary prototype, first flown October 4, 1942, with Griffon 61; five-bladed propeller; extended-span, pointed-tip wings (as on Spitfire VII); broad-chord rudder and revised canopy. Full Mk 21 prototype (PP139) flown on July 24, 1943, with modified wing planform to incorporate larger ailerons; more fuel in wing, increased u/c track and longer mainwheel oleo legs, and four 20-mm cannon armament. Name Victor provisionally adopted, but dropped before first production **Spitfire F Mk 21** flown on March 15, 1944, externally similar to PP139. The extended 'high-altitude' wing-tips were not used on subsequent production aircraft, a few of which had Griffon 85 engines with contra-props. Deliveries began early-1945 to equip No 91 Sqn, operational by April 1945. Production total, 120 by CBAF.
Max speed, 450 mph (724 km/h) at 19,600 ft (5,975 m). Initial climb, 4,850 ft/min (24.79 m/sec). Service ceiling, 43,000 ft (13,105 m). Range (clean), 580 mls (933 km). Empty weight, 7,160 lb (3,247 kg).

Below left: Spitfire FR Mk XIVE, MV247, in April 1945, showing 'clipped' wings and fuselage camera installation. Below right: A Spitfire FR Mk XVIII, with standard-span wings.

Above: The first production Spitfire F Mk 21, LA187, in interim configuration, with extended-span Mk VII-type wings and four cannon.

Above: Second production F Mk 21, LA188, with definitive wing. Left: The first production Spitfire F Mk 22, showing the all-round vision cockpit hood with cut-down rear fuselage.

Gross weight, 11,290 lb (5,121 kg). Span, 36 ft 11 in (11.26 m). Length, 32 ft 11 in (10.04 m). Wing area, 243.6 sq ft (22.63 m²).

Spitfire F Mk 22: Similar to Mk 21 but with cut-down rear fuselage, 360-deg vision hood and enlarged vertical and horizontal tail surfaces. One prototype (with Mk 21 tail unit) and 287 production aircraft, deliveries starting March 1945 too late for wartime service.

Spitfire 23: Intended variant based on Mk 22 with improved 'laminar flow' wing. Prototype wing development (Supermarine Type 372) using Griffon-engined Spitfire VIII (JG204), first flown January 1944, and Mk 21 prototype (PP139). Production plans cancelled.

Spitfire F Mk 24: Post-war development of Mk 22.

SUPERMARINE S.24/37

Carrier-borne torpedo dive bomber/reconnaissance aircraft designed in response to Specification S.24/37 to meet OR.53. Two prototypes of Supermarine Type 322 design ordered in May 1939 for competitive evaluation with Fairey design (Barracuda). Powered by a 1,300 hp Rolls-Royce Merlin 30 (in R1810) or 1,645 hp Merlin 32 (in R1815), the Type 322 – nicknamed Dumbo – featured a high-mounted wing with variable incidence and full-span leading-edge slats, large slotted flaps and (later) slotted ailerons. With a crew of three, it was to have an armament of two 0.303-in (7.7-mm) machine-guns, one in the wing and one in the rear cockpit, and to carry a Mk XII torpedo or up to 1,500 lb (680 kg) of bombs. The first prototype flew on February 6, 1943, and the second soon after, but no production took place, as the Barracuda was by then already in service.

Max speed, 279 mph (446 km/h) at 4,000 ft (1,219 m). Gross weight, 12,000 lb (5,454 kg). Span, 50 ft 0 in (15.2 m). Length, 40 ft 0 in (12.1 m).

SUPERMARINE SPITFIRE
(Griffon, photo-reconnaissance)

Spitfire PR Mk XIX: Final photo-recce variant, based on Spitfire F Mk XIV, with additional provision for pressurised cockpit. Starting April 1944, 22 aircraft delivered without pressurisation, and with Griffon 65 engines and same wing tankage as Merlin-engined PR Mk XI. Prototype definitive PR Mk XIX (Supermarine Type 389) completed October 1944 with pressurisation, Griffon 66 and extra 20-Imp gal (91-l) fuel tankage in each wing. Provision for 90- or 170-Imp gal (409- or 773-l) tank under fuselage. Total of 225 built (Supermarine Type 390), production continuing until mid-1945. Service use began May 1944 with No 542 Sqn.

Max speed, 445 mph (716 km/h) at 26,000 ft (7,925 m). Gross weight, 10,450 lb (4,740 kg). Span, 36 ft 10 in. Length, 32 ft 8 in (9.96 m).

Above: Spitfire PR Mk XIX PS925, completed late-1944, in the post-war codes of the Photographic Reconnaissance Development Unit. Below: Second of the two S.24/37 prototypes (Experimental Aeroplane 189), R1815, with definitive taller fin and rudder.

SUPERMARINE SEAFIRE
(Griffon, fighter)

Naval interest in a Griffon-engined Seafire emerged early in 1943 and a contract was placed in March that year for three prototypes, with three more ordered in May. Operational Requirement OR.113 set out the performance targets and Specification N.4/43 indicated that the aircraft should combine Griffon VI engine and forward fuselage of Spitfire XII with rear fuselage, tail unit and u/c of Spitfire VIII and wings of Seafire III.

Seafire F Mk XV: Designation of first Griffon-engined Seafire variant (Supermarine Type 377), conforming to Specification N.4/43. Prototype (NS487) completed December 1943 with Griffon VI and 'A'-frame hook, as standardised for early-production type. Second prototype (NS490) tested 'sting'-type arrester hook, adopted for final production batches. Production total 434 by Westland (250) and Cunliffe Owen (184). Deliveries began March 1945; no wartime service.
Max speed, 383 mph (616 km/h) at 13,500 ft (4,115 m). Gross weight, 8,000 lb (3,629 kg). Span, 36 ft 10 in (11.23 m). Length, 32 ft 3 in (9.90 m).

Seafire F Mk XVII: Similar to F Mk XV, with cut-down rear fuselage and 360-deg vision canopy. Second Mk XV prototype converted to Mk XVII prototype, early

Above: The third Seafire Mk XV prototype, NS493, after conversion to serve as the prototype F Mk XVII, with tear-drop cockpit canopy and curved windscreen. Below right: A Westland-built Seafire F Mk XVII, SW991, with sting hook, in June 1945.

1945. Production (Supermarine Type 386) switched from Mk XV to Mk XVII, and 232 built, but all service post-war, as was camera-equipped **Seafire FR Mk XVII**.

Seafire F Mk XVIII: Proposed armed photo-recce variant of F Mk XVII with Griffon 37 engine. One prototype ordered (Supermarine Type 395), not completed.

Seafire F Mk 45: Navalised variant of Spitfire F Mk 21, to meet OR.167 and as defined by Specification N.7/44. Three prototypes ordered August 1944, to be converted from Spitfire F Mk 21 airframes built by CBAF. First prototype (TM379) flown October 1944, with 2,035 hp Griffon 61 engine and five-bladed propeller; armament, four 20-mm cannon. Also flown with Griffon 87 and contra-prop. Production plans reduced to 50 aircraft (Supermarine Type 388) when war ended; first completed

Above: The first of six Seafire XV prototypes, NS487, in February 1944. Below: The second prototype, NS490, on trials with both types of arrester hook extended.

January 1945. No wartime service. **Seafire F Mk 46** and **F Mk 47** were post-war developments.

SUPERMARINE SPITEFUL

A single-seat high-performance fighter proposed by Supermarine team led by Joseph Smith in 1942 and subsequently developed to conform to Specification F.1/43 and OR.120. Used new laminar-flow wing (Supermarine Type 371) with four 20-mm cannon armament, matched to a Spitfire F Mk XIV fuselage with further refinements, and a 2,375 hp Rolls-Royce Griffon 69 engine. Orders for three prototypes and initial production batches placed in 1943. Prototype (NN660) flown on June 30, 1944, with Griffon 61 in modified Spitfire F Mk XIV fuselage. Second prototype

Above: The fourth of the Westland-built batch of Seafire XVs in late 1944; only the A-frame hook was fitted. Below: A Seafire F Mk XV – with wing-tips folded – is struck down on the carrier lift. This is believed to show NS487 aboard HMS Illustrious in March 1944.

Above: The first production Spiteful F Mk XIV: the mark number was adopted as the design was based on combining the Spitfire F Mk XIV fuselage with the new laminar-flow wing. Below right, top to bottom: The three prototypes of the Spiteful were NN660 (Experimental Aeroplane 228) which used the original Spitfire XIV fuselage and tail unit; NN664 which introduced the all-round view cockpit but retained the original tail, and NN667 with the definitive tail, and the carburettor air intake extended to just behind the spinner.

(NN664) flown on January 8, 1945, with modified fuselage and enlarged fin and rudder; third prototype (NN667) flown after war had ended. First production **Spiteful F Mk XIV** flown on April 2, 1945, but programme cancelled with only 16 production aircraft flown, and no service use.
Max speed, 483 mph (777 km/h) at 21,000 ft (6,400 m). Gross weight, 11,400 lb (5,170 kg). Span, 35 ft 0 in (10.67 m). Length, 32 ft 11 in (10.3 m).

TAYLORCRAFT PLUS C
Two-seat light aircraft based on American Taylorcraft Model B design built under licence by Taylorcraft Aeroplanes (England) Ltd at Thurmaston, Leics. First British-built example flown May 3, 1939 at Ratcliffe. Eighteen civil Plus Cs impressed

in July/August 1941 for service with No 651 AOP Sqn at Old Sarum, initially powered by 85 hp Lycoming O-145-A2 engines. Fourteen surviving aircraft modified late 1941/early 1942 to have 90 hp Blackburn Cirrus Minor Is, when redesignated Taylorcraft Plus C/2.
Cruising speed, 90 mph (145 km/h). Gross weight, 1,300 lb (590 kg). Span, 36 ft 0 in (10.98 m). Length, 22 ft 11½ in (6.99 m).

TAYLORCRAFT PLUS D
Two-seat light aircraft derived from Plus C, with 90 hp Blackburn Cirrus Minor I engine. Eleventh British airframe completed as first Model D (T9120) for Army trials at Old Sarum in December 1939 in AOP role. Five civil Plus Ds built late-1939, all impressed or allocated for use at School of

Army Co-operation by 'D' Flight (later, No 1424 Flight, RAF, and then 43 OTU), and evaluated in France, April/May 1940.
Cruising speed, 90 mph (145 km/h). Gross weight, 1,400 lb (636 kg). Span, 36 ft 0 in (10.98 m). Length, 22 ft 11½ in (6.99 m).

TAYLORCRAFT AUSTER
Two-seat (side-by-side) lightplane, developed from Plus C and Plus D to meet Army requirements for an Air Observation Post. Initial contracts placed 1941 for 101 Auster Mk Is and subsequent contracts for later marks kept the type in production throughout the war, as below; Mks 7 to 9 appeared post-war. Used by at least 19 AOP squadrons, and other Army formations.
   Auster AOP Mk I: Similar to Taylorcraft Plus D, with 90 hp Blackburn Cirrus Minor I. First flown early 1942 and entered service with No 651 Sqn, August 1952. Normally flown solo in service; 101 built.
   Auster AOP Mk II: Two prototypes with 130 hp Lycoming O-290-3 engines; otherwise as Mk I.
   Auster AOP Mk III: Improved AOP

Above: Seafire F Mk 45 prototype TM379, first flown with a Griffon 61 and five-bladed propeller, later had a Griffon 87 and contra-prop, as shown here, with additional fin area. Below: Early production Seafire F Mk 45 LA432 in standard configuration.

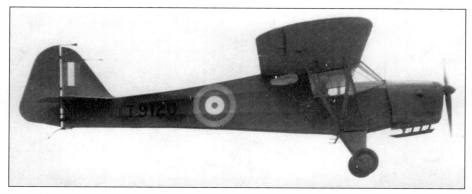

Left: T9120 was the first military Taylorcraft, a Plus D built for Army trials late-1939. Above: One of the production batch of Auster AOP Mk Is, LB296 went to No 653 Sqn and, later, 43 OTU.

with 130 hp DH Gipsy Major I engine. Fitted with wing flaps. Deliveries began early 1943 and total of 470 built. Used initially by Nos 655, 656 and 657 AOP Squadrons.

Auster AOP Mk IV: Similar to Mk III but with 130 hp Lycoming O-290-3 engine, third seat in rear of cabin and enlarged window area. Entered service in 1944 and 254 built.

Auster AOP Mk V: Similar to Mk IV but fitted with blind-flying panel. Total of 788 built, of which two fitted with floats for evaluation at the MAEE. Production ended January 1946.

Max speed, 130 mph (209 km/h) at sea level. Cruising speed, 110 mph (177 km/h). Range, about 300 mls (483 km). Gross weight, 1,700 lb (772 kg). Span, 36 ft 0 in (10.98 m). Length, 22 ft 5 in (6.84 m). Wing area, 167 sq ft (15.5 m²).

Auster AOP Mk VI: Based on Mk V, but with 145 hp DH Gipsy Major VII, new

Above: The Auster III (MT407 illustrated) featured increased cockpit transparencies aft of the wing, and a Gipsy Major engine.

undercarriage and auxiliary aerofoil flaps. Prototype flown on May 1, 1945; production and service use post-war.

TAYLORCRAFT MODEL H

One Taylorcraft airframe (actually a US-built Model B, imported pre-war as G-

Above: Most-produced of the war-time Auster variants, the AOP Mk V was powered by a Lycoming engine, had a blind-flying panel and, replacing the Mk III's skid, a tailwheel.

Above left: The Auster V TJ207 (ex Aero 241) was fitted with floats and evaluated at the MAEE in 1944. Several other float-equipped Austers were used post-war. Above right: First flown as the war in Europe ended, the Auster AOP Mk VI introduced auxiliary aerofoil flaps: prototype TJ707 is illustrated. Below: The private venture Model H glider, tested in 1943, is seen here at No 46 SLG Brinklow for ATC use in 1944. (Photo, courtesy M P Marsh).

AFKO) completed by Taylorcraft Aeroplanes (England) as a two/three-seat glider to investigate the practicability of using such an aircraft to train glider pilots. Forward fuselage lengthened to compensate for lack of engine. Testing began on July 6, 1943, but no official interest was shown and in 1944 the Model H (which carried neither serial number nor civil registration) was transferred to an ATC Gliding School at Bretford, Leics.

Take-off run (towed), 1,500 ft (457 m); rate of climb (on tow), 600 ft/min (3.05 m/sec). Full-flap stalling speed, 26 mph (42 km/h). Gross weight, 1,080 lb (490 kg). Span, 36 ft 0 in (10.98 m). Length, 24 ft 0 in (7.32 m).

VICKERS VIRGINIA

Twin-engined heavy night-bomber developed to meet D of R Type 4A requirement and produced in conformity with Specification 1/21. Production totalled 124 up to December 1932, all for RAF, in succession of marks up to Mk X, and in accordance with Specifications 28/23, 12/24, 10/26, 8/27, 13/28 and 5/31. Out of front-line service by early 1938, but several Virginia Xs (Vickers Type 268) remained in service at the Home Aircraft Depot's Parachute Training Flight at RAF Henlow. Powered by a pair of 580 hp Napier Lion VB engines, the final Virginia X was retired at Henlow in September 1941.

Max speed, 108 mph (173.8 km/h) at 5,000 ft (1,524 m). Gross weight, 17,600 lb (7,983 kg). Span, 87 ft 8 in (26.72 m). Length, 62 ft 2³/4 in (18.99 m).

Below: One of a handful of Virginia Xs that survived at Henlow into 1940/41 as parachute trainers, K2329 is seen here in pre-war service in the same role.

Above: One of the 11 Valentias tran-ferred to the SAAF in 1940, K2801 acquired the serial 265. Right: Vickers Valentia K5605 arrived in Hinaidi in March 1936 for service with No 70 Sqn, with which it remained until struck off charge in November 1940.

VICKERS VALENTIA I

Twin-engined troop and cargo transport, developed during 1933 as an enhanced derivative of the Victoria to Specification 25/33. Production of 28 to Specification 30/34 (Vickers Type 264) supplemented by conversion of 54 Victorias (Type 278). Powered by two 650 hp Bristol Pegasus IIL3 engines, the Valentia entered service with No 216 Sqn in the Middle East in September 1935 and was later used by No 70 Sqn and (with Pegasus IIM3 engines) by No 31 Sqn in India. Sixty Valentias were on RAF strength in September 1939 and were much used in North Africa until 1942, and with the Iraq and Persia Communications Flight until May 1944. The Valentia could carry up to 2,200 lb (998 kg) of bombs on wing racks and was sometimes used in the bombing role. Eleven Valentias transferred to SAAF in 1940.

Max speed, 120 mph (193 km/h) at 5,000 ft (1,525 m). Gross weight, 19,500 lb (8,845 kg). Span, 87 ft 4 in (26.62 m). Length, 59 ft 6 in (18.13 m).

VICKERS VILDEBEEST

Two/three-seat coastal defence biplane designed by RK Pierson to meet Specification 24/25 and first flown in April 1928. Production initiated late-1931 to Specification 22/31, with successive batches covering Mks I, II, III and IV to Specifications 20/33, 15/34 and 41/35, bringing the total for RAF to 173.

Vildebeest I: Vickers Type 244. 600 hp Pegasus IM3. Two-seat torpedo-bomber. 22 built; none on strength in 1939.

Vildebeest II: Vickers Type 258. 635 hp Pegasus IIM3 and detailed improvements. Two-seat torpedo-bomber. Thirty built for RAF.

Vildebeest III: Vickers Type 267. As Mk

II but with third seat added for observer. Total 193 built for RAF and 12 for RNZAF (latter with folding wings; Vickers Type 277).

Vildebeest IV: Vickers Type 286. 825 hp Bristol Pegasus VIII. Two-seat torpedo-bomber. Eighteen built for RAF; found unsuitable for overseas use through engine overheating.

Service use of Vildebeest Is began with No 100 Sqn at Donibristle in October 1932; four other front-line units, Nos 22, 36, 42 and 273, equipped with Vildebeests subsequently and all five still flying these biplanes operationally when war began, with 101 Vildebeests in RAF inventory. In the UK, No 22 with Mk IIIs and No 42 with Mks III and IV, flew on shipping reconnaissance and convoy escort duties until April 1940. Nos 36 and 100 Sqns had six Mk IIs and 46

Mk IIIs in Singapore in December 1941, used in torpedo and bombing roles until withdrawn to Java and finally retired in March 1942. Six Mk IIIs served with No 273 Sqn in Ceylon, also until March 1942. The RNZAF purchased 12 Vildebeest IIIs from Vickers in 1935, supplemented by 10 Mk IIIs and 17 Mk IVs, ex-RAF, in 1940-41. These were used by several general reconnaissance squadrons and by No 2 FTS for training, with a few surviving as target tugs into 1944.

Data for Vildebeest III: Max speed, 143 mph (230 km/h). Initial rate of climb, 630 ft/min (3.2 m/sec). Range, 630 mls (1,014 km). Service ceiling, 17,000 ft (5,182 m). Empty weight, 4,773 lb (2,165 kg). Gross weight, 8,500 lb (3,856 kg). Span, 49 ft 0 in (14.94 m). Length, 36 ft 8 in (11.18 m). Wing area, 728 sq ft (67.6 m²).

Above: The Vincent K4712 serving with No 8 Sqn, which was in Aden when the war began. The long-range tank, in place of a torpedo, was the principal feature distinguishing the Vincent from the Vildebeest.

Left: A Vildebeest IV – distinguished by the cowled engine – attached to No 42 Sqn at Bircham Newton in September 1939. Below: Vildebeest III K6402 of No 36 Sqn, with which it remained operational until the end of 1941.

Above: A late pre-war photograph of the Vickers G.4/31 biplane prototype whilst serving the Bristol company as an engine test-bed. The engine installation shown here is thought to be a Pegasus X.

VICKERS VINCENT I

Three-seat general purpose biplane evolved from Vildebeest as Vickers Type 266 in response to Specification 21/33. Fitted with long-range tank in place of external torpedo stowage, message pick-up hook and equipment for tropical operations. Production (including conversion of contracted Vildebeests to Specification 16/34) totalled 196 for RAF, delivered from 1934 to 1936. Vincents served at various Middle East and African bases with eight front-line squadrons. Of these, at the outbreak of war No 8 Sqn had 18 in Aden, No 244 had 23 in Iraq and No 47 Sqn and other miscellaneous units had 42 in Sudan and Egypt. Limited operational use was made until 1942, and Vincents remained on communications and 'hack' duties until 1944. From July 1939, the RNZAF received 60 ex-RAF Vincents, for use as trainers and in general reconnaissance squadrons until May 1943. The Vincent was powered by the 660 hp Bristol Pegasus IIM3 and was armed with one Lewis and one Vickers 0.303-in (7.7-mm) machine gun; bomb load was 1,100 lb (499 kg).
Max speed, 143 mph (230 km/h) at 5,000 ft (1,524 m). Gross weight, 7,745 lb (3,513 kg).

Span, 49 ft 0 in (14.94 m). Length, 36 ft 8 in (11.18 m).

VICKERS G.4/31

Single prototype K2771 purchased by Air Ministry for evaluation to meet Specification G.4/31. Vickers Type 253 biplane with 620 hp Bristol Pegasus IIM3 engine, first flown August 16, 1934. Requirement eventually satisfied by Vickers Wellesley based on Type 246 monoplane built as PV to same specification. K2771 then became engine test-bed for Bristol Aeroplane Co at Filton, surviving to 1940. Successively fitted with 690 hp Pegasus IIIM3 and 980 hp Pegasus X.
Max speed, 161 mph (259 km/h) at 4,500 ft (1,372 m). Gross weight, 8,350 lb (3,788 kg). Span, 52 ft 7 in (16.04 m). Length, 37 ft 0 in (11.28 m).

VICKERS WELLESLEY I

Two/three-seat medium bomber monoplane designed by RK Pierson to meet Operational Requirement (OR) 24 as defined by Specification 22/35. Prototype (Vickers Type 281) first flew early 1936 as modification of original Vickers Type 246 PV monoplane prototype to Specification

G.4/31 (OR.2). First production Wellesley (Type 287) flew January 30, 1937, with 835 hp Bristol Pegasus XX; strengthened wing structure (Type 294) after first eight aircraft; production total 176. Service use began in No 76(B) Sqn, RAF Finningley in April 1937, followed by seven more squadrons in UK and Middle East in quick succession. Wartime use restricted to three squadrons in North Africa, Nos 14, 47 and 223, making up No 203 Group's Advanced Striking Force operating against Italian forces in East Africa. Of these, No 47 continued flying Wellesleys until September 1942. Armament comprised one fixed forward and one flexibly mounted 0.303-in (7.7-mm) machine gun, and up to 2,000 lb (908 kg) of bombs.
Max speed, 228 mph (367 km/h) at 19,680 ft (6,000 m). Cruising speed, 180 mph (290 km/h). Time to 15,000 ft (4,572 m), 21 min. Service ceiling, 22,500 ft (6,858 m). Range, 1,335 mls (2,148 km). Empty weight, 6,760 lb (3,066 kg). Gross weight, 12,500 lb (5,670 kg). Span, 74 ft 7 in (22.74 m). Length, 39 ft 3 in (11.96 m). Wing area, 586 sq ft (54.4 m²).

VICKERS WELLINGTON
(Bomber variants)

Twin-engined day bomber to meet Operational Requirement OR.5 and conforming to Specification B.9/32, designed under Rex Pierson and Barnes Wallis. Initial studies (as Vickers Type 249) with R-R Goshawk or Bristol Perseus engines, but definitive prototype (Type 271) as ordered in September 1933 powered by 980 hp Bristol Pegasus X engines. Geodetic construction, gross weight of 21,000 lb (9,526 kg) and defensive armament of single 0.303-in (7.7-mm) guns in nose, tail and dorsal positions. Unarmed, prototype K4049 first flown at Weybridge on June 15, 1936; provisionally known as Crecy until name Wellington confirmed in September. Lost on April 19, 1937, during A&AEE trials at Martlesham Heath, by which time first production contract placed.

Wellington I: Initial production version, as defined by Specification 29/36, to be armed with pairs of Browning 0.303-in (7.7-mm) guns in Vickers nose and tail, and Frazer-Nash ventral (in place of dorsal) gun positions. Gross weight, 21,000 lb (9,527 kg) with up to nine 500-lb (227-kg) or two 2,000-lb (907-kg) bombs. First production aircraft flown with Pegasus X engines (as Vickers Type 285) on December

Above: Wellesley I K7775 operating in the Sudan with No 47 Sqn in 1940. Below: Wellesley I K8528, also in service with No 47 Sqn, flying off the Palestine coast in late 1942. This photo shows the little-used extended glazing between the two cockpits.

Above: Wellington IA P9299 did not reach No 115 Sqn until March 1940, yet carried the pre-war codes 'BK' rather than the wartime 'KO'.

Above: A late pre-war photograph of a Wellington I L4332, serving with No 37 Sqn, showing the original Vickers-designed nose and tail gun positions. Left: Wellington III Z1732 operating with No 12 OTU.

23, 1937, and with definitive 815 hp Pegasus XVIIIs (Type 290) on April 12, 1938. Total of 175 built at Weybridge (of which 61 with dual controls and two completed as Mks II and III prototypes) and three at Vickers-operated shadow factory at Broughton, Chester. RNZAF order for 30 Wellingtons (Type 403) placed in 1937 to be met by diversions from RAF contracts. First six (NZ300-NZ305) at RAF Marham for conversion training of New Zealand Flight handed back to RAF in September 1939 and re-acquired original RAF serials. Most or all Mk Is flown without planned FN9 ventral turret because of CG difficulties. Initial deliveries October 1938, to No 99 Sqn at Mildenhall; eight more squadrons equipped by September 1939. First operations September 4, 1939, by Nos 9 and 149 Sqns.

Wellington IA: Similar to Mk I, but with Frazer-Nash two-gun turrets – FN5 nose, FN10 tail and FN9 ventral – plus general airframe improvements designed for Mks II and III. Gross weight 28,000 lb (12,700 kg) and strengthened u/c. Deliveries began August 1939, and production (Vickers Type 408) totalled 170 from Weybridge and 17 from Chester. Replaced Wellington Is in initial squadrons and in service by December 1939. Balance of RNZAF order (see Wellington I) for 24 Mk IAs (Type 412) absorbed into RAF production, and No 75 (NZ) Sqn, with No 3 Group of Bomber Command, issued with Wellington IAs and ICs from RAF stocks. Designation **Wellington IB** reserved for Mk I with armament improvements; not built.

Wellington IC: Similar to Mk IA, but FN9 ventral turret deleted. Two belt-fed 0.303-in (7.7-mm) Brownings in beam mountings, one each side. Electrical system changed from 12 to 24-volt, and hydraulic system revised. Production (Vickers Type 405) totalled 1,056 at Weybridge (of which four completed as later marks), 1,583 at Chester and 50 at Vickers-operated shadow factory at Squires Gate, Blackpool. Bomb-load could include one 4,000-lb (1,814-kg) bomb on 33 Mk ICs with Vickers Type 453 modification. Deliveries from April 1940, and formed backbone of Bomber Command through 1941, primarily in squadrons of 3 Group. Operational in Middle East from September 1940, initially with No 70 Sqn, RAF, and in the Far East (India) from April 1942, initially with No 214 Sqn. One to

CLE in March 1942, with parachute exit in place of ventral turret.
Max speed, 234 mph (377 km/h) at 15,200 ft (4,633 m). Economical cruising speed, 165 mph (266 km/h) at 10,000 ft (3,050 m). Time to 10,000 ft (3,050 m), 25 min. Service ceiling, 16,000 ft (4,877 m). Range with max bombs, 1,055 mls (1,698 km). Empty weight, 18,800 lb (8,528 kg). Gross weight, 30,000 lb (13,608 kg). Span, 86 ft 2 in (26.26 m). Length, 64 ft 7 in (19.69 m). Wing area, 830 sq ft (77.11 m²).

Wellington II: Developed during 1938 as first major Wellington upgrade, in parallel with Mk III, to take advantage of uprated engines. Based on Mk I airframe with 1,145 hp R-R Merlin X engines; Frazer-Nash FN5 (nose) and FN10 (tail) turrets plus beam guns; 28,000 lb (12,700 kg) gross weight with strengthened u/c and – after early testing – wider-chord tailplane. One Mk I completed as Mk II prototype (Vickers Type 298), flown on March 3, 1939. Deliveries began October 1940 and 400 built (Type 406) at Weybridge. Gross weight increased to 33,000 lb (14,990 kg) and 22 with the Type 423 mod for 4,000-lb (1,814-kg) bomb, first used by Nos 9 and 149 Sqns on night of March 31/April 1, 1941. Also served in Middle East, with earlier marks.

Wellington III: Developed in parallel with Wellington II, with same new features but powered by Bristol Hercules engines. One Mk I completed as Mk III prototype

(Vickers Type 299), flown on March 19, 1939, with two-stage supercharged Hercules HE-1SM engines. Production Mk III (Type 417) powered by 1,400 hp Hercules II engines, as tested on second prototype (Mk IC conversion) early 1941, or 1,590 hp Hercules XIs. Four-gun FN20A tail turret in place of two-gun FN10, and gross weight increased to 34,500 lb (15,650 kg). Production total 780 at Chester and 737 at Blackpool, delivered 1942-43. Succeeded or supplemented Mk ICs in 3 Group in the UK, 205 Group in the Middle East and 221 Group in Far East. Also used by six Canadian-manned squadrons of 6 Group in UK during 1943, and for Special Duties units of 100 Group in 1943/44.
Max speed, 261 mph (420 km/h) at 12,500 ft (3,810 m). Economical cruising speed, 211 mph (340 km/h). Time to 15,000 ft (4,572 m), 25 min. Service ceiling, 22,750 ft (6,934 m). Range with max bombs, 1,200 mls (1,931 km). Empty weight, 25,100 lb (11,385 kg). Gross weight, 34,500 lb (15,650 kg). Dimensions as Mk IC.

Wellington IV: Similar to Mk III with 1,050 hp Pratt & Whitney R-1830-S3C4-G Twin Wasp engines. Prototype (Mk IC conversion) completed at Chester, December 1940, followed by 219 production examples (Vickers Type 410) delivered from June 1941. First operational use October 16, 1941.

Above right: An engine option for the Wellington was the R-1830 Twin Wasp, distinguishing the Mk IV variant. Below: Demand for Merlin engines for other programmes limited production of the Wellington II to only 400 aircraft; this one carries the markings of No 104 Sqn in 1941.

Wellington V and VI: High-altitude bomber variants using pressurised crew accommodation. See separate entry below.

Wellington VII: Designation reserved for Mk II derivative with 1,390 hp Merlin XX powerplants. Not built.

Wellington B Mk X: Final variant for Bomber Command, based on definitive Mk III but powered by 1,615 hp Bristol Hercules VI or XVI engines. Improved DTD646 aluminium alloy used throughout, with better strength-weight ratio, allowing gross weight to increase to 36,500 lb (16,556 kg). Two Mk IIIs with Hercules VI engines flown as prototypes (Type 440) at Blackpool. Production (Type 448) totalled 1,369 at Blackpool and 2,434 at Chester. Served in the Bomber Command Wellington squadrons that remained operational until October 1943; and in others on special duties and in Middle and Far East through 1944. Wellington production ended with delivery of a B Mk X at Blackpool on October 25, 1945, bringing overall total built to 11,461 – the most multi-engine aircraft of any single type ever built in Britain.

Above: The second prototype Wellington V, R3299, at the A&AEE in April 1942. Notice the small, off-set, cockpit hood and the engine-driven super-charger on the Hercules VIII engine. Right: The first Wellington V, R3298, with unsupercharged Hercules IIIs and larger canopy with D/F loop within. This was Experimental Aeroplane 130.

VICKERS WELLINGTON
(High-altitude bomber variants)

The Wellington IC airframe provided basis for adaptation as a high-altitude bomber, conforming to Specification B.23/39. Requirement was for a three-man crew, ability to bomb from 35,000 ft (10,668 m) or above, and to have an endurance of more than nine hours. Pressurisation was to begin at 15,000 ft (4,572 m), the altitude specified for cruise to and from the target.

Wellington V: Two prototypes (R3298, R3299) by conversion of Mk IC airframes, ordered in May 1939, as Vickers Type 407 with high-altitude Bristol Hercules VIII engines. Rear turret retained but pressure cell extended into nose, replacing forward turret, and accommodated rear gunner during high-altitude portion of flight. First prototype flown September 1940 with 1,400 hp Hercules IIIs (as Type 421); second prototype had 1,650 hp Hercules VIIIs and smaller 'blister' dome for pilot's head in place of longer canopy on first prototype. Production batch of 30 Mk Vs ordered to Specification 17/40, in compliance with Operational Requirement OR.94, to have Hercules VIII (Type 426) or Hercules 38 (Type 448) engines. One only (W5796) completed as Mk V; 20 as Mk VI (see below) and nine cancelled.

Wellington VI: Similar to Mk V, with 1,280 hp Rolls-Royce Merlin 60 engines.

First of production-batch Mk Vs (W5795, Vickers Type 431), completed as prototype Mk VI and flown in late 1941, followed by 19 more from Mk V contract and 44 from new production contract (for 100; others cancelled) placed in 1941. Standard FN20A turret retained, but gunner in pressure cell at all times, using periscopic sight in underside of fuselage. Basic type (28 aircraft) as Wellington VIA (Vickers Type 442), but final 35 were Wellington VIG (Type 449) without rear turret, and with Oboe blind-bombing aid. Two Wellington VIG used operationally by No 109(SD) Sqn, and others to train crews in use of Oboe.

Max speed, 300 mph (483 km/h). Service ceiling, 38,500 ft (11,735 m). Range, 2,275 mls (3,661 km) with 15,000-lb (6,804-kg) bombs. Empty weight, 20,280 lb (9,200 kg). Gross weight, 30,450 lb (13,812 kg). Span, 86 ft 2 in (26.26 m). Length, 61 ft 9 in (18.82 m). Wing area, 840 sq ft (78.04 m²).

VICKERS WELLINGTON
(Maritime variants)

The first of several major variants of the Wellington adapted to the maritime role was a highly-specialised mine sweeper, designated as the Wellington DWI, acronym for the deliberately misleading title Directional Wireless Installation. Subsequent adaptations for Coastal Command use took the GR role prefix for

Below: Built as a Wellington III, X3595 flew with No 75 Sqn and retained the latter's markings at the time of its conversion to a B Mk X as shown, although its subsequent deployment was only with various OTUs. Above left: The high-altitude Hercules 38 engine, intended for the production-model Wellington Vs flew only in this B Mk X, HF616.

Above: The third of the Wellington VIs, W5798 (ex Aero 196) on test at the A&AEE in November 1942. The configuration was in general similar to the Mk V, apart from the switch from Hercules to high-altitude Merlin 60 engines. Below: One of the later production Wellington VIs, with the tail turret removed, used as trainers for the Oboe bombing aid.

General Reconnaissance. The five GR marks were flown by a total of 22 squadrons based in the UK, Iceland and the Middle and Far East.

Wellington DWI: To combat the magnetic mines dropped around British shores early in the war, RAE and Admiralty Research Laboratory urgently developed a degaussing system comprising a ring of 51-ft (15.55-m) diameter, which when energised by electric current and flown at low speed and altitude above the mines, caused them to explode. A prototype installation fitted to Wellington IA (P2516) included a Ford V-8 in the fuselage to drive a 350 kW generator, and was first flown at Boscombe Down on December 21, 1939. Three further conversions were designated **Wellington DWI Mk I** (Vickers Type 418) and were in service by February 1940. Eleven **Wellington DWI Mk IIs** (Type 419) followed, based on ex-Bomber Command Wellington Is with DH Gipsy Six engine driving a 95 kW generator, and with degaussing ring reduced to 48 ft (14.67 m) diameter. After UK service, some Mk IIs transferred to Middle East for service with No 1 GRU, operating over Mediterranean and Suez Canal. Few additional conversions made in Middle East using components shipped from UK.

Wellington GR Mk VIII: Coastal Command variant based on Pegasus-engined Wellington IC airframe, for anti-submarine and anti-shipping patrol, initially identified as DWI Mk III. Combined ASV Mk II radar (with four 'stickleback' aerials on rear fuselage and 'yagi' aerials under wings) with searchlight to illuminate ships or U-boats at night. Initial comparative trials during 1941 of Wellington IC P9223 (an ex-DWI Mk I, using generator already installed) with Leigh light in retractable ventral installation, and Wellington IC T2977 with Helmore wide-angle searchlight in nose. Leigh light adopted, and production of Wellington VIII initiated later in 1941, initially by conversion of Mk IC airframes

already in production against bomber contracts. Wellington VIII (Vickers Type 429) had 30,000-lb (13,608-kg) gross weight, engine-generated electrical supply, provision to carry two 420-lb (191-kg) depth charges, crew of five or six, and ASV Mk II radar. Total of 394 delivered from Weybridge, of which 54 had the Leigh light and no nose turret; 49 (without Leigh light) had long-range tankage and (all but first 65) could carry two 18-in (45.7-cm) torpedoes in the bomb-bay. Squadron use began in No 172 Sqn; first 'kill' using Leigh light on July 6, 1942, against U-502.

Max speed, 235 mph (378 km/h). Service ceiling, 19,000 ft (5,791 m). Range, 2,550 mls (4,104 km). Empty weight, 21,118 lb (9,579 kg). Gross weight, 30,000 lb (13,608 kg). Span, 86 ft 2 in (26.26 m). Length, 64 ft 7 in (19.68 m). Wing area, 840 sq ft (78.04 m²).

Wellington GR Mk XI: Daytime torpedo bomber based on B Mk X airframe with Hercules VI or XVI engines, and FN20A four-gun rear turret. Initially with ASV Mk II 'stickleback' radar; later with ASV centimetric radar using disc-type scanner in radome under nose fairing (with nose turret replaced by Perspex fairing). Production total (Vickers Type 454 with ASV Mk II, Type 458 with ASV Mk III), 105 at Weybridge and 75 at Squires Gate, Blackpool. Served with Coastal Command squadrons in UK, Middle East and Far East, and with No 26 Sqn, SAAF, flying protective patrols from West Africa.

Wellington GR Mk XII: Night and daytime torpedo bomber, similar to Mk XI with ASV Mk III, with addition of retractable ventral Leigh light. Production total (Vickers Type 455), 50 from Weybridge and eight from Chester.

Wellington GR Mk XIII: As GR Mk XI, but with Hercules XVII engines, rated at 1,725 hp for low altitudes, better suited

Above right: Wellington IC HX682 was one of the first conversions to DWI Mk I mine-sweeping configuration, serving in North Africa with 1 GRU and later No 162 Sqn. Below: Wellington IC W5674 of No 221 Sqn, after conversion to GR Mk VIII in mid-1941, with ASV Mk II but, like the majority of this mark, without the Leigh light. Right: Wellington GR Mk XIII JA144, in full Coastal Command finish.

Above: A Wellington GR Mk XIV of No 38 Sqn, featuring ASV Mk III in the nose radome, and retracted ventral Leigh light. Below: One of the Wellington XIIIs, NC588, used – in day bomber colours – by No 69 Sqn for the visual observation role by night or day.

dummy guns. Eventually, designations **Wellington C Mk XV** and **C Mk XVI** adopted for freight and passenger transport versions respectively. Users included Nos 232 and 242 Sqns, as well as No 24.

VICKERS WELLINGTON
(Trainer variants)

Some of the earliest Wellingtons were fitted with dual controls to help crew conversion, without change of designation. More specific trainer variants emerged in 1944 and 1945 and were identified as follows.

Wellington T Mk X: Converted B Mk Xs for use as navigation trainers at No 6 Air Navigation School, principally post-war (when designation style changed to T Mk 10, service use continuing until March 1953).

Wellington T Mk XVII: Conversions of GR Mk XI to train night-fighter crews, with Hercules VI engines, fitted with SCR 720 radar in nose radome. Vickers Type 487.

Wellington T Mk XVIII: Conversions of GR Mk XIII to train radar operators, with Hercules XVII engines, SCR 720 radar as T Mk XVII, and provision for four pupils and instructor in fuselage. Vickers Type 490. Approximately 80 conversions, delivered from late 1944.

Wellington T Mk XIX: Early designation for B Mk X trainer conversion; see T Mk X.

to maritime patrol operations. ASV Mk III as standard. Production total (Vickers Type 466), 802 from Blackpool and 42 from Weybridge. In addition to service with Coastal Command squadrons, Mk XIIIs used to equip No 69 Sqn, RAF, in specialised night visual tactical reconnaissance role in 1944-45. ASV removed and clear Perspex nose fairing in place of turret, for visual observation. Stowage for 54 flares in fuselage (dropped from 3,000 ft/915 m) and open-shutter moving film camera fitted for use at 1,000 ft (305 m).

Wellington GR Mk XIV: As GR Mk XII but fitted with low-altitude Hercules XVII engines as in Mk XIII. Production total (Vickers Type 467), 538 from Chester, 250 from Blackpool and 53 from Weybridge.

VICKERS WELLINGTON
(Transport variants)

Plans for a troop-transport conversion of the basic Wellington bomber were drawn up initially to meet an urgent requirement in the Middle East, as Vickers Type 437. Designation **Wellington IX** assigned, but probably applicable only to converted Mk IC P2522, which served with No 24 Sqn in 1942-43. Further conversions for use by No 24 Sqn took designation **Wellington C Mk IA** or **C Mk IC**, depending on original bomber variant converted, and were of several configurations, some with rounded nose and tail fairings, others with turret-shaped fairings, suitably painted and fitted with

Above: The 'Duke of Rutland' was an example of the Wellington passenger transport conversion, used by No 24 Sqn. Note the nose and tail fairings in place of turrets.

Above: The 'Duke of Cornwall', N2990, was another of No 24 Sqns transport Wellington C Mk IAs, in this case a freighter, without cabin windows and with dummy nose and tail turrets.

Above: Wellington N2875 was a further example of the C Mk XVI – in this case with shorter cabin windows and no attempt to suggest turrets. Below: A late wartime Wellington conversion from bomber to T Mk X trainer, RP550 flew with No 1689 Flight.

Externally, the Wellington T Mk XVII (above) and T Mk XVIII (below) were virtually indistinguishable externally; both had SCR720 radar in the nose for the training of night-fighter observers.

VICKERS WARWICK

Advanced twin-engined heavy bomber designed to meet Operational Requirement OR.19 as expressed through Specification B.1/35 in mid-1935. Vickers proposed its Type 284 as essentially an enlarged Wellington with overload weight of 36,000 lb (16,330 kg) carrying 7,500-lb (3,402-lb) bomb-load over a range of 1,840 mls (2,961 km). One prototype (K8178) ordered October 1935, first flown August 13, 1939, powered by two 1,800 hp Rolls-Royce Vulture II engines, with twin-gun Frazer Nash nose (FN5) and tail (FN10) turrets plus provision for dorsal (FN9) and ventral (FN27) turrets. Second prototype (L9704) first flown April 5, 1940, with Bristol Centaurus engines; dorsal turret added later, and then re-engined with Pratt & Whitney R-2800 Double Wasp engines.

Warwick B Mk I: Subject of production order for 150 bombers placed in January 1941, to be powered by R-2800-S1A4-G engines (Vickers Type 422). First production aircraft flown April 1942, but bomber role for Warwick abandoned in January 1943 and only 17 completed in this configuration.

Warwick B Mk II: One hundred ordered at same time as B Mk Is, to be powered by 2,300 hp Centaurus IV engines (Vickers Type 413). None built as such; one B Mk I converted to have Centaurus engines in July 1943 served as engine test-bed, later with 2,500 hp Centaurus VIIIs.

Warwick C Mk I: Fourteen B Mk Is completed as mail/freight transports (Vickers Type 456), with all turrets deleted, cabin windows fitted and extra fuel tankage. First flight February 5, 1943. Intended to meet urgent BOAC need for service in Middle East and Africa, but not approved because of poor single-engine performance. Reverted to RAF and issued in 1944 to No 525 Sqn, later used by No 167 Sqn.

Warwick C Mk III: Definitive freight/passenger transport variant (Vickers Type 460) based on Warwick B Mk I, with nose and tail fairings in place of turrets, ventral paratroop exit, side door for stretcher loading, and freight pannier in bomb-bay. First C Mk III flown spring 1944 and 100 built. Gross weight up to 45,000 lb (20,412 kg) and small dorsal fin fitted retrospectively. Entered service with No 525 Sqn, June/July 1944.

Warwick C Mk IV: Reserved designation for transport variant similar to C Mk III, but with Centaurus engines as B Mk II. Not built.

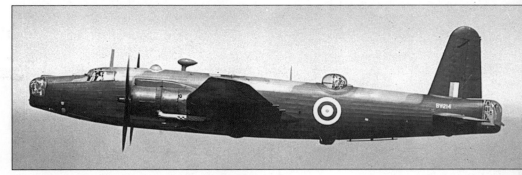

Above: The first production Warwick B Mk I, BV214, on test in May 1942. It carries nose, tail, dorsal and ventral turrets, but guns were yet to be fitted. Right: The Vulture-engined Warwick prototype K8178 in August 1939: Experimental Aeroplane 104 in the AP.1480X.

Warwick ASR Mk I: Version of Warwick B Mk I for 'deep search' air-sea rescue. Ventral turret deleted but nose, tail and dorsal turrets retained and Airborne Lifeboat Mk I fitted in/under bomb-bay. Airframes originally ordered and laid down as part of B Mk I production completed for ASR role (Vickers Type 462) included 40 as Warwick Bomber/ASR, able to carry two sets of Lindholme survival gear but not the lifeboat; 10 Warwick ASR (Stage A) able to carry either the 'boat or Lindholme gear; 20 Warwick ASR (Stage B) which added ASV radar and improved FN120A tail turret; and 149 Warwick ASR (Stage C). Last-mentioned had extra fuel tankage, and could carry improved Mk II Airborne Lifeboat (but not with Lindholme gear), and thus represented definitive Warwick ASR Mk I, of which 151 further examples built on new

Above: The first of 14 Warwick transports intended for, but not used by, BOAC. Left: Another of the 'civil' Warwicks, G-AGFJ, after its return to the RAF as BV255, operated as a C Mk I by No 525 Sqn.

Below: A Warwick C Mk III, HG215, one of the batch of 100 produced. A dorsal fin was added later. Right: Another of the C Mk IIIs, HG224, on test from the A&AEE with pannier removed.

contracts placed in May 1943. Engines in the ASR Mk I were R-2800-S1A4-G initially, and R-2800-47 in the final 95 examples (known to Vickers, but not to the RAF, as ASR Mk VI). Service use initiated late-1943 in No 281 Sqn, joined in 1944 by Nos 282 and 279 in the UK, and No 292 in India for a few months in 1945.

Warwick ASR Mk II: Reserved designation for ASR variant of B Mk II with Centaurus VII engines. Not built, but one ASR Mk I fitted with Centaurus as engine test-bed.

Warwick GR Mk II: Torpedo-bomber version for Coastal Command, based on B Mk II, with ability to carry three 18-in (46-cm) or two 24-in (61-cm) torpedoes or 12,250 lb (5,557 kg) of bombs. Fitted with ASV Mk III or VIB radar in radome under nose, which had single 0.50-in (12.7-mm) Browning gun in multi-faceted Perspex fairing; dorsal and tail turrets retained as in original bomber. Powered by 2,400 hp Bristol Centaurus VII engines but several used by Bristol's Centaurus Development Flight to test Centaurus XII and Centaurus 130. Production total 132 (Vickers Type 469); few used at OTUs but end of war precluded operational deployment.

Warwick GR Mk V: As GR Mk II, but with ventral Leigh light in retractable installation, and with dorsal turret removed in consequence. ASV Mk III or, later, AI Mk VIB or XVII radar. Gross weight increased to 51,250 lb (23,247 kg). First flown April 1944 and 210 built (Vickers Type 474). Issued to No 179 Sqn as the war ended, when further development then cancelled. Nos 17 and 27 Sqns, SAAF, each equipped

Above: Warwick ASR Mk I Stage C, HF944, with the short Mk IA lifeboat, in service late-1944 with No 282 Sqn. Left: The Warwick ASR Mk I BV403, from the original production order for bombers, on test with the long Mk II lifeboat.

with 16 GR Mk Vs in mid-1945, but disbanded upon return to South Africa later that year.

Max speed, 298 mph (480 km/h) at 3,500 ft (1,067 m). Cruising speed, 264 mph (425 km/h) at 9,500 ft (2,896 m). Rate of climb, 1,250 ft/min (6.35 m/sec). Service ceiling, 19,000 ft (5,791 m). Max range, 3,050 mls (4,908 km). Empty weight, 35,400 lb (16,057 kg). Gross weight, 51,250 lb (23,247 kg). Span, 96 ft 8½ in (29.46 m). Length, 73 ft 0 in (22.25 m). Wing area, 1,019 sq ft (94.67 m²).

VICKERS WINDSOR

High-performance long-range bomber evolved from 1941 onwards by Rex Pierson's design team, initially as pressurised Warwick III in accordance with Operational Requirement OR.106 and Specification B.5/41. Two prototypes ordered September 1942 to revised OR.115 and Specification B.3/42; two further proto-

types and two pre-production Windsor Is ordered later and plans for production batch of 300 (Vickers Type 483) drawn up, but only three prototypes eventually completed. Windsor designed to have four crew in pressure capsule within fuselage using geodetic construction, but pressurisation abandoned before first flight of prototype DW506 (Vickers Type 447) on October 23, 1943, at Farnborough. High aspect ratio wing of elliptical planform carried four 1,315 hp Rolls-Royce Merlin 65s, and four individual main undercarriage legs, one in each nacelle. Second prototype DW512 (Type 457) had 1,635 hp Merlin 85s in annular cowls and first flew on February 15, 1944. Third prototype NK136 (Type 480) had Merlin 85s and introduced remotely-controlled barbettes in tails of inner engine nacelles, each mounting a pair of 20-mm cannon, aimed from the (gunless) tail turret. With two 0.303-in (7.7-mm) Brownings in the nose, this prototype flew on July 11, 1944, and, with DW512, continued on test until after war ended, when further development and production were cancelled.

Max speed, 317 mph (510 km/h) at 23,000 ft (7,010 m). Gross weight 54,000 lb (24,495 kg). Span, 117 ft 2 in (35.71 m). Length, 76 ft 10 in (23.43 m).

Above: Warwick GR Mk II HG348, with dorsal turret, and below, a pair of GR Mk Vs serving as the war ended with No 179 Sqn at Chivenor, Devon. A ventral, retractable Leigh light replaced the dorsal turret in this mark.

VICKERS F.7/41

High-altitude single-seat fighter, initially in compliance with Specification F.22/39 to meet OR.76, but successively revised and redesigned to Specifications F.16/40 and F.7/41 (OR.108). Two prototypes ordered, but only one, DZ217 (Vickers Type 432) completed and flown, starting on December 24, 1942, at Farnborough. Powered by two 1,060 hp Rolls-Royce Merlin 61 engines, the Type 432 was to be armed with six 20-mm cannon in a ventral pack, and have a pressure cabin for the pilot, but the latter feature was never completed and development was abandoned at the end of 1943. Fewer than 30 flights made by single proto-type.

Max speed (design estimate), 440 mph (708 km/h) at 28,000 ft (8,534 m). Gross weight, 20,168 lb (9,148 kg). Span, 56 ft 10¹/₂ in (17.34 m). Length, 40 ft 7¹/₂ in (12.38 m).

WEIR W.5

Single-seat helicopter built as private venture by G & J Weir, which had previously built four prototype autogyros based on

Above: The second of the Windsor prototypes (ex Aero 215), DW512 continued to test for a few months after the end of the war. Below: The third Windsor, NK136, with provision for gun barbettes in the outer nacelle tails.

Cierva principles. Featured side-by-side two-bladed rotor configuration (inspired by Focke work in Germany) and a 50 hp Weir Pixie engine. First flown at Dalrymple on June 7, 1938 (first practical British heli-copter to fly) and believed to be still extant when war began, but probably not flown after September 1939.

Max speed, 70 mph (112.6 km/h). Gross weight, 860 lb (390 kg). Rotor diameter (each), 24 ft (7.3 m). Length of fuselage, 16 ft (4.9 m).

WEIR W.6

Single prototype two-seat helicopter ordered by Air Ministry to Operational Requirement OR.66 in 1938 after successful testing of W.5. Specification 28/38 written around Weir proposal and issued early 1939, calling for helicopter capable of hovering over fixed spot in 20-mph (32-km) wind for at least 15 minutes at height of at least 500 ft (152 m), with a rate of climb of 800 ft/min (4.06 m/sec) and service ceiling of 12,500 ft (3,810 m). Side-by-side three-bladed rotor configuration and powered by a 205 hp DH Gipsy Six Srs 2 engine. Tandem seating with provision for dual controls. Prototype R5269 first flown on October 27, 1939, and subsequently lifted three occupants (first helicopter in world to do so). Testing stopped in June 1940 after about 70 hrs completed, and aircraft stored for remainder of war. Second prototype reportedly planned as Z2130, not built.

Max speed, 90 mph (149 km/h). Gross weight, 2,360 lb (1,070 kg). Rotor diameter (each), 26 ft (7.92 m). Fuselage length, 22 ft (6.7 m).

Above: The sole Vickers F.7/41, DZ217, was identified as ex Aero 183. Below left: The Weir W.5, Britain's first practical helicopter and, below right, the W.6 (ex Aero 119), which continued on test until mid-1940.

WESTLAND WIDGEON

Light two-seat monoplane, designed by Arthur Davenport, originally to compete in Air Ministry Light Aeroplane Competition at Lympne in 1924, and first flown on September 22, 1924. Considerably redesigned for production as Widgeon III, first flown March 1927. Nineteen Widgeon IIIs of all-wood construction followed by five Widgeon IIIAs with metal fuselages. Of the latter, final example G-AAGH with a 105 hp Cirrus-Hermes I engine, built in 1930, retained as Westland's 'hack' and flown throughout war, in civil marks, for communications by Harald Penrose. One Widgeon III (VH-UHU) and one Widgeon IIIA (CF-AIQ) survived the war in Australia and Canada respectively, but were not used by the military.

Max speed, 104 mph (167 km/h). Gross weight, 1,650 lb (748 kg). Span, 36 ft 4¹/₂ in (11.07 m). Length, 23 ft 5¹/₄ in (7.16 m).

WESTLAND WESSEX

Six-seat, three-engined light transport, originating as Westland IV which first flew on February 21, 1929, with 95 hp ADC Cirrus III engines. Wessex featured uncowled 145 hp AS Genet Major IA engines and some detail refinements, and first flew in 1930. Both Westland IVs converted to Wessex standard and eight Wessex built as such, by 1933. Two aircraft, G-AAGW

Above: A South African-built, Jaguar-engined, Wapiti IIA of the SAAF, in wartime camouflage for service in a training and support role. Below: A British-built Wapiti II A serving at No 1 SFTS of the Indian Air Force in 1940.

(converted Westland IV) and G-ACHI in service in 1939 with No 3 E & RFTS operated by AST Ltd at Hamble, transferred to No 11 AONS in November 1939 and remained in service as navigation trainers until Cs of A expired in 1940. The last production Wessex went to Egyptian Air Force in 1934 and was still serving as a VIP transport in 1939 or later.

Max speed, 122 mph (196 km/h). Gross weight, 6,300 lb (2,858 kg). Span, 57 ft 6 in (17.53 m). Length, 38 ft 0 in (11.58 m).

WESTLAND WAPITI

Two-seat general purpose biplane developed to meet Specification 26/27 as D.H.9A replacement. Designed by Arthur Davenport to use many D.H.9A components, first prototype powered by 420 hp direct-drive Bristol Jupiter VI and flown March 7, 1927. Production of 25 mixed-construction Wapiti Is initiated in 1927, for service with RAF squadrons in India. Ten all-metal Wapiti IIs with 480 hp geared Jupiter VIII engines delivered in 1930 led to definitive Wapiti IIA. Variants that survived to serve during war were as follows:

Wapiti IIA: Major production version for the RAF, originating in 1928 as variant of Wapiti II. Armament of one 0.303-in (7.7-mm) Vickers forward and one similar calibre Lewis on Scarff ring in rear cockpit; up to 580 lb (263 kg) bombs. Detachable control column in rear cockpit for emergency use. Provision for operation as seaplane using twin Short floats. Total of 413 built for RAF to Specifications 1/29 and (final

70) 16/31; delivered 1929-32. Entered service in India early 1929 with Nos 11 and 39 Sqns. Also served in Iraq and with the AAF at home, equipping 20 squadrons in all. About 70 Wapitis still flying in India in 1939, of which majority soon passed to Indian Air Force (which had acquired four as its initial equipment for No 1 Sqn in 1933). Used operationally by IAF Coastal Defence Flights until 1942 and by second-line units (training, target-towing, army co-operation) until 1943. Starting 1929, RAAF acquired 28 new-build Wapitis (nine as Mk IAs, later updated, and remainder Mk IIAs) supplemented in 1937 by six ex-RAF Mk IIAs. In use at No 1 FTS in Australia until 1943, and as tugs for DHA-G2 gliders. From 1936, RCAF received 24 ex-RAF Wapiti IIAs, of which a few served with No 10 (BR) Sqn for anti-submarine patrols off Canada's east coast until May 1940, and others flew on support duties until 1944.

Max speed, 135 mph (217 km/h) at 5,000 ft (1,524 m). Rate of climb, 1,140 ft/min (5.8 m/sec). Time to 10,000 ft (3,050 m), 9¹/₂ min. Service ceiling, 20,600 ft (6,279 m). Range, 530 mls (853 km). Empty weight, 3,810 lb (1,728 kg). Gross weight, 5,400 lb (2,450 kg). Span, 46 ft 5 in (14.15 m). Length, 31 ft 8 in (9.65 m). Wing area, 488 sq ft (45.33 m²).

Wapiti V: A long-fuselage derivative of the Mk IIA, with 2-ft (61-cm) increase, for army co-operation service in India, with message pick-up hook. Production of 35 for RAF in 1930, allocated to squadrons serving in India, of which about a dozen still operational in 1939, transferred to IAF.

Wapiti IIA (South Africa): Four Wapitis to Mk IIA standard but fitted with 480 hp geared AS Jaguar VI engines, purchased by SAAF in 1929, followed by 27 built in SAAF Workshops at Roberts Heights, Pretoria, powered by 550 hp AS Panther IIA or Jaguar VI engines. A few survived as trainers and 'hacks' into the wartime period.

Above: A post-war photo of the Widgeon IIIA G-AAGH, which was flown throughout the war as a communications 'hack' for Westland Aircraft. Below: The Wessex W202 in service with the Egyptian Air Force.

Left: Wallace II K6050 after conversion for target-towing, photographed in March 1943. Above: three Wallace Is and (farthest from camera) a Mk II in service with No 2 ATS shortly before war began.

WESTLAND WALLACE

Light bomber and army co-operation biplane derived from Wapiti, with split-axle undercarriage and Bristol Pegasus engine. Private venture prototype (Westland P.V.6) first flown October 31, 1931, leading to adoption by RAF. To Specification 19/32, 57 Wapiti IIA airframes (mostly in store, and unflown) converted to Wallace I, as well as two Westland prototype and development aircraft; eight more built as new. Then to Specification G.31/35, the RAF bought 107 Wallace IIs (including three Wapiti conversions) differing principally in having a totally enclosed canopy over the two cockpits, with a revised mounting for the Lewis gun in the rear cockpit. Wallace I had 550 hp Bristol Pegasus II engine, replaced by supercharged 665 hp Pegasus IV in Wallace II, with larger diameter propeller. Wallaces were used to equip RAF Special Reserve and, later, AAF squadrons in UK, starting with No 501 (City of Bristol) in January 1933. In September 1939, some 125 Wallaces were still on strength (41 of them Mk Is). They flew on until mid-1943, serving as trainers at Bombing and Gunnery Schools, and in other support roles including target-towing.

Data for Wallace II:
Max speed, 158 mph (254 km/h) at 15,000 ft (4,572 m). Gross weight, 5,750 lb (2,608 kg). Span, 46 ft 5 in (14.14 m). Length, 34 ft 2 in (10.41 m).

WESTLAND LYSANDER

Two-seat artillery-spotting and reconnaissance monoplane defined by Specification A.39/34 in response to Operational Requirement OR.18. Designed under the direction of W E W 'Teddy' Petter as Westland P.8 and two prototypes ordered in June 1935. First prototype (K6127) flown on June 15, 1936, powered by 840 hp Bristol Mercury IX and second (K6128) on December 11, 1936, with 905 hp Mercury XII. Production ordered in September 1936 to Specification 36/36, with name Lysander and in Mk I and Mk II versions, respectively powered by Mercury XII and 905 hp Bristol Perseus XII engines. Perseus first flown in K6127 during 1938. Three squadrons of Mk Is and three of Mk IIs equipped during 1938/39 moved to France with BEF in 1939; about 50 Lysanders shot down and 30 destroyed on ground in May 1940. Other squadrons operational, 1938-39, in Egypt, Palestine and India; later served in Greece, North Africa and Western Desert, and Gibraltar. Up to 12 squadrons flying Lysanders in UK in 1940, when provision made for one 20-mm cannon to be fitted on each wheel fairing, for anti-invasion role, as alternative to one 250-lb (113.5-kg) SCI (Smoke Curtain Installation, which could also imply the use of poison gas as response to enemy use of such weapons) on each stub wing. Prototype K6127 modified in 1941 to Westland P.12 configuration with shortened fuselage ending in Frazer Nash four-gun turret for rear defence and large-span tailplane with end-plate fins based on Delanne tandem-wing principle. First flown July 27, 1941, with mock-up turret, and scrapped in 1944.

Lysander I: Initial production run, with Mercury XII engine and armament of two forward-firing 0.303-in (7.7-mm) Browning machine guns in wheel fairings and one pintle-mounted Lewis or Vickers of same calibre in rear cockpit. Provision for up to 500-lb (227-kg) of bombs on stub wings (when fitted) and four 20-lb (9-kg) bombs under rear fuselage. First production Mk I (of 169 delivered to RAF), flown spring 1938 and service deliveries began May 1938 to No 16

Below: Lysander II N1273 in service with No 28 Sqn, based at Lahore in the second half of 1942. Supply canisters are carried on the stub wings. Above right: Lysander I P1687 of No 16 Sqn fitted in 1940 with a pair of 20-mm cannon on the wheel fairings for potential anti-invasion use.

Above: Lysander IIIA(SD) V9289, with long-range tank and long access ladder to rear cockpit, operated in 1945 by No 357 Sqn in Burma; note the SE Asia blue/white insignia. Below: Canadian-built Lysander IIIA target-tug, which served with No 4 Bombing and Gunnery School.

Sqn; one early aircraft with dual controls for conversion training. About 20 later converted to Mk I.TT (TT Mk I later) target tugs. One extra aircraft built to French order crashed in 1939 before delivery. Eighteen built for Egyptian AF delivered 1938/39, with one more ex-RAF (and one Mk III) later. Three ex-RAF Mk Is released to Finland, some operating on skis during Continuation War of 1941-44.

Max speed, 229 mph (369 km/h) at 10,000 ft (3,050 m). Cruising speed, 150 mph (241 km/h). Rate of climb, 1,650 ft/min (8.4 m/sec). Time to 10,000 ft (3,050 m), 6.8 min. Service ceiling, 26,000 ft (7,923 m). Range, 600 mls (966 km). Empty weight, 4,065 lb (1,844 kg). Gross weight, 7,500 lb (3,402 kg). Span, 50 ft 0 in (15.24 m). Length, 30 ft 6 in (9.30 m). Wing area, 260 sq ft (24.5 m²).

Lysander II: Similar to Mk I but powered by Bristol Perseus XII engine. First deliveries to No 4 Sqn, 1938, and total of 399 built (including 47 originally ordered

Above: Lysander V9817 serving in the UK with the USAAF's 3rd Gunnery & Tow Target Flight. Right: The Westland P.12 was the Lysander prototype K6127 with a Delanne-style tail unit and (mock-up) tail turret. This was identified as Experimental Aeroplane 136.

for Indian AF, which eventually received 48 on transfer from RAF). Six built for Irish Air Corps, and 36 for Turkey in early 1940. About 25 transferred ex-RAF to Free French Air Forces in North Africa, late 1940. Some 20 later converted to Lysander II.TT (TT Mk II later) target tugs, and at least 22 converted to Mk III. Mk IIs served alongside Mk Is as already described. One Mk II (P9105) modified in 1940/41 to fly with Stieger-designed forward-sweep high-lift wing of parallel chord and with full-span flaps and slots, and wing-tip spoilers in place of ailerons. Orders from Latvia for 12 Mk IIs and Yugoslavia for two Mk IIs not fulfilled. One Mk II, ex-RAF, to Canada as pattern aircraft for local production.

Lysander III: As Lysander I and II, but powered by 870 hp Bristol Mercury XX or 30 engine. Deliveries began July 1940 and production totalled 350 for RAF (plus 22 Mk II conversions) before switch to **Lysander IIIA**, which introduced a twin-gun installation in the rear cockpit, using 0.303-in (7.7-mm) Lewis guns. Westland built 347 Mk IIIAs at Yeovil and 17 more at shadow factory at Doncaster, where remainder of 500-aircraft batch cancelled. Production ended with 100 **Lysander IIIA.TT** (TT Mk IIIA later) target tugs, with armament removed, attachments for drogue targets and a winch in the rear cockpit. Many Mk IIIs also converted to target tugs. Eventually, four squadrons in Fighter Command flew Lysander target tugs; others were used in India. Sixty-seven Lysander III and IIIA target tugs were transferred to the FAA in the UK from 1941 onwards, and about 25 Lysanders went to the USAAF in the UK, also primarily for use as target tugs. Eight Mk IIIAs to Portugal in September 1943. From initial Lysander III production, nine diverted to Finnish Air Force and one to Egypt, these being aircraft originally ordered for Estonia but absorbed into RAF contracts. In Finland, Lysanders flew briefly with L1v.14 in the Winter War and then with L1v.16 in the Continuation War until 1944, frequently on skis. Lysander IIIs supplemented earlier marks in overseas units including those in North Africa, Madagascar and India/Burma. In the UK, they were adopted for Air-Sea Rescue role from mid-1940 onwards, carrying M-type dinghies and other survival gear on the stub wings, and eventually equipping four full squadrons. Another major role was in support of SOE operations to deliver and collect agents in enemy-occupied territory. Starting in August 1940, Special Duty Lysanders were modified to have all armament removed, a 150-Imp gal (682-l) tank fitted under the fuselage and a long access ladder provided for the rear cockpit. The **Lysander III(SD)** and **IIIA(SD)** had a gross weight of 10,000 lb (4,536 kg) and endurance of over eight hours with a pilot and two passengers. They were flown successively by No 419 Flight, No 1419 Flight, No 138 and No 161 Sqns in the UK, by No 149 Sqn in North Africa and by No 357 Sqn in the Far East.

Above: One of the Lysander IIIs transferred by the RAF to Finland in February 1940, LY-118 is seen here in partial winter camouflage, and locally-designed and manufactured skis. Below: Lysander II P9105 with the Stieger-designed high-lift wing.

Whirlwind P7062 was one of the 114 production Whirlwind Is. Initially issued to No 137 Sqn, it is shown here after it had been transferred to No 263, with which it was serving when destroyed on February 19, 1943, on a training flight.

Max speed, 212 mph (341 km/h) at 5,000 ft (1,525 m). Time to 10,000 ft (3,050 m), 8.0 min. Service ceiling, 21,500 ft (6,553 m). Empty weight, 4,365 lb (1,978 kg). Gross weight (SD), 10,000 lb (4,536 kg). Dimensions as Mk I.

Lysander (Canada): Production of Lysander II initiated for RCAF in March 1938, in newly-constructed facility at Malton managed by National Steel Car Corp Ltd. One Mk II supplied ex-RAF as pattern aircraft and first of 75 built at Malton flown on August 16, 1939. Deliveries began September 1939 and used by three RCAF squadrons. Six transferred to RAF, and one converted to prototype target tug, with electric winch in rear cockpit. Further production of 150 Lysander IIIA target-tugs from December 1941. RCAF also received 103 Lysander IIIAs, ex-RAF, from Britain, virtually all converted to target tugs before or after reaching Canada. One Canadian Lysander II was fitted experimentally with skis.

WESTLAND WHIRLWIND I
Single-seat twin-engined fighter to meet OR.31, calling for four 20-mm cannon armament, and complying with Specification F.37/35. Designed during 1936 under direction of W E W 'Teddy' Petter as Westland P.9, and selected for prototyping by Air Ministry early 1937, with an order for two. Unarmed, the first of the two prototypes flew on October 11, 1938, and the second in 1939, each powered by a pair of liquid-cooled 860 hp Rolls-Royce Peregrine I engines, radiators for which were buried in the inner wing sections. Production of 200 ordered in January 1939 and first production Whirlwind I flew in June 1940. Service introduction began in No 263 Sqn in July 1940 and first 'kill' claimed January 12, 1941. Second, only other, squadron, No 137, operational October 1941 and both squadrons switched to ground-attack duties, for which Whirlwinds fitted to carry two 250-lb (113.5-kg) or 500-lb (227-kg) bombs underwing. Production limited to 114, all of which served with one or other of the two squadrons until re-equipment in 1943. One Whirlwind went to US for evaluation after serving with No 263 Sqn.

Max speed, 360 mph (579 km/h) clean and 270 mph (435 km/h) with bombs, at 15,000 ft (4,575 m). Rate of climb, 1,300 ft/min (6.6 m/sec). Time to 20,000 ft (6,100 m), 8.6 min. Service ceiling, 30,000 ft (9,150 m). Range, 800 mls (1,287 km). Empty weight, 8,310 lb (3,770 kg). Max take-off, with two 500-lb (227-kg) bombs, 11,388 lb (5,165 kg). Span, 45 ft 0 in (13.70 m). Length, 32 ft 3 in (9.83 m). Wing area, 250 sq ft (23.2 m²).

WESTLAND WELKIN
Single-seat twin-engined high-altitude fighter of similar configuration to Whirlwind, designed by Petter as Westland P.14 in response to OR.81 and conforming to Specification F.4/40 and further developed to F.7/41. Specification called for armament of 20-mm cannon and use of RM.6SM version of Rolls-Royce Merlin, but Merlin 61s were used in' unpressurised first prototype flown on November 1, 1942. The second prototype flew early in 1943 followed in mid-year by first of production batch. Production Welkin I used Merlin 72/73 or Merlin 76/77 combinations, odd-numbered marks with cabin blower attachment. In May 1944 two Welkins supplied to Fighter Interception Unit at Wittering, but RAF interest had already come to an end. Production ended with 101 airframes, of which final 26 delivered less engines, and all but a handful going to MUs for ultimate disposal. In line with OR.125, one Welkin I was modified, in conformity with Specification F.9/43, to become **Welkin NF Mk II** prototype, with AI Mk VIII radar, a modified nose to accommodate the scanner as well as cannon, and aft-facing observer in modified cockpit covered by new one-piece canopy. First flight was made on October 23, 1944, but the night-fighter was not ordered for production.

Max speed, 387 mph (623 km/h) at 26,000 ft (7,930 m). Rate of climb, 3,850 ft/min (19.6 m/sec). Time to 40,000 ft (12,200 m), 20 min. Service ceiling, 44,000 ft (13,420 m). Range, about 1,500 mls (2,414 km). Empty weight, 14,375 lb (6,526 kg). Gross weight, 19,775 lb (8,978 kg). Span, 70 ft 0 in (21.35 m). Length, 41 ft 6 in (12.66 m). Wing area, 460 sq ft (42.73 m²).

Above: Welkin DX282 was the fifth production Mk I. Issued to the A & AEE, it was photographed on November 25, 1943, during a handling flight that ended in a belly landing. Repaired, it was destroyed in a further accident, in January 1944. Right: The sole Welkin NF Mk II PF370 (Ex Aero 230) acquired the new serial WE997 post-war.

COMMONWEALTH AIRCRAFT AT WAR

Providing an Appendix to the main contents of this volume, these pages illustrate, and summarise the wartime service of, those aircraft types that originated in the countries of the British Commonwealth. Included are those types of indigenous design in Australia, Canada and India. Also included are details of some aircraft types that were designed in the USA but were subject of extensive development by licensees in Australia and Canada; excluded are those US types that were built without modification to supplement US production. British designs that were built in Australia, Canada, New Zealand and South Africa are fully covered in the main body of the book.

AUSTRALIA

COMMONWEALTH AIRCRAFT WIRRAWAY

In April 1938, the North American NA-16 advanced trainer was adopted for manufacture in Australia, becoming the first project for Commonwealth Aircraft Corporation. Named the Wirraway, first Australian-built example flew on March 27, 1939, and production by CAC totalled 755, with deliveries spread from July 1939 to June 1942 and then from November 1943 to July 1946. Total included 233 funded by Britain to support Empire Air Training Scheme. Production batches identified by different CAC charge numbers, but with few external changes and mostly minor improvements. Mark numbers seldom used, but comprised: **Wirraway I**, 40 CA-1; **Wirraway II**, 60 CA-3, 32 CA-5, 100 CA-7, 200 CA-8 and 188 CA-9; and finally **Wirraway III**, 135 CA-16. The Wirraway was powered by 600 hp Pratt & Whitney R-1340-S1H1G Wasp (most of which were built by CAC) and basic specification included two Vickers Mk V 0.303-in (7.7-mm) machine guns in the upper front fuselage and a third (Mk I) gun on a mount in the rear cockpit. Up to 1,000 lb (454 kg) of bombs (or 1,500 lb/ 680 kg in Wirraway III) carried on wing racks, and practice bombs under centre section. Classified as a general purpose type, Wirraway served in numerous roles, including light/dive bombing, coastal patrol and advanced training. Service use with RAAF began with No 12 Sqn in September 1939 at Darwin, engaged on coastal patrols, and then No 21 (GP) Sqn in 1940 in Singapore, seeing service against Japanese forces invading the Malayan Peninsula in December 1941. Six more squadrons flying Wirraways operationally by January 1942, including No 24 engaged in defence of Rabaul. Army co-operation added to Wirraway's roles in 1942, and No 4 (AC) Sqn operated in New Guinea in 1942/43. In training role, Wirraways equipped several Service Flying Training Schools as part of EATS throughout war.

Max speed, 220 mph (354 km/h) at 5,000 ft (1,524 m). Rate of climb, 1,950 ft/min (9.9 m/sec). Service ceiling, 23,000 ft (7,010 m). Range, 720 mls (1,158 km). Empty weight, 3,992 lb (1,811 kg). Gross weight, 6,595 lb (2,991 kg). Span, 43 ft 0 in (13.1 m). Length, 27 ft 10 in (8.48 m). Wing area, 255.8 sq ft (23.8 m²).

Above: CA-1 Wirraway Is of No 21 Sqn flying from Laverton early in 1940; the letter 'R' was the squadron code. Left: CA-6 Wackett A3-180 in overall yellow finish, 1941.

COMMONWEALTH AIRCRAFT WACKETT

Tandem two-seat *ab initio* trainer designed to meet RAAF Specification 3/38. Two prototypes (CA-2) ordered October 1938, with 130 hp de Havilland Gipsy Major in-line engines, first flown September 19 and early November 1939 respectively. Both converted to have 175 hp Warner Super Scarab radial engines in May/July 1940 and production order for 200 similarly-powered CA-6 Wackett Trainers placed June 1940 to comply with RAAF Specification 1/40. First production CA-6 flown February 6, 1941, and delivery of 200th completed April 1942. Served in RAAF as intermediate trainer (between Tiger Moth and Wirraway) primarily at Nos 1, 3, 8 and 11 EFTSs, and at 1 Air Observer's School, 1, 2 and 3 Wireless Air Gunner's Schools and 5 OTU.

Cruising speed, 115 mph (185 km/h) at 4,000 ft (1,219 m). Rate of climb, 700 ft/min (3.55 m/sec). Service ceiling, 16,000 ft (4,877 m). Max range, 425 mls (686 km). Empty weight, 1,910 lb (866 kg). Gross weight, 2,590 lb (1,175 kg). Span, 37 ft 0 in (11.28 m). Length, 26 ft 0 in (7.92 m). Wing area, 184 sq ft (17.1 m²).

Below: CA-13 Boomerang A46-126 'Sinbad II' in service with No 5 Sqn at Mareeba, Queensland, early 1944. Right: The sole CA-14, A46-1001, showing the supercharger in the fuselage side.

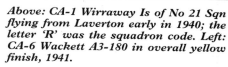

Above: CA-4 Woomera prototype A23-1001, carrying two torpedoes, on test over RAAF Point Cook in June 1942. Above right: The only other Woomera, CA-11 A23-1, in 1945. Right: First prototype DHA G1 at RAAF Laverton in November 1942. Below right: First of six DHA G2 gliders on test over RAAF Laverton.

COMMONWEALTH BOOMERANG

Single-seat 'stop-gap' fighter initiated late 1941 to make good RAAF's foreseen lack of imported fighters of better performance. Design based on using components of Wirraway trainer, combined with 1,200 hp Pratt & Whitney R-1830-S3C4-G radial engine and two-speed supercharger. Initial five CA-12 aircraft built early 1942, followed by first production batch of 100 ordered February 1942. First CA-12 flown May 29, 1942, and deliveries began July 1942. Further production comprised 95 CA-13, delivered from August 1943, 49 CA-19, delivered from May 1944, and single CA-14, making total of 250 by early 1945. Differences between variants minor. Armament comprised eight 0.303-in (7.7-mm) Browning guns in first five CA-12s, changed to four Brownings with two 20-mm Hispano cannon in production aircraft. CA-13s had metal (instead of fabric) covered ailerons and CA-19s had single F.24 camera in rear fuselage for tac-R role. Single CA-14 had General Electric B-2 turbo-supercharger in rear starboard fuselage side and R-1830-S1C3-G engine; it first flew on January 13, 1943. Boomerangs entered service at 2 OTU late 1942, and flew operationally with Nos 4, 5, 83, 84 and 85 Sqns. Of these, Nos 4, 5 and 84 saw service against Japanese forces in New Guinea and Borneo; other two squadrons remained in Australia.
Max speed, 305 mph (491 km/h) at 15,500 ft (4,724 m). Cruising speed, 190 mph (305 km/h) at 15,000 ft (4,572 m). Rate of climb, 2,940 ft/min (14.9 m/sec). Time to 25,000 ft (7,620 m), 13.2 min. Service ceiling, 34,000 ft (10,363 m). Range (internal fuel), 930 mls (1,496 km). Range (drop tank), 1,600 mls (2,575 km). Empty weight, 5,373 lb (2,437 kg). Gross weight, 7,699 lb (3,492 kg). Max overload, 8,249 lb (3,742 kg). Span, 36 ft 0 in (10.97 m). Length, 25 ft 6 in (7.77 m). Wing area, 225 sq ft (20.90 m²).

COMMONWEALTH WOOMERA

Twin-engined three-seat bomber designed to RAAF Development Specification 2/41 under direction of L J Wackett. Design work initiated April 1940 and single CA-4 prototype (A23-1001) flown at Fishermen's Bend on September 19, 1941. Powered by two 1,200 hp Pratt & Whitney R-1830-S3C4-G radial engines, CA-4 was armed with four 0.303-in (7.7-mm) machine-guns in the nose, two each in remotely-controlled barbettes at rear of nacelles above the wings, and single similar gun in ventral position. Provision for four 250-lb (113-kg) bombs in bays in nacelles and up to 4,000 lb (1,815 kg) on three external fuselage stations, or two Mk XII torpedoes. CA-4 lost on test flight on January 15, 1943, by which time production order placed (early 1942) for 105 developed CA-11 version. First

(and only) CA-11 (A23-1) completed mid-1944, first flown July 7, 1944, with nose armament of two 20-mm cannon and two 0.303-in (7.7-mm) Brownings. Programme cancelled September 1944 when next six aircraft in final assembly stage. Data for CA-11:
Max speed, 282 mph (454 km/h). Rate of climb, 2,090 ft/min (10.62 m/sec). Service ceiling, 23,500 ft (7,168 m). Max range, 2,225 mls (3,580 km) with one torpedo. Empty weight, 12,756 lb (5,791 kg). Gross weight, 22,885 lb (10,390 kg). Span, 59 ft 1 in (18.02 m). Length, 39 ft 6³/₄ in (12.06 m). Wing area, 440 sq ft (40.88 m²).

DE HAVILLAND DHA G1

Seven-seat experimental glider to meet RAAF requirements, designed by Martin Warner. Two prototypes built by DH Aircraft Pty in Australia, first flown June 14 and early November 1942. First flights behind Wapitis, subsequently towed by Fairey Battle and Supermarine Spitfire.
Max speed, 185 mph (298 km/h). Gross weight, 2,800 lb (1,272 kg). Span, 59 ft 0 in (17.99 m). Length, 35 ft 0 in (10.68 m).

DE HAVILLAND DHA G2

Developed DHA G1, to meet RAAF Specification 5/42. Contract for six placed in 1942. First flown at Mascot on March 20, 1943, towed by Fairey Battle. First

DHA G2 used 1944/45 for trials and pilot conversion at No 1 APU; other five into storage August 1943.
Max speed, 200 mph (322 km/h). Gross weight, 3,250 lb (1,476 kg). Span, 50 ft 6 in (15.40 m). Length, 33 ft 0 in (10.07 m).

WACKETT GANNET

Seven-seat utility transport, originally produced by Tugan Aircraft; name Wackett Gannet adopted when Tugan absorbed by CAC late-1936. Six examples acquired by RAAF from late 1935 and served in air ambulance role, two surviving to war's end. Powered by two 200 hp de Havilland Gipsy Six engines.
Max speed, 150 mph (241 km/h). Gross weight, 5,400 lb (2,449 kg). Span, 52 ft 0 in (15.85 m). Length, 34 ft 6 in (10.51 m).

CANADA

CANADIAN VICKERS VEDETTE

Two/three-seat single-engine pusher forestry protection biplane designed in UK by R K Pierson early 1924 for development in Canada. Prototype Vedette I flown November 4, 1924, powered by 200 hp Rolls-Royce Falcon III. RCAF acquired one Wright J-4-engined Vedette I in 1925 and 18 Armstrong Siddeley 210 hp Lynx IV-engined Vedette IIs from 1926 onwards; all of these

Below: One of the RAAF's six Gannets, acquired in 1935/36 for photo-survey duties and used from 1942 onwards by No 2 Air Ambulance Unit. Serials ran to A14-7, but the latter was A14-1 renumbered.

Above: Canadian Vickers Vedette VA No 816 at Vancouver in early 1940 when still serving with No 4(BR) Sqn, wearing the codes FY:F. Below: Vancouver IIS 903 similarly served with No 4(BR) Sqn before joining the S & BRT School in May 1940.

three open cockpits in nose and amidships; external racks for up to four 250-lb (113-kg) bombs. The Vancouvers served primarily with No 4 Sqn at Vancouver, two surviving to join the Seaplane and Bomber Reconnaissance Training School on its formation at Sea Island, Vancouver, in May 1940.

Max speed, 94 mph (151 km/h). Gross weight, 10,000 lb (4,540 kg). Span, 55 ft (16.76 m). Length, 40 ft (12.19 m).

FAIRCHILD SUPER 71P

Between 1927 and 1930, the RCAF acquired some 59 Fairchild high-wing monoplane single-engined transport aircraft in a variety of models including the FC-2, FC-2L, FC-2W, Model 51/51A and 71/71B/71C. Although a few of these were built by Canadian-Vickers and by Fairchild Aircraft in Canada, most were imported from the US and all were designed by the American Fairchild company. The Super 71, on the other hand, was designed by Fairchild Aircraft in Canada to meet specific requirements for a 'bush' freighter in northern Canada. Despite the designation, it bore only a superficial resemblance to the Fairchild 71. The prototype Super 71 flew on October 31, 1934, powered by a 525 hp Pratt & Whitney Wasp R-1340-T1D1, but no production ensued.

In 1936, two examples of a modified version, known as the Super 71P, were built for the RCAF, powered by the 600 hp Pratt & Whitney Wasp R-1340-S2H1-G and with the original parasol wing faired into the top of the fuselage. Flown both as landplanes and floatplanes, the Super 71Ps were intended for photo-survey and ambulance duties but achieved little success. One was destroyed early in 1938 and the other was taken out of RCAF service in April 1940.

Max speed, 142 mph (228 km/h) at 10,000 ft (3,050 m). Gross weight, 7,090 lb (3,219 kg). Span, 58 ft 0 in (17.67 m). Length, 36 ft 2 in (11.02 m).

out of service before war began. Starting 1929, RCAF then acquired 13 Vedette Vs with higher gross weight and Lynx IV engines, and 11 Vedette VAs featuring Handley Page wing slots. A single Vedette VI, with Wright J-6 engine, featured a metal hull. Seven Vedette VAs and the Mk VI survived into wartime service, flying with No 4(BR) Sqn and the Seaplane and Bomber Reconnaissance Training School (later No 13 OT Sqn) in Vancouver until May 1941.

Max speed, about 95 mph (153 km/h). Gross weight, 4,000 lb (1,816 kg). Span, 42 ft 2³/₄ in (12.86 m). Length, 42 ft 0 in (12.8 m).

CANADIAN VICKERS VANCOUVER

Twin-engined flying-boat developed to RCAF Specification C.12/28 as a forest fire-suppression aircraft. Single Mk I with two 200 hp Armstrong Siddeley Lynx IVB engines flown April 1929, followed by five improved Vancouver IIs to Specification C.18/29 delivered to RCAF in 1930. Three were powered by 225 hp Lynx IVC engines but later re-engined with 340 hp Armstrong Siddeley Servals (Mk IIS/S) and other two with 300 hp Wright J-6 Whirlwinds (Mk IIS/W). Armament comprised single 0.303-in (7.7-mm) machine guns in each of

Left: Fairchild Super 71P 665, the only one of two acquired by the RCAF to survive into the wartime period but struck off strength in April 1940. Above: The unusual Model 50K freighter, 799 was one of a pair in service until 1944.

Below: Fleet Fawn I 206 was used by No 118 (B) Sqn as a 'hack' before becoming an instructional airframe in December 1942. Right: Finch 1027 was the last of 27 Mk Is built, serving until 1942.

Above: The last of the 100 Fleet Forts, which served throughout the war after conversion for use as wireless trainers. Below: The sole example of the HAL glider completed bore the RAF serial HW885; planned production of a further 99 was cancelled.

FLEET FAWN and FINCH
As a subsidiary of Consolidated Aircraft Corp set up in 1928, Fleet Aircraft Inc had factories at Buffalo, NY, and across the border at Fort Erie in Ontario. The Canadian company produced a series of single-engined two-seat training aircraft, based on US designs but including some variants adapted specifically to RCAF needs. The latter purchased 20 Fleet Model 7B (with 125 hp Kinner B-5 engine) and 31 Model 7C (with 140 hp Armstrong Siddeley Civet I engine), known respectively as **Fawn I** and **Fawn II** in service. Many remained as station 'hacks' into wartime. The improved Model 16 was designed to meet RCAF requirements for an aerobatic trainer, and 27 were delivered in the closing months of 1939, with 160 hp Kinner R-5 engines. Known as **Finch I**, they were followed by 404 of the **Finch II** version, first flown on March 12, 1940, and powered by the 125 hp Kinner B-5. Finches were used to equip, wholly or partly, 12 Elementary Flying Training Schools within the British Commonwealth Air Training Plan until 1942, and many continued on miscellaneous duties until after war ended. Data for Finch II:
Max speed, 104 mph (167 km/h). Gross weight, 2,000 lb (908 kg). Span, 28 ft 0 in (8.53 m). Length, 21 ft 8 in (6.6 m).

FLEET MODEL 50K
Twin-engined 'bush' freighter designed for wheel or float operation, with optional accommodation for up to ten passengers. Prototype first flown on February 12, 1938, and of five Model 50s built, two acquired by RCAF in 1942 for potential use as Army paratroop trainers. One served in ambulance role and both retired in second half of 1944. They were powered by 330 hp Jacobs L-6MB engines.
Max speed, 150 mph (241 km/h). Gross weight, 8,326 lb (3,780 kg). Span, 45 ft 0 in (13.7 m). Length, 36 ft 0 in (10.97 m).

FLEET MODEL 60 FORT
Intermediate training monoplane designed in Canada in 1938, with tandem seating and raised rear cockpit. PV prototype, with 330 hp Jacobs L-6MB engine, first flown at Fort Erie on March 22, 1940. RCAF production order for 200 placed and name Fort adopted, but contract cut to 100 when need for intermediate trainer dropped. First production Fort I flown April 18, 1941, and deliveries completed June 1942. Role changed to wireless trainer, and trial installation of R.1082 receiver/T.1083 transmitter in rear cockpit, with aft-facing seat for trainee operator, flown at Rockliffe Air Station in February 1942. Identified as Fort IIs, converted aircraft used at No 2 Wireless School, Calgary, for remainder of war.
Max speed, 162 mph (261 km/h). Rate of climb, 1,100 ft/min (5.6 m/sec). Service ceiling, 15,000 ft (4,572 m). Empty weight, 2,601 lb (1,181 kg). Gross weight, 3,650 lb (1,657 kg). Span, 36 ft 0 in (10.97 m). Length, 26 ft 10¼ in (8.18 m). Wing area, 216 sq ft (20.07 m²).

NOORDUYN NORSEMAN
Single-engined six/nine-seat monoplane designed for Canadian 'bush' operation, first flown (on floats) on November 14, 1935, powered by 420 hp Wright Whirlwind. RCAF acquisition began early 1940 with purchase of 47 **Norseman IV**, powered by 550 hp Pratt & Whitney R-1340-S3H1 Wasp engine, for general transport duties. A further 30 **Norseman IVW** wireless trainers followed, equipped to seat five students and an instructor. RCAF also acquired one Mk III and the sole Mk II, ex-civil, both converted to Mk IV standard. Starting 1940, USAAF acquired total of 749 **C-64A Norseman** utility transports with R-1340-AN-1 Wasp engines, similar to the Mk IV, plus seven service trial **YC-64s** and six interim-standard **UC-64Bs**. Of this total, 20 supplied to RCAF as **Norseman VI** and three transferred to USN with designation **JA-1**. USAAF also supplied 14 C-64As to RAAF in 1943, two to Britain for RAF evaluation and, in March 1945, eight to R Norwegian AF to form Norseman Flight before transfer from UK to Norway. Data for Norseman IV:
Max speed, 160 mph (257 km/h) at 5,000 ft (1,525 m). Time to climb to 5,000 ft (1,525 m), 6.25 min. Service ceiling, 22,000 ft (6,706 m). Range (standard fuel), 600 mls (966 km). Empty weight (landplane), 3,675 lb (1,667 kg). Gross weight, 6,450 lb (2,926 kg). Span, 51 ft 6 in (15.7 m). Length (landplane), 32 ft 4 in (9.95 m). Wing area, 325 sq ft (30.19 m²).

INDIA

HINDUSTAN TROOP GLIDER
India's single aircraft-manufacturing company, Hindustan Aircraft Ltd, chose as its first indigenous design project a nine-seat troop-carrying glider. Of wood-and-fabric construction, a prototype of the glider was flown in August 1941. With no clear IAF requirement, and the availability of British and US gliders, planned production of 100 was cancelled, and HAL's priorities changed to major aircraft overhaul and repair work for the remainder of the war.

Above: Ski-equipped Norseman IV 691 photographed at RCAF Camp Borden in February 1940 when serving with No 1 Wireless School. Below: A Norseman serving the USAAF in India in 1945. The original C-64A designation had by then changed to UC-64A.

Index